WALLS

A HISTORY OF CIVILIZATION
IN BLOOD AND BRICK

DAVID FRYE

SCRIBNER
NEW YORK LONDON TORONTO SYDNEY NEW DELHI

Scribner
An Imprint of Simon & Schuster, Inc.
1230 Avenue of the Americas
New York, NY 10020

First Scribner trade paperback edition August 2019

SCRIBNER and design are registered trademarks of The Gale Group, Inc.,
used under license by Simon & Schuster, Inc., the publisher of this work.

For information about special discounts for bulk purchases,
please contact Simon & Schuster Special Sales at 1-866-506-1949
or business@simonandschuster.com.

The Simon & Schuster Speakers Bureau can bring authors to
your live event. For more information or to book an event, contact the
Simon & Schuster Speakers Bureau at 1-866-248-3049
or visit our website at www.simonspeakers.com.

Interior design by Kyle Kabel
Maps by David Lindroth Inc.

Manufactured in the United States of America

3   5   7   9   10   8   6   4   2

Library of Congress Control Number: 2018022463

ISBN 978-1-5011-7270-0
ISBN 978-1-5011-7271-7 (pbk)
ISBN 978-1-5011-7272-4 (ebook)

For Noelle, the muse of everything but history

Contents

PART THREE: The World in Transition

PART FOUR: A Clash of Symbols

Selected Timeline

Because few historical walls can be dated with precision, and many can't be dated at all, the following timeline includes only a small set of prominent rulers and events highlighted in the text. All dates are AD unless otherwise indicated. The designation *c.* indicates "circa."

	NEAR EAST AND CENTRAL ASIA	EUROPE	CHINA	AMERICAS
c. 2000 BC	Shulgi, king of Ur, builds the Wall of the Land			
c. 1900s BC	Pharaoh Amenemhat I builds the Wall of the Ruler			
c. 1600–1100 BC		Mycenaean Greece		
c. 800 BC			Border wall of Nan Chung	
500s BC	Nebuchadnezzar, king of Babylon, wall builder	Spartan reforms, rejection of walls		Walls of El Mirador, Guatemala
c. 450 BC		Athenian Long Walls		
214 BC			First Emperor constructs Long Wall	
141–87 BC			Emperor Wu of Han, wall builder	
c. 78		Earliest literary reference to Alexander's Gates		

SELECTED TIMELINE

	NEAR EAST AND CENTRAL ASIA	EUROPE	CHINA	AMERICAS
100s		Roman emperor Hadrian, wall builder		
c. 280–380	Shah Shapur II, wall builder	Roman emperor Diocletian, wall builder	Western Jin dynasty walls	
c. 400s	Oasis walls at Samarkand, other cities	Fall of Western Roman Empire	Northern Wei dynasty walls	
c. 500s	Shah Khosrow I, Persia, wall builder	Byzantine emperor Justinian, wall builder	Northern Qi and Sui dynasty walls	
c. 600s			Emperor Yang of Sui, wall builder	
c. 700s	Various Central Asian border walls			
c. 900–1200		Dragon Walls, Ukraine	Liao and Jin dynasty walls	
c. 1200s	Mongol invasions	Mongol invasions	Mongol invasions	Extensive palisades at Cahokia, Illinois
c. 1400s		Fall of Constantinople and construction of Irish Pale	Ming dynasty begins construction of Great Wall	Great Wall of the Inca, Bolivia
1989		Fall of Berlin Wall		

Introduction:
A Wall against the Wasteland

An ancient wall, at least four thousand years old, sits abandoned in a desolate region of Syria. To its west lie cities, some ancient, some modern, many now ruined by wars, also both ancient and modern. To its east lies only wasteland, a vast dry steppe that becomes progressively drier as one follows it farther east until it finally ends in desert. The wall stretches well over one hundred miles, and at its southernmost tip it turns sharply west, as if to cut off the mountains to its south. It briefly climbs the Anti-Lebanon Range, where it ends abruptly on a crest.

The Syrian wall is a tumbled ruin now, so unremarkable as to have gone completely undiscovered for thousands of years. Even in its heyday, it wouldn't have been especially impressive. The dry stones that sprawl across the sunbaked ground couldn't have been stacked much higher than a few feet. An additional layer, consisting of dirt, might once have extended the height of the structure, but only by another foot or so.

Historians, frustrated by the lack of inscriptions on the stones, find the monument a bit of a cipher. They study a map whose design has changed little in four thousand years: civilization on one side of the structure, barren waste on the other. It's as if some ancient king had ordered the construction of a wall against the wasteland. But who builds a wall against wasteland?

* * *

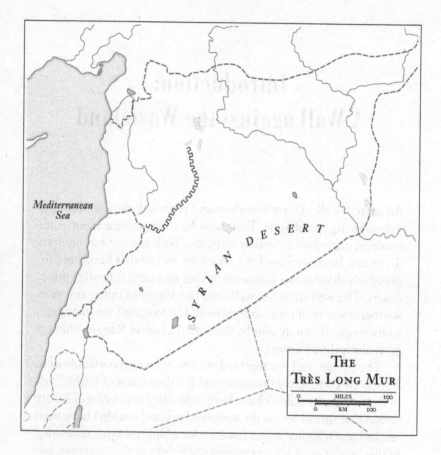

Mediterranean
Sea

SYRIAN DESERT

THE
TRÈS LONG MUR

MILES
0   100

KM
0   100

Well north of Syria, a far more famous wasteland sprawls across two
continents, where interconnected meadows and deserts form the
dominant physical feature of the Eurasian landmass. The immense
Eurasian Steppe—the Great Steppe, to many—extends some five
thousand miles from its western end in the Carpathian Mountains
to its eastern end in Manchuria. It is a forbidding place. In many
areas, its vast oceans of grassland appear only seasonally, before
the summer sun roasts the hardy weeds and nearly extinguishes
plant life altogether. Scorching winds then blow across the dusty
landscape like the hot air released by the opening of an oven door.

Eventually, winter arrives, bringing not relief but another kind of hell. Unbearable cold prevails, along with a layer of snow frozen so hard that grazing animals bloody their muzzles trying to poke through the icy shell for something to eat.

The steppe reveals its history only grudgingly. Immense monuments hint at its ancient past, but they are stubbornly difficult to find. Nature seeks to hide them. Endless cycles of hot and cold have cracked open the man-made structures, allowing them to become overgrown with vegetation long after most of their original glory has eroded away. To make matters worse, these monuments survive mostly in places few Westerners could even find on a map: Uzbekistan, Turkmenistan, Azerbaijan, Ukraine, Bulgaria, the Crimea, the Golestan province of Iran, Inner Mongolia. Together, they form a ruined blockade, facing the steppe from the south: walls, more than ten thousand miles of them, undefended, unguarded, and forgotten.

The walls lying south of the Eurasian Steppe are somewhat less ancient than their Syrian cousin—most are "only" fifteen hundred or so years old—but they evoke just as much mystery. Nearly all of them straddle the marginal zones that once divided the world into civilization and wasteland. In some cases, only wasteland remains. The locals who live closest to the walls have invented all manner of legends to explain their existence. Baffled by the long and unnatural mounds, they attribute them to gods, monsters, or famous conquerors. They relate fanciful stories about them. They give them quaint and colorful names.

For the most part, the folk names confound the mystery of the walls, tantalizing us with misleading clues to their origins. In southeastern Europe, a whole series of "Trajan's Walls" take the name of a second-century Roman emperor who probably played no role in their construction. To their west squat the remains of the so-called Devil's Dykes, and to their north the even more imaginatively named Dragon Walls. In Central Asia, the locals have acquired the peculiar habit of dubbing most of their long ruins Kam Pirak—"the old woman"—in reference to a legendary queen who built great fortifications to protect her people. Shorter barriers on both sides of the Caspian Sea invariably carry the name Derbent—Persian for "locked gate"—and nearly every pass through the Caucasus Mountains features some ancient ruin known as the Caucasian Gates. Most of these have been attributed at one time or another to Alexander, who almost certainly never paused anywhere long enough to build a wall.

Ruined walls appear all over the world. The materials—sometimes brick, sometimes stone, sometimes simply tamped earth—vary with the locale, but everywhere we find the same pattern: obscure barriers, adorned only by their colorful nicknames, nearly always facing desolate wastes. In Iraq, birthplace of the world's first civilization, ancient walls once formed barricades against the Syrian steppe in one direction and the even harsher wastelands of Arabia in another. Iraqi villagers dimly acknowledge these structures when they speak of the String of Stones, Nimrod's Dyke, and the Moat of Shapur. In Jordan, yet another barricade—the so-called Khatt Shebib, wrongly attributed to a medieval Arab ruler—once divided civilization from the Arab wastes.

The long wall in Syria takes pride of place for being the oldest. Perhaps for this reason it has no colorful nickname. No locals recall its history. The task of naming the structure eventually fell to the French archaeologists who discovered it. Amazed by the wall's length, they dubbed it simply Très Long Mur (French for "very long wall"). The modern label reeks of practicality more than poetry—the archaeologists were clearly determined not to attribute the barrier to the wrong king—and it's no wonder that most authors prefer the abbreviated form, TLM.

The physical remains of the TLM offer few clear indications of its origins, or, for that matter, anything else. Archaeologists puzzle over the wall's every detail. They wonder how a fortification only three or four feet tall could have been defended. They argue about who built it. Was it Bronze Age Ebla, so famous for its massive cache of cuneiform tablets? Or perhaps the lesser known city of Hama? They agree only that the TLM once functioned as a type of structure that, depending on your point of view, is either all too common in the modern world or not common enough. They have determined that the TLM was a border wall, the earliest ever built and the first of many such predecessors to our modern border defenses.

*   *   *

Hadrian's Wall, or what is left of it, lies more than two thousand miles from Syria, in the much greener countryside of northern Britain. It was constructed about two thousand years after the TLM, and it was nearly another two thousand years after that before archaeologists started poking around the Wall in earnest. By then, the concept of a massive barrier, stretching for miles along a border, seemed ancient and obsolete.

When I joined my first archaeological dig at a site near the Wall in 2002, walls never appeared in the nightly news. Britain was still many years away from planning a barrier near the opening of the Chunnel in Calais. Saudi Arabia hadn't yet encircled itself with high-tech barricades. Israel hadn't started reinforcing its Gaza border fence with concrete. Kenya wasn't seeking Israel's help in the construction of a 440-mile barrier against Somalia. And the idea that India might someday send workers high into the Himalayas to construct border walls that look down on clouds still seemed as preposterous as the notion that Ecuador might commence construction on a 950-mile concrete wall along its border with Peru.

No one chatted about walls while we cut through sod to expose the buried remains of an ancient fortress in northern Britain. I doubt that anyone was chatting about walls anywhere. The old fortress, on the other hand, was generally considered the crown jewel of British archaeology. For more than thirty years, sharp-eyed excavators at the Roman fort of Vindolanda had been finding writing tablets—thin slivers of wood upon which Roman soldiers had written letters, duty rosters, inventories, and other assorted jottings. At first, the tablets had represented something of a technical challenge; their spectral writing faded almost immediately upon exposure to air, almost as if written in invisible ink. But when the writings were recovered through infrared photography, a tremendous satisfaction came from the discovery that Roman soldiers complained about shortages of beer while the wives of their commanders planned birthday parties. The Romans, it turned out, were a lot like us.

Archaeology, even at such a special place, was tiring business, but after work I enjoyed taking hikes along the Wall. It was beautiful countryside—well lit by an evening sun that lingered late during the Northumbrian summer—and as I ambled over the grassy hills, occasionally enjoying the company of sheep, I sometimes imagined I was a lonely Roman soldier, stationed at the end of the world, scanning the horizon for barbarians while I awaited a resupply of beer. I'm ashamed to say that I took no detailed notes on the Wall itself. It made for beautiful photographs, the way it stretched languidly over the countryside, but my real interest lay in other things: the Roman soldiers, the barbarians, the letters. If anything I saw in Britain was to hold any significance for my research, it seemed obvious that I would find it in the wet gray clay of Vindolanda. There I hoped only to discern tiny clues about a particular period of Roman history. Such are the modest goals of the academic. For the duration of my stay, my focus was on the clay. All the while, I was standing right next to a piece of a much bigger story, a fragment of the past that was about to rise up from its ancient slumber to dominate contemporary politics on two continents. I was leaning against it, resting my hand on it, posing for pictures by it. I just didn't see it.

It was my interest in the barbarians that finally opened my eyes to the historical importance of walls. The barbarians were, in the main, inhabitants of every North African or Eurasian wasteland— the steppes, the deserts, the mountains. Civilized folk had erected barriers to exclude them in an astonishing array of countries: Iraq, Syria, Egypt, Iran, Greece, Turkey, Bulgaria, Romania, Ukraine, Russia, Britain, Algeria, Libya, Azerbaijan, Uzbekistan, Afghanistan, Peru, China, and Korea, to give only a partial list. Yet somehow this fact had entirely escaped the notice of historians. Not a single textbook observed the nearly universal correlation between civilization and walls. It remained standard even for specialists to remark that walls were somehow unique to Chinese history, if not unique to Chinese culture—a stereotype that couldn't possibly be any less true.

The reemergence of border walls in contemporary political debates made for an even more surprising revelation. Like most people my age, I had watched the fall of the Berlin Wall in 1989 with great excitement. To many of us it looked like the beginning of a new era, heralded by no less towering an international figure than David Hasselhoff, whose concert united both halves of Berlin in inexplicable rapture. More than a quarter century has passed since then, and if it had once seemed that walls had become a thing of the past, that belief has proven sorely wrong.

Border walls have experienced a conspicuous revival in the twenty-first century. Worldwide, some seventy barriers of various sorts currently stand guard over borders. Some exist to prevent terrorism, others as obstacles to mass migration or the flow of illegal drugs. Nearly all mark national borders. None faces the great Eurasian Steppe. By some cruel irony, the mere concept of walls now divides people more thoroughly than any structure of brick or stone. For every person who sees a wall as an act of oppression, there is always another urging the construction of newer, higher, and longer barriers. The two sides hardly speak to each other.

As things turned out, it was the not the beer or the birthday parties that connected the past to the present in northern England. It was the Wall. We can almost imagine it now as a great stone timeline, inhabited on one end by ancients, on the other by moderns, but with both always residing on the same side facing off against an unseen enemy. If I couldn't see that in 2002, it was only because we were then still living in an anomalous stage in history and had somehow lost our instinct for something that has nearly always been a part of our world.

How important have walls been in the history of civilization? Few civilized peoples have ever lived outside them. As early as the ninth millennium BC, the builders of Jericho encircled their city, the world's first, with a rampart. Over time, urbanism and agriculture spread from Jericho and the Levant into new territories: Anatolia, Egypt, Mesopotamia, the Balkans, and beyond. Walls inevitably followed. Everywhere farmers settled, they fortified their villages. They chose elevated sites and dug ditches to enclose their homes. Entire communities pitched in to make their villages secure. A

survey of prehistoric Transylvanian farming villages determined that
some fourteen hundred to fifteen hundred cubic meters of earth
typically had to be moved just to create an encircling ditch—an
effort that would have required the labor of sixty men for forty days.
Subsequently, those ditches were lined with stone and bolstered
by palisades. If a community survived long enough, it might add
flanking towers. These were the first steps toward walls.

The creators of the first civilizations descended from generations of
wall builders. They used their newfound advantages in organization
and numbers to build bigger walls. More than a few still survive. In
the pages that follow, I will often describe these monuments with
imposing measures—their heights, their thicknesses, sometimes
their volumes, almost always their lengths. The numbers may begin
to lose their impact after a while. They can only tell us so much.
We will always learn more by examining the people who built the
walls or the fear that led to their construction.

And what about these fears? Were civilizations—and walls—
created only by unusually fearful peoples? Or did creating civilization cause people to become fearful? Such questions turn out
to be far more important than we've ever realized.

Since 2002, I've had ample time to reflect on the Roman soldiers
who once guarded Hadrian's Wall. They certainly never struck
me as afraid of anything. Then again, they weren't exactly Roman
either. They came chiefly from foreign lands, principally Belgium
and Holland, which were in those days still as uncivilized as the
regions north of the Wall. Everything they knew of building and
writing, they had learned in the service of Rome.

As for the Romans, they preferred to let others fight their battles.
They had become the definitive bearers of civilization and as such
were the target of a familiar complaint: that they had lost their
edge. Comfortable behind their city walls and their foreign guards,
they had grown soft. They were politicians and philosophers, bread
makers and blacksmiths, anything but fighters.

The Roman poet Ovid knew a thing or two about the soft life,
but he also had the unusual experience of learning what life was

like for Rome's frontier troops. The latter misfortune came as a consequence of his having offended the emperor Augustus. The offense was some peccadillo—Ovid never divulges the details—compounded by his having penned a rather scandalous book on the art of seduction. "What is the theme of my song?" he asked puckishly, in verse. "Nothing that's very far wrong." Augustus disagreed. Reading Ovid's little love manual, the moralistic emperor saw plenty of wrong. He probably never even made it to the section where Ovid raved about what a great ruler he was. Augustus banished the poet from Rome, exiling him to Tomis, a doomed city on the coast of the Black Sea, sixty-odd miles south of the Danube. This Tomis was a hardscrabble sort of place, a former Greek colony already some six hundred years old by the time of Ovid's exile in the first century AD and no shinier for the wear. Its distinguishing characteristics were exactly two: First, it was about as far from Rome as one could be sent. Second, it lay perilously close to some of Rome's fiercest enemies, in an area that didn't yet have a border wall. Like northern Britain, the region of Tomis would one day receive its share of border walls, but in Ovid's day the only barriers to invasion were the fortifications around the city itself.

Ovid suffered in his new home. It was one thing to live in a walled city, quite another to be completely confined within those walls. In his letters to Rome, Ovid complained that the farmers of Tomis couldn't even venture out onto their fields. On the rare occasion when a peasant dared to visit his plot, he guided the plow with one hand while carrying weapons in another. Even the shepherds wore helmets.

Fear permeated everyday life in Tomis. Even in times of peace, wrote Ovid, the dread of war loomed. The city was, for all intents and purposes, under perpetual siege. Ovid likened the townspeople to a timid stag caught by bears or a lamb surrounded by wolves.

Occasionally, Ovid reminisced on his former life in the capital, where he'd lived free from fear. He wistfully recalled the amenities of Rome—the forums, the temples, and the marble theaters, the porticoes, gardens, pools, and canals, above all the cornucopia of literature at hand. The contrast with his new circumstances was complete. At Tomis, there was nothing but the clash and clang of weapons. Ovid imagined that he might at least content himself by gardening, if only he weren't afraid to step outside. The enemy was quite literally at the gates, separated only by the thickness of the city's wall. Barbarian horsemen circled Tomis. Their deadly arrows, which Ovid unfailingly reminds us had been dipped in snake venom, made pincushions of the roofs in the city.

There remained a final indignity for Ovid: the feeble, middle-aged author was pressed into service in defense of Tomis. Pitiably, he described his unique distinction as being "both exile and soldier." His reduced material comfort and constant anxiety already provided sufficient fodder for his misery, but how much more miserable was he when asked to guard the city wall? As a youth, Ovid had avoided military service. There was no shame for shirkers back in Rome, a city replete with peaceniks and civilians. Now aging, Ovid had finally been forced to carry a sword, shield, and helmet. When the guard from the lookout signaled a raid, the poet donned his armor with shaking hands. Here was a true Roman, afraid to step out from behind his fortifications and hopelessly overwhelmed by the responsibility of defending them.

From time to time, a Chinese poet would find himself in a situation much like Ovid's. Stationed at some lonely outpost on the farthest reaches of the empire, the Chinese, too, longed for home while dreading the nearness of the barbarians. "In the frontier towns, you will have sad dreams at night," wrote one. "Who wants to hear the barbarian pipe played to the moon?" Sometimes, they meditated on the story of the Chinese princess who drowned herself in a river rather than cross beyond the wall. Even Chinese generals lamented the frontier life.

Oddly, none of these sentiments appear in the letters written by the Roman soldiers at Vindolanda. Transplanted to a rainy land far from home, they grumbled at times about the beer supply, but had nothing to say about shaky hands or sad dreams. It was as if these barbarian-turned-Roman auxiliaries had come from another world, where homesickness and fear had been banished. Perhaps they had.

Almost anytime we examine the past and seek out the people most like us—those such as Ovid or the Chinese poets, people who built cities, knew how to read, and generally carried out civilian labor—we find them enclosed behind walls of their own making. Civilization and walls seem to have gone hand in hand. Beyond the walls, we find little with which we can identify—warriors mostly, of the sort we might hire to patrol the walls. The outsiders are mostly anonymous, except when they become notorious.

The birth of walls set human societies on divergent paths, one leading to self-indulgent poetry, the other to taciturn militarism. But the first path also pointed to much more—science, mathematics, theater, art—while the other brought its followers only to a dead end, where a man was nothing except a warrior and all labor devolved upon the women.

This book isn't intended to be a history of walls. It is, as the subtitle indicates, a history of civilization—not in the comprehensive sense, but with the limited goal of exploring the unrecognized and often surprising influence of walls. I refer specifically to defensive walls. No invention in human history played a greater role in creating and shaping civilization. Without walls, there could never have been an Ovid, and the same can be said for Chinese scholars, Babylonian mathematicians, or Greek philosophers. Moreover, the impact of walls wasn't limited to the early phases of civilization. Wall building persisted for most of history, climaxing spectacularly during a thousand-year period when three large empires erected barriers that made the geopolitical divisions of the Old World all but permanent. The collapse of those walls influenced world history almost as profoundly as their creation, by leading to the eclipse of one region, the stagnation of another, and the rise of a third. When the great border walls were gone, leaving only faint traces on the landscape, they still left indelible lines on our maps—lines that have even today not yet been obscured by modern wars or the jockeying of nations for resources. Today, a newer set of walls, rising up on four continents, has the potential to remake the world yet again.

The walls that have shaped human history have spawned many mysteries. Solving them, even in part, hasn't been easy. It has required the accumulated efforts of hundreds of detectives working in long-dead languages or troweling dirt in the summer sun. Those researchers, mostly archaeologists and historians, have toiled at their task for generations. They have kept at it through World Wars and revolutions, deciphering dead languages, discovering new walls, and exploring lands without histories. Gradually, brick by brick and tablet by tablet, they have unlocked the stories behind the walls.

I owe inestimable gratitude to those pioneering archaeologists and historians. Their efforts have made my work possible. However, in constructing this broad history, I am also aware that I have, from time to time, parted ways with specialists. I hope that my occasional dissents have some value. In my defense, I can only say that they are almost certainly the result of the unusual perspective from which I have approached this project. It is, in many ways, the only perspective that the historian can ever have of the distant past—that of a barbarian outsider, peeking in, peering over countless high and fiercely defended walls to gaze upon a curious and unfamiliar world.

PART ONE

BUILDERS AND BARBARIANS

Midwife to Civilization:
Wall Builders at the Dawn of History

THE ANCIENT NEAR EAST, 2500–500 BC

The great wall of Shulgi has not survived, but then, how could it? Time lay heavily across the landscape of Mesopotamia. Like some relentlessly pressing weight, it sought to smother everything that would rise up out of the flat alluvial plains of ancient Iraq. Its effects there were uncharacteristically swift, almost impatient; it destroyed things before it could age them. As early as the third millennium BC, the Mesopotamians already had a word—*dul*—for the shapeless lumps of dead cities that even then dotted the horizons, having long ago melted like wax under the sun. *Dul* eventually gave way to an Arabic word, *tell*, which reflected the growing obscurity shrouding the region's past. To the Bedouins whose animals meandered around the unsightly mounds, the tells were nothing more than insignificant heaps of dirt. Only later did archaeologists realize that every one of those strange landmarks represented the ruins of a lost world.

In Shulgi's day, some four thousand years ago, Mesopotamians battled ceaselessly against the work of time. They lived as if in sand castles, forever building and rebuilding a world that would inevitably be washed away. Nothing endured. The great fertile fields that fed the cities were a mirage. If the workers neglected the cleaning and repair of their vast irrigation systems for even a few seasons, the ditches would silt up, and the land would return to desert. Their buildings were no more permanent. For construction materials, the Mesopotamians had little more than the dirt beneath their feet. In this hot land made of silt deposited by the Tigris and Euphrates Rivers, there were no stones and few trees. Lacking sufficient fuel to bake all their mud bricks, the Mesopotamians settled for drying them in the sun, a process that created building blocks of such dubious quality that they could not withstand even occasional rain. To protect their brick walls, the Mesopotamians slathered them with a plaster of mud, and when that first outer coat washed away, they slathered them with mud again. If they were diligent at maintaining their walls, the resulting accumulation of washed-off plaster would eventually clog the streets, forcing them to knock down the buildings and start over. If they were interrupted in their maintenance, the result was much the same as for the unirrigated fields: temples, palaces, and even city walls crumbled away. Another city became a tell.

The impermanence of their mud-built world clearly troubled the Mesopotamians. A popular legend—possibly the most popular, judging from the variety of copies that have survived—tells of a king who refused to accept that he, like all mortals, must someday die and return to clay. The mythical Gilgamesh searched far and wide for a way to cheat death, but his efforts went for nothing. The Mesopotamian storytellers couldn't conceive of any ending for their hero that didn't require him to sink back into the soil.

In the end, the Mesopotamians defeated time in only one activity. The clay tablets upon which they inscribed their cuneiform writing have survived the passing centuries completely unchanged. If the planet endures another million years, those tablets will also endure, remaining in exactly the same condition.

Successful, therefore, in overcoming time only in their record keeping, the Mesopotamians naturally developed the bureaucratic urge to assign dates to events, and this led to the habit of kings giving names to years. Though perhaps not so elegant a system of chronology as our current one, it did serve a second purpose that has become quite useful to historians. It allowed the kings to commemorate their achievements—including the building of structures that they surely realized could not last.

Shulgi—who, as king of Ur around 2000 BC, ruled over much of Mesopotamia—was a builder of many things that didn't last, and he was a few other things besides. It's probably best to let his own words speak for him. The long-reigning monarch composed several extant hymns of self-praise, and these tell us a great deal about him, if we can shake the nagging suspicion that he has padded his résumé somewhat. Shulgi clearly wrestled with the constraints of modesty. In one hymn, he described himself as "a powerful man who enjoys using his thighs." This was the sort of boast that probably shouldn't have been committed to a medium that could still be read after four thousand years. Then again, Shulgi also referred to himself as the "god of manliness," so it would seem he wasn't easily embarrassed. He assures us that, as a youth, he excelled all other students. Grown to manhood, he slew every lion in Mesopotamia and defeated every human enemy as well. He mastered all weapons and musical instruments, and in a rare feat of athleticism, he once delighted his cheering subjects by running over two hundred miles in a single day. These, at least, are Shulgi's claims, whether or not we choose to accept them. He was no stranger to boasting, and so it should come as no surprise that his year names comprise a rather predictable list of triumphs.

In the twentieth year of his kingship—"The Year the Citizens of Ur Were Drafted as Spearmen"—Shulgi apparently instituted a general draft, and this led to a particularly impressive series of victories. From that time forward, the bombastic monarch had Ur's enemies on the run. The region was experiencing its great revival, duly reflected in the names of years, and the triumphal march seemed poised to continue indefinitely.

However, Shulgi's year list reveals a conspicuous absence of military successes immediately after his defeat of Anshan in the thirty-fourth year of his reign. Three years later, after what might have been merely a brief pause in the litany of conquests, we sense for the first time that something has gone terribly wrong. In his thirty-seventh year, Shulgi failed to record a victory yet again. For a notable achievement, he could highlight only a different sort of enterprise, one that seems oddly uncharacteristic, at least for someone with such splendid and busy thighs. It was the sort of achievement that would soon enough crumble and be washed away, returned to the soil and smothered by time. Shulgi's thirty-seventh year was officially designated "The Year the Wall of the Land Was Built."

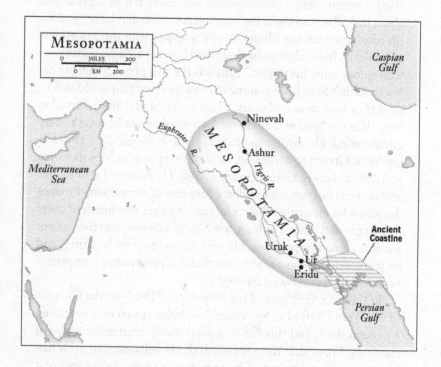

In retrospect, Shulgi's decision to build a wall was no great innovation. For a people such as the Mesopotamians, who were accustomed to the constant chore of construction and reconstruction, the first solution to any problem was building. They built temples to fend off the wrath of their gods and walls to fend off the wrath of their enemies. They built canals, dams, and irrigation channels so they could live.

Like early farming communities everywhere, cities in Mesopotamia focused their greatest efforts on surrounding themselves with fortifications. Massive bulwarks protected the people, their food supplies, their wealth, and their animals. Walls engulfed all man-made structures, swallowing up ziggurats and cities with equal appetite. Uruk, the city of Gilgamesh, was defined by its "all-encircling wall," allegedly built by the great king himself. This may well have been an instance of art imitating life. Nearly every Mesopotamian king advertised having raised up at least one city wall, and many built more than one. They knew their works wouldn't last for any great period, but the prospect of repeating the labors of their ancestors didn't deter them. At least five different kings provided walls for Babylon, and at least four built walls for Ur. An individual born in Isin at the right time could have seen his city surrounded by three successive sets of walls—sand castles every one.

For the Mesopotamians, building was a sacred duty. On the first day of a new construction project, the king blessed a brick mold, then packed it with mud. Songs and the beating of kettledrums filled the air. The king brushed a brick stamp with honey, butter, and cream, then struck his mark on the wet clay. When the brick dried, the king himself ceremoniously lifted it out of the mold. Subsequently, the moment might be memorialized in a year name or even in art. Many of the greatest Mesopotamian kings—including Shulgi—were depicted in their official propaganda carrying baskets of bricks on their heads.

The drudgery required by all these enterprises must have been awful, but the Mesopotamians accepted it as their lot. An ancient Mesopotamian flood myth describes how the gods set out to dig the first irrigation ditches and wells. The work didn't suit them. First, they complained; then they burned their tools and baskets. Finally, they created mankind to take over their chores. Someone had to move all that mud.

Not every Mesopotamian enjoyed a good wall raising. The words of a Bronze Age shepherd have come down to us, describing his feelings about life behind walls. Shepherds were the freest members of Near Eastern society. They inhabited Mesopotamia in great numbers, but unlike farmers they spent long periods far away from the city, accompanying their flocks to pasture. For much of the year—especially when crops were growing—shepherds had to steer clear of all sown land, and the obsessively bureaucratic administrators of the palaces and temples for whom the shepherds worked hardly kept track of them at all. To individuals such as these, the limited horizon of the walled city was worse even than a cage. "If I leave myself inside just one day," our Bronze Age herdsman remarked, "until I leave the city walls to renew my vigor, my vitality ebbs away."

It's worthwhile taking a closer look at those particular Mesopotamians who had so little use for walls. They weren't the most refined inhabitants of the plains. For the most part, the shepherds were illiterate, known to us only by the scribblings of city dwellers. The two groups were connected by kinship but little else. In the eyes of the townsfolk, the shepherds were quite distinct, a rough and somewhat fearless lot, skilled with slings, throw sticks, and staffs, inured to loneliness, dark, and the hazards of outdoor living. The daily life of the shepherd contrasted sharply with that of the farmer or factory worker. Shepherds contended with fierce sheep-stealing carnivores, whereas farmers merely fended off placid, skittish herbivores. Like the biblical David of 1 Samuel 17:34–36, shepherds lived with weapons, killing, and the mortal dangers of the steppe:

Your servant used to keep sheep for his father; and whenever a lion or bear came, and took a lamb from the flock, I went after it and struck it down, rescuing the lamb from its mouth; and if it turned against me, I would catch it by the jaw, strike it down, and kill it. Your servant has killed both lions and bears; and this uncircumcised Philistine shall be like one of them.

In contrast to the people who dwelled behind walls, shepherds accepted little in the way of governance. Even those herders directly employed by the temple or palace had to report to their overseers only twice a year. For them, the temptation to drift away must have been strong. The authors of Genesis, writing in the first millennium BC, certainly saw nothing extraordinary about the idea that shepherds might head off with their flocks and never return. In biblical tradition, Abraham, a possessor of flocks, herds, and tents, simply abandons his original home in the Mesopotamian city of Ur and sets off with his animals and women and over three hundred fighting men. Abraham's band subsequently wanders about, living wherever they pitch their tents, and forcing the urban kings of Canaan and the Jordan Valley to acquiesce to their presence on the land. They help themselves to water from city wells or, less frequently, dig new wells, which become such flash points for violence that they're given names such as Contention and Enmity. They negotiate for women and occasionally slaughter whole cities for them. A generation removed from Abraham, his herding descendants are remembered mostly for their hotheadedness. Jacob, lying on his deathbed, fondly describes his sons: Simeon and Levi are angry, violent, and quick to sword. Judah's hands are on the neck of his enemies. Gad is a raider, Benjamin a ravenous wolf, and so forth.

In Mesopotamian myth, the goddess Inanna is asked to choose between a farmer and a shepherd, both of whom seek to marry her. In her deliberations, she rudely criticizes the herder. He is too brash and his clothes are coarse. Without the gods of civilization, she declares, the shepherd would live roofless in the steppes, a mere nomad. It's a rather harsh assessment, but in the end, she marries him anyway. Apparently, she prefers a bad boy.

Inanna's decision—the sort that has baffled countless generations of "nice guys" left alone on a Friday night—would have raised few eyebrows in Shulgi's day. Shepherds were widely admired in the ancient Near East. They occupied a place in the imagination much like the cowboys of the Old West. "I am a hero!" a king such as Shulgi would boast. "I am a shepherd!" But, of course, Shulgi was no such thing, and neither were any of those other Sumerian kings who carried baskets of mud bricks on their heads. The shepherds, who disdained walls, were rootless, rough, unpredictable, and often violent. They were the sort of men who could defend a city—and they were often asked to do so—but they could never build one. On the other hand, nothing in the description of the shepherd applies particularly well to their cousins who raised a civilization out of mud. Mesopotamian townspeople were as monotonously reliable as they were settled. In the city, survival depended on the unwavering commitment of citizens to their wearisome chores—the digging of wells, the constant removal of silt from the irrigation ditches, and the building and rebuilding of walls. They enlivened the tedium of this work with music and festivals and prostitution, but these diversions did not compromise their efficiency.

The townspeople's acceptance of a life of labor—replete with governors, supervisors, rules, and records—had innumerable implications for Mesopotamian society. The most obvious was that it rendered men less capable as protectors. Workers, bound by their day-to-day responsibilities, couldn't go off on hunts that might have honed their fighting skills. Ensconced behind their walls, they became accustomed to a life of comfort and security. They exhausted their energies in labor rather than saving it for bursts of violence. Those few townsmen who were forced into battle fought like men unaccustomed to war, being perhaps the first soldiers anywhere to protect themselves by donning rudimentary armor that fortified the spirit more than the body. Like the timid amateurs that they were, they fought in tightly packed rows of infantry. Slow moving, inflexible, and easily targeted or pursued, these early phalanxes embodied a natural tendency to seek safety in numbers and for the weak to crouch behind the strong. Few men were willing to brave military service at all. The men who carried baskets had not been socialized to embrace battle, and they had no taste for it. They preferred instead to contribute to the defense of their cities by doing what they did best: build things out of mud. In a world of farmers, priests, sculptors, surveyors, drummers, prostitutes, master builders, silo managers, throne bearers, accountants, masons, musical-instrument makers, general laborers, and scribes, the profession of arms was all but forgotten. "I have men enough to carry baskets," one general complained. "What I need are soldiers."

The Mesopotamians concluded that a grand bargain lay at the heart of civilization: the basket carriers had sacrificed strength for comfort. It was an idea at least as old as the Gilgamesh epic. The mighty Gilgamesh could find no equal among the weaklings who dwelled inside Uruk's massive walls; only the wasteland outside the walls could spawn a primitive brute such as Enkidu, who ran with the animals and could match the great king's strength. And what had Uruk's city dwellers gained in return for their helplessness? The harlot who seduced Enkidu described the life of the townspeople: they dress in gorgeous robes; every day is a holiday; they even smell good. This was the perspective of a sensualist. If she'd thought about the question more deeply, she might have added that some of her fellow urbanites were also adept at writing or mathematics or architecture or music.

The notion that the civilized life of the walled cities had softened men and left them less fitted for war was widespread in the ancient Near East. Occasionally, an Old Testament prophet would voice a similar idea while exhorting his countrymen to abandon walled Jerusalem and return to their tents. It was one way to recapture the favor of a god who, like Inanna, preferred his men a little rough. A few clans of ancient Israel took this advice to heart, electing to abstain from such civilized amenities as alcohol, agriculture, and regular haircuts. Their most famous representative, Samson, burst with rough-hewn strength, but only as long as he remained shaggy and uncivilized.

Cooped up inside their massive fortifications, the creators of the world's first civilization come across as a rather timid lot, ever eager to escape into their grand festivals, ever fearful that outsiders were about to burst in and ruin it all. They didn't look upon the broader world with confidence—and for good reason: they could not have known that their grand experiment of cities, farms, priests, scribes, and walls would even succeed. The world outside their walls was not exactly uninhabited, but it was, in the eyes of the basket carriers, dangerous. This was civilization in its infancy: every city its own frontier, never far from hostile neighbors in the mountains, desert, or steppe. The Mesopotamians had but to walk out from behind the security of their city walls and they would soon enough find themselves in the company of outsiders who saw them as little more than a ready source of loot, land, animals, or women. They lived, in the memorable phrase of one anxious Bronze Age king, "like birds in a cage."

Viewed from afar, the civilized nations of the ancient Near East—Sumer, Egypt, Israel, Assyria, and the like—were clusters of these birdcages. Even their gods and heroes were wary of what lurked outside. In Mesopotamian myth, a Guardian of the Sown kept watch at the edge of the farmlands, around which he'd placed a barrier. Dumuzi, the shepherd and protector, died at the hands of highland nomads when he ventured too far. The legendary king Lugalbanda survived a similar journey but lost his nerve. "A lost man is terrible," he despaired. "On the unknown path at the edge of the mountains . . . Don't let me flow away like water in a violent death! Don't let me be thrown away into the desert unknown to me like a throw stick!"

An Egyptian writer once described a journey that took him outside the lands of the walled cities. He knows he must traverse a countryside that teems with robbers menacing from every side. When he passes through a narrow defile, he panics. The hairs on his head stand up. He begins to shudder. His soul, he writes, is in his hand. Making his way over boulders and pebbles, he sees that his path leads between a ravine and a mountain. His heart now heavy with fear, his imagination racing, utterly convinced that the robbers are behind him, he begins to run. This was what happened to birds that ventured outside their cages.

In the late third millennium BC, nearly all the cages of mud collapsed. Barbarian highlanders descended from their mountains and swept aside the world's first empire, the Akkadian, which encompassed all of Mesopotamia, with astonishing rapidity. Royal records speak of how the attackers "acted with violence against the gods . . . took away the wife from the one who has a wife . . . took away the child from the one who had a child." The destruction was thorough. Agade, the imperial capital, has still never been found, not even as a tell. Mesopotamia's political structure was left in a chaos famously reflected in the Sumerian King List: "Who was king?" the author asks. "Who was not king?"

An ancient text chronicles the terror that these invasions struck in the hearts of the basket carriers: Heralds avoided the roads. Boatmen were afraid to take to the river. Even shepherds dared not search for lost sheep, or cowherds for lost cattle. Fields, gardens, and fish ponds went untended. Farmers were forced to relocate gardens within city walls, while the price of everyday items, such as oil, grain, wool, and fish, soared. Watches were posted everywhere—in trees and on riverbanks—and a cowed populace huddled inside city walls, afraid to venture out long enough even to bury the dead.

Another text, the so-called *Cuthean Legend*, purports to represent the hard-earned wisdom of Naram-Sin, the king whose ill-advised mountain campaign precipitated the disaster. Here the attackers are known as Umman Manda, a "forlorn, fugitive race" who grew to manhood in the mountains. So monstrous are the Umman Manda (they're said to look like "cave birds") that Naram-Sin is reported to have sent out an officer to determine whether they bled like men or were "evil spirits, specters, ghosts, and fiends." Such was the usual stereotype of those who lived in the mountains, deserts, and steppes beyond the walls. The Umman Manda advance inexorably from the northwest, wiping out settlements along the way. Three times, Naram-Sin sends out enormous armies against them only to see them annihilated. "I am a king," he despairs, "who brings no prosperity to his country, a shepherd who brings no prosperity to his people." The Akkadian king bemoans the futility of sending troops against highlanders: "How could I have been so precipitous to have gone forth? Now panic, night, death, plague, shivers, terror, chills, financial losses, hunger, famine, insomnia—innumerable ills—have come down on my people."

Naram-Sin speaks for all the inhabitants of the walled cities when he proffers his advice to future kings: Strengthen your walls. Keep your trenches filled with water. Make sure all your goods are safely stored away. And when the barbarians come, don't provoke them. Even though they will trample your land and slay your cattle, don't dare meet them or even take up your weapons. Better to stay behind your walls, respond to their wickedness with kindness, and address them as lords.

Strengthen your walls. Stay behind your walls. Now here was advice that even a traumatized population of basket carriers could embrace.

Civilization nearly perished completely during the great invasions of the late third millennium. The record of destruction is

astonishing: Egypt, Syria, Canaan, Akkad, Sumer, Troy, Elam, the
Indus Valley, and Anatolia alike all suffered. Empires collapsed.
Kingdoms crumbled. Cities burned. Economies broke down, and
whole populations of survivors struggled to adapt to an insecure
world in which their gods no longer guaranteed protection. In that
fertile composting of determination, industriousness, and fear grew
the first fantastic dreams of a walled kingdom.

By the time of Shulgi, there was already some precedent for the
idea of a wall that could protect an entire kingdom. Syria's enig-
matic TLM predated Shulgi's fortifications by several centuries,
and its reputation may have reached Ur. At least in their myths, the
Mesopotamians had contemplated similar designs. A poem from
the twenty-second century BC described a struggle between the
god Ninurta and the demon Azag, a "killer out of the highlands"
who had been raiding cities with his warriors. Ninurta ultimately
prevailed in the story, and in the aftermath of his victory the god
took steps to ensure that Sumer would never again be harassed
by mountain men: he brought agriculture and civilization to the
mountains, then built "a bank of stones against the highland . . .
like a great wall."

Late in Shulgi's reign, warlike invaders from the highlands
of Syria arrived to terrorize Mesopotamia. The newcomers represented everything the basket carriers feared most: a mountain
people who roamed about ceaselessly, forever causing turmoil.
The Syrian Amorites had no homes other than their tents. They
neither constructed cities of mud nor lived in cages. As they moved
south toward the great cities, a pervasive gloom settled over the
Land between the Rivers.

According to legend, one of the earliest Mesopotamian kings
had constructed a great wall across the desert "like a net" to keep
the Syrian Amorites at bay. Shulgi either repaired that ancient wall
of King Lugalbanda's or constructed an entirely new one. In his
typically pompous manner, Shulgi boasted that his fortifications
had finally brought peace to the hard-set kingdom. The people, he
said, could at last live in green meadows and in peaceful dwelling

places. The Year the Wall of the Land Was Built came more than fifteen hundred years before the first earth was tamped in place for any of the great walls of China, and with it we might mark the formal beginning of the idea of an enclosed kingdom in which civilians need not fear the raids of outsiders.

The idea would prove considerably more durable than the wall itself. As could only be the case in an impermanent, mud-brick world, the impact of Shulgi's fortifications was marginal and temporary. Shulgi's surviving correspondence is chiefly concerned with the urgent need to restore a key fortress that was apparently in no condition to deter an invasion. He orders his master builder to work day and night and chastises his generals for not repairing his forts quickly enough. Meanwhile, news reports trickle in: the enemy has risen up in great strength; Shulgi's commanders can no longer guard the cities; the canals have been destroyed; the enemy waits outside in the hills.

Shulgi's successor fared no better at walling out the nomads from Syria. Like Shulgi, Shu-Sin focused on the building and repair of a fortified border—an assemblage of mud bricks and trenches known by the excruciatingly clumsy phrase "That Which Keeps the Amorites at a Distance." His troops labored under great duress to extend the defensive barrier to the mountains, but their efforts came to nothing. Shu-Sin's correspondence betrays a growing anxiety. The Amorites, his general informs him, have invaded the land. Observing Shu-Sin's construction work, they have encamped menacingly nearby, harassing the workers. The army has begun to run short of soldiers. Word soon arrives from outlying areas: the cities themselves can no longer be protected.

In literature, it is not Amorites but other highland barbarians—Gutians and Elamites—who bring down the walled kingdom created by Shulgi. A god is said to have dispatched the Gutians in an irresistible invasion. The mountain men smash the heads of their victims and fill the Euphrates with floating corpses. At Adab, they sic their dogs on the refugees, stampeding them like goats. "The Gutians, the Vandals," cry the people, "they are wiping us out." A terrible famine has left no food or beer even for the king. Meanwhile, other barbarians strike at Ur, where the famine inside the city walls kills as many as the highlanders outside: "Inside Urim [Ur] there is death, outside it there is death." Once the barbarians breach the walls, they smash the people's heads like clay pots.

To the west, the pharaohs made their own attempts at walling off their state. Recently, archaeologists have completely overturned conventional opinion on early Egyptian society. Egyptian cities were not open, as previously assumed, but girded by mud-brick walls. All along the Nile, the cities and their guardians, the pharaohs, maintained a careful watch over the wastelands of Libya, Nubia, and the east. Foreign invasion was a standard theme in Egyptian literature. One early second-millennium text, the *Admonitions of Ipuwer*, despairs that so many outsiders have flooded the country that there are no real Egyptians left. Another work, the *Prophecy of Neferty*, reveals the panic spread by invasions of nomads who brought "terror to the hearts of those who [were] at harvest . . . seizing the teams as they ploughed." Here the barbarians have overrun the kingdom's fortresses, and the pharaoh's soldiers, afraid to sally forth, are taken during their sleep. Nomads' animals drink from the Nile. The Egyptians, previously unaccustomed to weapons, have taken up arms and begun making arrows of metal. Terror and hopelessness pervades Egyptian thought: "I go to rest saying, 'I must stay awake!'"

The Egyptian response to insecurity was typical for a people who, like the Mesopotamians, raised up walled cities out of mud: they fortified their borders. Pyramid texts speak of defenses against desert peoples from both the west and the east. The pharaoh Amenemhat I constructed a fortification called the Wall of the Ruler. No trace of this wall has survived, its mud bricks undoubtedly having long ago eroded away and been buried by sand. However, Egypt's fortifications in the more arid south stood for nearly four thousand years, until they were finally destroyed in the flooding caused by the Aswan Dam. There the pharaoh's mud-brick forts once sprawled over 250 miles, overlooking the frontier from atop islands, cliff tops, and steep hills. Longer fortifications, including a four-mile wall flanking the Nile, supported the forts, and Egyptian patrols regularly fanned out to the desert edge searching for evidence of nomads and sending back all except the traders.

Nearly fifteen hundred years later, Near Eastern kings still hadn't let go of the idea that a great border wall might keep nomadic raiders out. In the mid-first millennium BC Nebuchadnezzar II (r. 605–562 BC) became the first ruler to establish a defensive circuit around an entire country.

Nebuchadnezzar is a bit better known than Shulgi. He has inspired every sort of legend. Some ancient authors assert that he built the wondrous Hanging Gardens for his Median wife, a comely hillbilly who longed for home. In the Bible, he's said to have put his fortune-tellers, magicians, sorcerers, and wizards to death for having failed to guess the contents of his dreams.

Nebuchadnezzar spent thirteen years laying siege to the city of Tyre, and if the experience taught him nothing else, it apparently impressed upon him the value of well-built fortifications. During the siege, he made his men carry so many loads that their heads were rubbed bald and their shoulders worn raw. The walls never fell. Returning home around 573 BC, Nebuchadnezzar surrounded his capital with fortifications that would dwarf even those of Tyre. Thousands of slaves toiled away for Nebuchadnezzar, making the bricks, baking them (an expensive and unusual step), and stacking them into walls so thick that chariot races could be run on the tops. When they were finished, three massive walls surrounded Babylon, its more than one thousand temples, its aqueducts, canals, and gardens.

Babylon's city walls were just a start. Relying on rivers to defend the eastern and western approaches to Babylonia, Nebuchadnezzar could completely enclose the core of his kingdom, by adding long walls to the north and south. The northern wall, whose ruins are known today as Habl as-Sahr ("string of stones"), extended some thirty-one miles. A staggering 164 million bricks were used in its construction. The southern wall connected Babylon on the Euphrates to Kar-Nergal on the Tigris.

Nebuchadnezzar believed that his walls had immunized Babylonia against invaders. He had his name stamped on every brick. Inscriptions as far afield as Lebanon announced to the world his great achievement:

> So that no enemy and troublemaker should reach the territory of Babylon . . . I piled up a great earthwork and surrounded the city with mighty waters. So that no flood should break into it, I loaded its sides with a strong embankment of bitumen and baked brick. . . . I piled up a great earthwork, and I surrounded the land with mighty waters, like an uprising of the ocean. . . . I reinforced the defenses of Esagil and Babylon and I made Babylon a mountain of life for the people.

The prophet Jeremiah was skeptical. He prophesied that the walls of Babylon would be razed and burned: "The peoples exhaust themselves for nothing," he wrote. "The nation's labor is only fuel for flames."

For at least another thousand years after Nebuchadnezzar, Mesopotamian rulers would carry on with efforts to translate the labor of nations into defense. The so-called Umm Rus wall, for example, once guarded the Mesopotamian plain from the desert to the north. Similarly, the massive mud-brick wall known as either El Mutabbaq or Nimrod's Dyke defended the Tigris plain against Bedouins. The basket carriers kept busy, but at least they held off the barbarians for a while.

History shows that the basket carriers had good reason for their fear. From the middle of the third millennium BC to the middle of the first, urban settlements in Mesopotamia declined, in the aggregate, to just one-sixteenth their former size, and that wasn't the end of it. The heartland of civilization would suffer another two thousand years of invasions from the wastelands before the great cities and canals were finally destroyed. As the world of the civilized Mesopotamians became ever smaller and less secure, the immense early promise of Mesopotamian civilization was never realized. Fearful of venturing too far beyond their defenses, the Near Easterners largely contented themselves with remembering past glories—their scholars endlessly assembling the data collected by earlier generations and their artists endlessly reproducing the same formulaic images they had inherited from their forebears. Mostly they repeated the rituals they hoped would placate the gods who periodically sent barbarians against them.

Perhaps what finally doomed the basket carriers was their stubborn disinterest in reconsidering a defensive strategy that was inextricably tied to their way of life. They were, with few exceptions, civilian populations resigned to being defended only by brick walls, small numbers of soldiers, and mercenaries. They insisted on remaining that way even as they were being driven to extinction. Generation upon generation elected to build walls rather than take up arms. Their commitment to this vision could be characterized as either admirable or pathetic, depending on one's point of view; however, it was not the universal resolution of all ancient peoples. In Greece, the heartland of another ancient civilization, a city would soon come to reject the logic of the basket carriers and re-create urban life in a wholly new form, without walls, and, incredibly, without civilians. The story of a city without walls—a thing almost unheard of in ancient history—must occupy our attention next.

To Wall or Not to Wall?

GREECE, 600–338 BC

When the German American businessman Heinrich Schliemann commenced excavations near the Turkish village of Hisarlik in 1871, he brought with him all the patience of a visionary—which is to say none at all. Never one to be constrained by the rigors of archaeological method, Schliemann hired some 80 workers—later expanded to 150—and immediately set them to work uncovering what he'd dreamed of finding since childhood: Troy, the great city of the *Iliad*, surrounded, just as Homer had described it, by walls. Following Schliemann's imprudent orders, the workers ignored all antiquities deemed insignificant as they cut through layers of history. They smashed ancient structures and tossed aside relics with abandon. Centuries flew by in shovelfuls of dirt. In just three years Schliemann cleared away over three hundred thousand cubic yards of earth, all of it impregnated with the detritus of the ages. This was archaeology at its worst and most primitive—amateurish, unscientific, and utterly tainted by confirmation bias—but the results were straight out of Hollywood. To the chagrin of careful practitioners ever since, Schliemann and his mercenary crew found exactly what they were looking for. A ring of walls, six and a half feet thick, emerged from underneath the ruins of the Roman city once known as New Troy.

The buried walls were impressive but not, in Schliemann's mind, sufficiently Homeric, and so the self-made millionaire promptly committed yet another in his long series of methodological sins and continued digging. He renewed the excavations with all the reckless haste of a true believer. Eighty workers once more plunged into the ancient hillside, clattering with mattocks and shovels and making a proper hash of the site until they had found yet another set of walls, this time more than eight feet thick. Here Schliemann might well have stopped, but he didn't. He remained at Hisarlik for another two years, finding walls beneath walls beneath walls beneath walls. More than a century later, another German archaeologist would suggest something that never even occurred to Schliemann: the ancient ramparts at Hisarlik, he argued, represented nothing more than Troy's royal citadel, itself enclosed within a far larger fortified perimeter that defended a larger ancient city.

Schliemann departed Troy without exploring the surrounding plain. Temporarily barred from Hisarlik for having smuggled out the cache of gold jewelry he'd discovered there—it was last seen on the neck of his young Greek bride—the pioneering archaeologist turned his attention to another Homeric target: Troy's ancient enemy, Mycenae. There his task was considerably easier. The massive stone walls of Mycenae were still plainly visible. That was all the luck he needed. Schliemann knew next to nothing about the painstaking craft of archaeological excavation, but he was intuitive enough to realize one key thing: that if he wanted to find a forgotten city, all he needed to look for was the wall.

The Greeks of the classical era (479–338 BC) were, like Schliemann, separated from the heyday of Mycenae by more than a few centuries. Unlike Schliemann, they were somewhat bemused by the ruins of Agamemnon's city. They imagined that Mycenae's massive limestone fortifications were the work of monsters. Their own cities were considerably more refined. In Athens and other places, townspeople enjoyed all those institutions that were conspicuously lacking even in the great capitals of the ancient Near East—marketplaces, gymnasiums, sports stadiums, theaters, artists' workshops, and schools. The building blocks of Western society had at long last made their splashy debut in Greece, although not without the accompaniment of their older chaperones: temples and, of course, walls.

The Greeks had been building walls at least since the Bronze Age, when their ancestors established the civilization that historians call Mycenaean (flourishing roughly 1600–1100 BC). However, this prologue is not well understood. Greek poets remembered their Bronze Age forebears as fearless heroes—chariot-borne warriors and freebooters, such as Achilles and Odysseus—yet whatever swagger these mighty champions once felt when they steered their boats toward Troy or Egypt clearly gave way to trepidation when they turned their attentions north to the barbarian lands beyond Greece. In the late thirteenth century BC, the Mycenaeans of the Peloponnesian peninsula constructed a fortified wall to separate them from the rest of the Balkans. Panic was also evident north of the Peloponnesus. There, the ancestors of the Greeks first built their famous wall at Thermopylae some seven centuries before a Persian threat even existed. The ingenious defenders even channeled water over the pass to erode away the ground and create untraversable gullies. Cities throughout Greece prepared for attacks by enclosing and securing their water supplies.

Inevitably, trouble found its way past the border walls and into the urban areas of Bronze Age Greece. Mycenaean civilization came to a violent end during the twelfth century. In the space of just a few decades, virtually all the cities of southern Greece were abandoned or destroyed. Mycenae itself fell around 1150 BC, burned in an inferno that melted even stone.

It took several centuries for civilization to revive in Greece. When new cities finally arose on the ashes of the old, they, too, had walls. The new fortifications rested on foundations of limestone masonry, but they otherwise differed little from their Mesopotamian, Trojan, or Mycenaean predecessors. This much had not changed since Jericho. A city was a thing with walls, just as it had always been—except in the extraordinary case of Sparta.

The Spartans repudiated nearly ten thousand years of urban tradition in their rejection of walls. But then, this was for them a matter

of principle. Spartan men, unlike their rivals from Athens—or anywhere else for that matter—viewed the habit of sleeping securely
behind walls as a demonstration of cowardice. They saw nothing
admirable about a peaceful population of civilian basket carriers
refusing to come out and fight. Indeed, more than once a Spartan
is said to have quipped that city walls were nothing more than
"women's quarters."

Women's quarters? Now there's a phrase packed with meaning.
To be sure, the Spartans were renowned for their economy of
expression. They honed it through long years of practice, beginning
in childhood. Spartan elders regularly prompted young boys with
hard questions just to see if the lads could respond laconically—that
is, with the proper pithiness of someone from the Spartan country
of Laconia. Spartan women also learned to restrain any natural
garrulity. Their penchant for crisp, clever speech eclipsed even
that of their husbands, and more than a few screenwriters have
poached a zinger from Plutarch's *Sayings of the Spartan Women*.
Still, it's a bit of a shock to see the venerable concept of walls
dispatched so summarily. Two words—*women's quarters*—and an
ages-old institution lies wounded and bleeding, as if stabbed by
a Spartan spear.

The Spartan perspective contradicts nearly everything we know
about early attitudes toward walls. The Mesopotamians had viewed
walls as sacred features of their environment. They took great pride
in fortifications that "gleamed like copper" or had been raised
"as high as the mountains." A particularly massive set of fortifications might give rise to boasting, but never shame. Defensive
barriers—and most especially the walls surrounding cities—were
everywhere accepted as a necessary and god-ordained fact of civilized life. Homer tells us that Troy's ramparts were the work of
Poseidon and Apollo. Even the Israelites, who claimed descent from
wandering shepherd clans, established the principle that houses
in walled cities belonged to their owners in perpetuity, whereas
houses in unwalled villages belonged to the open country. Little
wonder, too, that the Egyptian hieroglyph for *city* depicted two
crossroads meeting inside a set of walls. During peacetime, those
walls made it possible for an unwarlike populace to go about its

proper business of making shoes or painting pots in relative security, and if the people were ever to graduate to writing plays, novels, or poems, then that would require security, too. How, then—or why—would the Spartans alone have conceived this nonsense of a city without walls?

Naturally, the Spartans discarded any notion that they might have descended from the Mycenaean wall builders of the Bronze Age. The latter were, in their eyes, the very weaklings whom their ancestors had conquered and subjugated. As for those ancestral conquerors, they could be none other than the sons of Heracles, a mighty clan of invading warriors. The Spartans thus imagined themselves an invincible nation of champions. They could not envision their ancestors as civilians who took shelter during periods of danger. If they feared anything, it was that they might some-day become fearful. The conservative element in Spartan society resisted any institution that might weaken Sparta's men. Inspired by an unwavering belief in the primitive vigor of their ancestors, they embarked on one of the most extraordinary social experiments in history—the complete repudiation of walls and, with walls, all things civilized.

The Spartan economy, in its early days, could have supported the loftiest ambitions of civilization. Spartan citizens owned land yet were generally freed from the burden of toiling in the fields. They possessed abundant leisure that might have been turned toward literature, mathematics, art, philosophy, or theater. In fact, the early Spartans may well have dabbled in many of these activities. Traces of a Spartan literature survive, most notably in a martial poetry that inspired generations of Greeks to hold their positions in battle without flinching. In the end, however, the Spartans would not pursue literary or artistic excellence. They opted for a forced, artificial barbarism over high culture. Like so many radical thinkers before and after them, they concluded that the fruits of civilization itself had weakened them and they could only regain their strength by abstaining from those fruits altogether. It was this conviction that prompted their rejection of walls.

The archaeology of Sparta is rather straightforward. At some point during the sixth century BC, the Spartans looked about at their fine Laconian pottery, their imported amber and ivory, their bronze and wooden statues, their tens of thousands of objets d'art, and chose to do away with it all. Henceforward, Sparta would not evolve like other Greek states. The city would not feature grand monuments, walls, or even a planned urban center but would remain an unprepossessing collection of villages. At least one Greek author, the historian Thucydides, reckoned that future generations of Greeks, surveying the remains of Sparta, would have a hard time believing such a city could have once dominated Greece. They might not realize it had ever been a city at all.

The powers that remade Sparta in the sixth century, stifling its cultural development and rejecting the construction of walls, did so in the name of the city's legendary lawgiver, Lycurgus. Unfortunately, his life is now more or less a cipher. He comes down to us only in confusing and contradictory reports as a kind of Spartan Moses, a quasi-historical legislator who allegedly received divine assistance in his work. Even the sixth-century reformers knew him only as a figure of myth.

A Spartan king was once asked what gain the laws of Lycurgus had brought to Sparta. "Contempt for pleasures" was his reply. He might as well have said, "Contempt for civilization." The Lycurgan reforms were thorough and pervasive. Anything that hinted of civilization, anything that might dazzle the eye or tickle the intellect, was banished from the city. All at once, the Spartans expelled those goods that they regarded as superfluous because they brought only pleasure. Henceforward, Spartans could no longer possess gold or jewelry. They were required to keep their homes simple, the wood beams crudely fashioned with axes rather than fine carving tools. The interiors, the reformers insisted, were left so plain that beds with silver legs or extravagant purple bedspreads would look entirely out of place.

Spartan clothing developed a reputation all its own. Athenian playwrights, being constitutionally incapable of passing up a good insult, ridiculed Spartan visitors for their ragged, filthy cloaks. Thucydides, a more evenhanded observer, was somewhat more kind. He credited Spartans for being the first to dress simply—rich and poor alike. They were the first, too, he said, to play games naked and to take off their clothes in public. Perhaps this helped with the odor.

Not that the Spartans smelled of potpourri. The Lycurgans (if we might coin a name for the reformers) banned perfumes, which were deemed wasteful, and dyes because they were thought to pander to the senses. The ears were treated no better than the eyes and the nose. One Spartan leader famously took an adze and cut away two of the nine strings of a musician's lyre. Who needed the rest of the scale?

The rejection of walls didn't make the Spartans any more open or cosmopolitan; if anything, it intensified their xenophobia. The reformers took great pains to ensure that none of the products of civilization would creep back into their unwalled, primitivist paradise. They denied citizens the right to travel lest they acquire from abroad a taste for luxury. They banished gold and silver currency from the city to deter the importation of foreign goods. No Eastern trader would peddle his exotic wares in Sparta, knowing that he would receive in return only the heavy iron pieces that the Spartans used for currency.

It wasn't enough that Spartans should deny themselves the luxuries that they feared softened them. From cradle to grave their lives were reshaped to provide the benefits of a more primitive, barbarian experience. Do primitives wear fine gowns or take frequent baths? No? Then neither should a Spartan. Spartan babies were denied swaddling clothes and left alone in the night, so as to grow accustomed to cold and dark. As children, Spartans learned the rudiments of reading and writing, but such education was kept to a minimum. It was considered far more important that the boys get used to going about barefoot and naked because shoes cause children's feet to grow soft, and changing clothes to suit the weather creates a delicate constitution.

The great experiment encompassed women as well as men. A proper Spartan recoiled at the thought that women should enjoy sheltered upbringings or develop feminine characteristics. The reformers mandated that young women walk nude in processions, showing off the bodies they had developed by working out, running, wrestling, and throwing the discus and javelin. They talked tough, too. The famous Spartan saying "Come home either with your shield or on it," a warning to those who would toss aside their shields to flee faster, originated as a parting message from mothers to their sons. One mother, upon hearing that her son had committed an act of cowardice, murdered him. In her defense, she remarked that he had been raised to die for Sparta and had now done so.

For meals, the Spartans established mess halls where citizens were expected to dine communally. They reasoned that it would do no good to allow men to return home at the end of the day, lie on expensive couches, and fatten themselves up, undoing their physical and moral training. Eating alone was considered a gateway to far worse behavior: sleeping in, taking a warm bath, napping. Spartans were instructed to eat plain foods, without wine. Table talk was jocular—teasing and, of course, laconic. Not only were citizens trained to remain taciturn, responding to questions only with pithy answers, but the teaching of rhetoric was forbidden as well. They left the talking to the Athenians.

The purest signal of the reformers' intentions can be seen in their drive to eliminate all civilian careers from the city. The list of professionals expelled from Sparta is long: teachers of rhetoric, fortune-tellers, pimps, prostitutes, mimes, conjurors, dancing girls, harpists, and craftsmen of all sorts. Once, a Spartan king is said to have addressed soldiers from Sparta and its allies, asking first that the potters stand, then the metalsmiths, the carpenters, the builders, and the rest of the craftsmen. By the end, virtually every allied soldier was on his feet, but not a single Spartan. Sparta had become an entirely militarized state.

Greek writers record that Sparta inevitably loosened its strict discipline. After the Peloponnesian War at the end of the fifth century BC, an influx of gold and silver allegedly reintroduced all the evils that the Lycurgans had sought to expel. The newly wealthy indulged a growing taste for the civilized life, while the mass of the population continued to squat in the city, more interested in revolt than defense. More than once a king would arise and, like some prophet of Israel exhorting his people to return to the wilderness, demand that Sparta revive its primitivist experiment. In the late 240s BC, the Spartan king Agis IV convinced the city's young men to support his plan for a complete restoration of the Lycurgan system. The king and his supporters stripped off their clothes to show that they would sacrifice anything to return Sparta to what it had once been. The defeat of Agis's reforms was only temporary. Within a decade, yet another young Spartan king had taken up the cause of revitalizing the Spartan experiment. Cleomenes III began with a ruthless purge of the opposition. He then restored the system of physical training, as well as the old mess halls.

The Lycurgan constitution of Sparta experienced its cyclical ups and downs, but the central premise of Spartan society endured for hundreds of years. The Spartans possessed a clear vision of what it meant to be a man, and sleeping inside "women's quarters" formed no part of it. Sparta didn't require fortifications of limestone blocks because it was defended by "walls of men." Three concepts—walls, civilization, and effeminacy—were inextricably linked in the Spartan mind, where they formed an unholy trinity of weakness, but why? What did the Spartans see that led them to conclude that this seemingly unconnected threesome was, in reality, a unity?

The Greek historian Thucydides was frequently given to marvelous moments of insight, not the least of which came when he divided Greek societies into two types: those that went about armed at all times and those in which the men had set aside their weapons and devoted themselves to other aspirations. The former weren't terribly evolved, in Thucydides's eyes. They harkened back to an earlier age when the Greeks still viewed raiding and robbing as acceptable, even honorable activities. However, the latter weren't above criticism, either. Having abandoned their warrior ways, the men of these civilian societies had devolved into dandies, wearing linen underwear and golden hair clasps.

It was the Athenians, according to Thucydides, who were first among the Greeks to take the initial step of setting aside their weapons in everyday life. The accuracy of this statement cannot be tested, but the Athenians certainly played a key role in spreading the more civilized form of Greek society. The Athenians were also Greece's most prolific builders of walls. They erected ramparts for themselves and then sometimes for their allies and colonies.

The Athenians weren't weak, but neither were they Spartans. Military service in Athens was an occasional duty, discharged by amateurs. Athenian men underwent no real training for war and ridiculed those peoples who did. Athenian children were shielded from war, and not until the fourth century did Athenian teenagers receive any preparation for battle—a brief period of mandatory exercise preparatory to receiving arms. Even this experiment proved short-lived, going against the spirit of an age in which philosophers were proposing that civilians should be relieved of all military duties and that a separate class of soldiers should fulfill all combat roles. The training of eighteen-year-olds was quickly converted into a system of general intellectual, moral, and physical education.

To a man, the great leaders of classical Athens were wall builders, and this observation applies even to that redoubtable hero of the second Persian War, Themistocles. To be sure, Themistocles was more of a statesman than a soldier. His political skills were formidable. Like politicians in every age, Themistocles believed in democracy just as long as he could dupe the people into following his lead, and he didn't care how he made that happen. When he wanted the populace of Athens to approve his naval strategy, for example, he invoked bogus omens and prophecies and even employed theater machines to fool the people into believing that the gods were on his side. Eventually he resorted to spreading the rumor that the goddess Athena had fled the city for the sea, and this proved fairly effective at convincing the founders of Western civilization to support his plan.

Themistocles led the drive to fortify Athens in the fifth century BC. To obtain funding for the new walls, he sailed about the Aegean, demanding tribute from all of Athens's allies. He told them he'd brought with him two goddesses: Persuasion and Force. The inhabitants of one island replied that they, too, had two goddesses and that theirs—Poverty and Impossibility—prevented them from making payments. In the end, Themistocles had his walls.

The culmination of Athens's great fortifying enterprise came in the mid-fifth century with the construction of the Long Walls. Designed to protect the city's lifeline to the outside world, the Long Walls stretched several miles from the center of Athens to its seaports on the Aegean. Cimon, the driving force behind the construction of the Long Walls, carried on proudly in Themistocles's tradition of duping the populace. He once announced that he had found the bones of the mythical hero Theseus, news that the Athenians celebrated by erecting three of the head-and-penis statues, or herms, that they thought conferred good luck.

By following Cimon's plan and extending the city's walls all the way to the sea, Athens could maintain its maritime umbilical cord even under siege. Pericles—yet another politician who possessed a knack for getting his way, although he preferred straightforward bribery to hocus-pocus—even convinced his fellow Athenians that they could dispense with farming altogether and supply their needs entirely by sea. The Athenians thus sealed themselves off from enemy armies without cutting themselves off from the world.

By the mid-fifth century, Athens was more physically secure than it had ever been. An Athenian golden age dawned behind the new walls. The walled Athenians were as open to the outside world as the unwalled Spartans were closed. Philosophers poured into the city. Theater flowered, along with sculpture, mathematics, architecture, and painting. Protected by walls that simultaneously sealed off the city from attack while keeping its ports open, the Athenians experienced war in an entirely new way. Year after year, even with the city under siege, the playwrights composed new works, entered them into contests, and staged them at the theater. Philosophers delighted their pupils and annoyed rivals. Artists carried on their work with exquisite skill.

The clearest picture of Athenian society behind the fifth-century walls comes from the plays of Aristophanes, who spent nearly his entire career trapped in the city by a conflict he viewed as unnecessary. Aristophanes, at least judging from his works, must have been some character, well suited to the city that had produced Themistocles, Cimon, and Pericles. He took his humor broad. He appreciated the value of a well-timed fart. And if ever an author enjoyed repeatedly thrusting a double entendre into the right spot until his audience convulsed in ecstasy, it was he. In his most famous play, the women of Athens—still wearing fine gowns, cosmetics, perfumes, and slippers, even during the war—complain that their husbands are too often absent and the supply of foreign dildos has dried up. Elsewhere, Aristophanes satirizes a besieged populace that does little more than argue over politics, gamble on horse racing, or engage in fruitless philosophical speculations. Most incredibly, he was able to satirize the city's political leaders with impunity. Business as usual behind the Long Walls.

An apparent irony presents itself: the Spartans, who lived openly, without walls, possessed not even a modicum of freedom. Their elders taught them what to do and how to do it. They were instructed in how to speak; how, what, and where to eat; how to interact with sons, wives, husbands, and daughters; and what they could and could not possess. The Athenians, by contrast, built walls and behind those walls became the freest people on earth. Secure in their enclosed city, they argued politics, discussed philosophy, attended theater, and developed mathematics and science. As for the notion that art might weaken men, they were having none of it. "Our love of what is beautiful does not lead to extravagance," declared Pericles. "Our love of the things of the mind does not make us soft."

These differences were reflected on every level. The Spartans in their wide-open country were wholly dependent on slaves. Sparta's open borders required that the men remain in constant military preparedness, relegating all productive labor to the unfree. In walled Athens, meanwhile, slavery was already fading. The city produced the first openly abolitionist sentiments in world history.

To the teacher or professor of ancient history, it is all but irresistible, when the lessons turn to Greece, to ask for a show of hands: Whom do you admire more—the Spartans or the Athenians? Invariably, an enthusiastic contingent prefers the Spartans. A few tentative hands rise in support of Athens, but these votes are cast without conviction, as if the students suspect that the teacher has asked a trick question. I suspect that this general Spartaphilia is widespread, even if it hasn't been fully thought out. How many students, given the option, would voluntarily go a year without bathing or changing clothes, all the while dining on black broths and owning nothing, their security entirely dependent on their own strength?

In the end, the Spartan solution to the problem of security—though widely romanticized today—was no solution at all. It was simply not possible to defend a civilized people by demanding that they toughen up by becoming uncivilized. The lure of money and material comfort repeatedly overwhelmed the Spartan constitution, and in the long run, Sparta's enemies would, too.

Yet whatever merits the Athenian model might have had, the citizens themselves could never agree on it. The Athenians were good at nothing if not debating, and for more than fifty years politicians and philosophers argued over the wisdom of fortifications. Plato took the Spartan position. In his eyes, the crumbled walls of Athens, torn down joyfully, to the music of flutes, by the victorious Spartans at the end of the Peloponnesian War, were best left sleeping in the ground. Walls make men soft, he argued, lulling them into a false sense of security and tempting them to seek refuge rather than fight. Aristotle wasn't so sure. He considered it "old-fashioned" to believe like the Spartans that a city could not have both courage and walls.

A middle position soon emerged. The perfect state, concluded Plato, should defend its entire border, not merely its urban core. In the case of Athens, he argued that guards should be sent out to dig moats and build walls to block passes through the mountains in the Attic countryside. Athens should be defended by border walls, defending every entry into Athenian territory. The philosopher knew that this would require fundamental changes in Athenian society. City walls, such as those built by Themistocles and Cimon, were compact and easily accessed by a ready population of instantly available defenders. Border walls were too far from the town center to be defended by ad hoc forces. They necessitated the formation of professional troops who could garrison the border at all times.

For a while at least, Plato had his way. The Athenians fortified the borders of their country rather than their city. Unfortunately—

for historians at least—the Athenian experiment with border walls didn't last long enough to provide any evidence as to the wisdom of the strategy. After the invading Macedonians defeated the defenders of Greece in 338 BC, Athens abruptly rediscovered its ardor for traditional city walls. As one Athenian observed, "Some set themselves to building walls, others to make ditches and palisades. Not a man in the city was idle."

Idleness seems never to have been a problem for wall builders, although some walls were built voluntarily and others at the crack of a whip. In our next chapter, we encounter forced labor on a scale that was never even imagined by the Greeks. An emperor with a magic whip is said to have overseen the construction of China's first border wall. The stories of the First Emperor are often fanciful in that way. But they contribute as much to our understanding of history's greatest wall builders as do the careful records of scribes, and perhaps much more.

"Cries of Pain and Sadness"

CHINA, 214 BC

___

The earliest of the great walls of China has mostly disappeared, washed away by a widow's tears. Or at least that is how the wall's demise was remembered by Chinese peasants. They should know a thing or two about the First Emperor's Long Wall. They built it.

In the original version of the tale, the widow hasn't yet been assigned a name. We know her simply as a woman who is "good at weeping." Her husband has been drafted to work on the Long Wall. He is apparently not a man who is "good at working," as he flees the work site, unable to bear the cruel conditions of life as a conscript laborer. When he returns, he's beaten to death by his supervisor and buried inside the wall. His wife travels far in search of him. Upon learning his fate, she weeps for ten straight days, washing away the wall and revealing the bones of all the workers who had died during its construction.

Many years later, a Chinese monk reflected on the Long Wall: "For a myriad of miles," he wrote, "they built it of men and of mud." His recipe for the wall had only two ingredients, and the first was manpower. The Chinese would never forget how much labor went into their walls. The workers' recollection of their conscription and relocation, their separation from their families, and the cruelty of their supervisors stretches across the nation's collective memory like a scar. According to one legend, the First Emperor multiplied the number of suns so that night would never fall and allow his workers to rest. He is said to have ordered that anyone found napping during the wall's construction should be buried inside it. "The Wall was built with cries of pain and sadness," went one Chinese song. Poets lamented not only the plight of those constructing the wall but also of those on the home front who had to churn out clothes to supply the wall's workers and defenders.

A fifth-century AD imperial adviser, well versed in history but apparently possessing little insight into the mind of the common Chinese worker, once made a lengthy case for new border walls. He concluded his argument on this note: "And because the men would understand the long-term advantages of a wall, they would work without complaining." That was some wishful thinking. In all the folk culture that has come down to us, those workers viewed their great walls as testimony to imperial folly. Why suffer to construct something that will fall on its own? The Chinese worker, like the Mesopotamian, understood the impermanence of work. By the time the first Chinese great walls were being constructed, they'd already built countless lesser walls and seen them washed away or blown away or both. They had their own way of doing things, but the results were scarcely more durable than the mud brick of Mesopotamia. Chinese wall builders typically shoveled windblown silt, or loess, between great wooden frames, then tamped it down layer by layer until it became almost rock hard. Earthen walls such as these made for formidable obstacles—at least to an enemy who lacked the power of weeping—but never possessed the permanence of actual rock.

The myth of the weeping widow washing away the Long Wall was already widespread within two hundred years of the wall's construction. Evidently, the wall had started breaking down long before that. Over the next fifteen hundred years, the Chinese had plenty of opportunities to watch tamped-earth walls disappear into the landscape. An official from the Jin dynasty (AD 1115–1234) once became so frustrated that he urged the court to abandon a wall before it was even finished. "What has begun is already being flattened by sandstorms," he observed, "and bullying the people will simply exhaust them." An adviser to the sixteenth-century Ming, whose subjects were constructing the latest in a long series of Chinese long walls, expressed similar pessimism: "Walls made of sandy earth could easily collapse," he warned. Within a century, most of the Ming walls stood no higher than a man's shoulder. Windblown sand had filled the moats as well.

The Long Wall, and its most famous successor, the Great Wall, had many ancestors. Walls played midwife to civilization in China, much as they had in Greece, Mesopotamia, and Egypt. Insecurity came from the usual quarters, too; the mountains from which China's rivers descended were home to highland barbarians who posed a frequent menace to the cultivators of the valleys, and in time, the barbarians of the steppes were even more menacing. Chinese farmers, just like their counterparts in Egypt and Mesopotamia, converted their capacity for labor into defenses that alleviated the need to remain on a perpetual war footing. Even Neolithic Chinese villagers dug ditches and erected walls around their communities. As the settlements expanded, these defenses grew to impressive dimensions. Third-millennium walls sometimes reached a width of eighty feet.

A breathtaking amount of labor went into the construction of even the earliest Chinese walls. Whole communities pitched in to tamp down layer upon layer of dirt into forms. When they were finished, they had created the germ of a city—a partnership of wall and community that lasted throughout Chinese history. Many centuries later, when they had developed writing, the Chinese would adopt the same symbol for both city and wall. Some centuries after that, they developed the belief that each city had a protective city god—the *Cheng huang shen*. The name literally means "god of the wall and moat."

There is no evidence that the early Chinese resented the building of city walls, just as there is no evidence of such resentment among the Mesopotamians, Egyptians, or Greeks. Where the Chinese eventually distinguished themselves, however, was in the construction of massive *border* walls—the great walls—which inspired a resentment nearly as great as the monuments themselves. This was the sort of greatness that, to borrow a cliché, the Chinese weren't exactly born to but had thrust upon them. The thrusting, in this instance, came from the Eurasian Steppe, where a new way of life emerged in the first millennium BC.

The steppe peoples distinguished themselves from earlier barbarians only in the style of their warfare and the mobility of their lifestyle, but the impact of those innovations was such that the entire map of Eurasian civilization was transformed. Nearly two thousand years elapsed between the first great invasions of the Scythians in the seventh century BC and the Mongol invasions of the thirteenth century AD. During that period, the capacity of steppe peoples to wreak havoc upon Old World civilizations approached the apocalyptic. Vast empires channeled their energies and resources into walling off this threat, but the first to do so was China.

The Chinese had no interest in conquering the steppe. It was as unappealing to them as it was forbidden. They saw the lands to their north as dry, uninhabitable waste covered with towers of ice and snow. Frontier poets spoke of how the wind howled at night, cutting their faces "like a knife." The wasteland to their west was even worse. Authors described it as a thundering abyss, a desert where nothing grew and where floating sands swallowed up animals, vehicles, and men. Geographers confirmed these accounts with their colorful descriptions of Mount Scorched and River Coldhot. They described lakes so hot that the water seemed to boil and sands so hot that birds dared not fly over them. The worst thing about these descriptions was how much truth was in them. Windstorms regularly deposit thick layers of dust in northern China. Even modern journalists have observed mules drowning in the sand. In 1920, an earthquake wiped out 90 percent of the population of Gansu. It was said that the soft soil rolled like waves on the sea.

The burning summers and bitterly cold winters of the lands beyond China did not beckon the builders of walled cities. Pastoralism, a way of life that depended on animals, always made for a better fit. The herds of the pastoralist could take native grasses that were indigestible to humans and convert them into meat and dairy, which provided perfectly edible fats, carbohydrates, and proteins, as well as water. The pastoralist could survive where the farmer could not, but only as long as he kept moving.

Steppe pastoralists roamed constantly in search of untapped pasture and seasonal warmth. They acknowledged no boundaries. Whatever the shortcomings of this lifestyle, its satisfaction was undeniable, for the nomads of the steppe remained for thousands of years stubbornly uninterested in urban development, even in those areas where rivers crossed the steppe, making city life feasible. Theirs was a practical way of life. Pastoral nomadism provided fully for all their needs and offered something else besides: the warriors of the steppe could be organized into the greatest armies on earth.

The rise of the steppe armies began with two prehistoric technological advancements, neither of which is well understood. These were the wheel, which allowed for the unprecedented mobility of a people who could pack all their belongings into wagons, and the chariot, which brought about the first great leap forward in battlefield mobility. Of the first development, which dates to the fourth millennium BC, we know relatively little. However, the second makes for rather interesting prehistory. Charioteers first streamed southward from the steppes in the early second millennium BC, when the steppe hadn't yet been fully transformed by pastoral nomadism and was perhaps as settled as it would ever be. In those days, the homeland of the steppe charioteers was dotted with well-established villages that churned out chariots and weapons in large numbers. Almost every home contained a metallurgical oven. The migrations of the charioteers southward overwhelmed the cities of Central Asia as well as the mysterious civilization of the Indus Valley.

The manufacturing centers of the Bronze Age steppe never grew into cities. Instead, a revolution in warfare rendered the chariot, and the centers that manufactured them, vulnerable and obsolete. At some point, perhaps around 1000 BC, the erstwhile charioteers became adept at fighting from horseback. Scholars still speculate as to what brought about this change—possibly developments in the tack that makes horses more easily controlled or perhaps the invention of more compact bows that could be wielded from horseback. Either way, the effects were revolutionary. Cavalry had every advantage over charioteering. Compared to the clumsy chariot, a cavalry mount provided a faster, more maneuverable firing platform, capable of traveling longer distances and able to traverse rougher terrains. Cavalry dispensed with all the limitations of charioteering: broken wheels and axles, the need for manufacturing centers, the drain on scarce metals, and the necessity for two-man teams in which only one man fights while the other steers. The steppe warriors who entered history in the first millennium BC were therefore, without exception, equestrians.

The spread of cavalry effectively ended the burgeoning village life of the early steppe. All across the vast plains, a single style of life soon prevailed—mobile, horse based, and aggressive. The nomadic equestrians lived in great tents that they packed up and moved whenever the weather worsened or pastures became depleted. Although in some areas they might grow crops on a modest and temporary basis, they were far more efficient in their use of animals. They collected the dung for fuel, the flesh for meat, the hair for clothes, the bones for tools, and the milk for yogurt, cheese, and that infamous fermented beverage known as koumiss. They herded and hunted on horseback, and during wartime, they each gathered several horses to serve as remounts, then formed into massive, self-sustaining forces that could campaign over vast reaches.

From time to time, a charismatic leader would forge the men of several steppe tribes into a horde. It was as close as the premodern world ever came to the atom bomb. These larger armies necessitated rapid, predatory campaigning. Horde formation upset the natural order of pastoralism, in which herds dispersed so that animals didn't compete for pasture. A horde concentrated hundreds of thousands or even millions of animals into a single, massive pasture-devouring entity that had to move constantly to find feed. Unlike civilized militaries, which were tethered to their homelands by supply chains limiting their reach, the horde had no option except to campaign ever farther from its homeland. Moreover, the horde had to travel at a far faster clip than that maintained in peaceful pasturing movements. Killing was a necessity, too: the longer the horsemen campaigned, the more horses died and had to be replaced by seizing the livestock of settled peoples.

By the middle of the first millennium BC, the steppe north of China had given rise to the Hsiung-nu, a nomadic nation of warriors who fought from horseback. The more common English term for Hsiung-nu is Hun.

There may have been fifty times as many Chinese as Huns, but numbers brought the Chinese neither comfort nor security. Hun warriors terrorized the Chinese. Hun chieftains built their status on the economic exploitation of Chinese leaders, who would pay them all manner of tribute in the hopes of being left alone. The Chinese, meanwhile, developed an extensive vocabulary to describe the various sorts of attacks they suffered at the hands of nomads. Autumn was an especially dreadful time for the Chinese—the season of raiding, when nomads would appear from nowhere to strike at workers exposed in the fields.

A delightfully jaunty folk song recalls an early Chinese campaign against the barbarians of the steppe. Almost in passing, it refers to a new feature of the landscape:

> The King had thus charged Nan-Chung:
> "Go and build me a frontier wall."
> So rattled our cars along
> Our war-flags fluttering all.
> The royal command had we
> To wall and defend the north;
> And dread was Nan-Chung to see
> As he swept the Hîn-Yuns forth.
>
> At first when we took the track
> The millets were all in bud;
> And now for the journey back
> 'Tis snowing and all is mud.
> O hard for the King we've slaved,

With never a moment free;
And often for home we craved
But feared that royal decree.

Here, then, is the birth announcement of the first Chinese border
wall. Already the familiar themes are present: the defensive posture,
the exhaustion and homesickness, the dread of a monarch who has
drafted the men for a thankless task. The campaign and perhaps
the song, too, date to around 800 BC. Hardly a word of the lyric
would need to be changed over the next twenty-five hundred years.

Nothing more is known of Nan-Chung's wall. Perhaps it kept
the barbarians out for a while. At the very least, it seems to have set
a precedent. During China's Warring States period (471–221 BC),
border walls proliferated. Walls separated Chinese from Chinese
as well as from Huns and other barbarians. Several kingdoms built
walls over three hundred miles long. The new fortifications were
on a scale the world had never seen, dwarfing even the defenses
Nebuchadnezzar had built for Babylonia. Yet they were but a prelude to the immense works of the First Emperor.

The First Emperor, as he was known, cut quite a swath through
history. Robert Ripley, writing more than two thousand years later
and with no special concern for accuracy, even maintained that you
could see that swath from the moon. He was wrong about that. You
can't even see much of it from earth. The First Emperor's Long
Wall survives only in fragments, and even these have been eaten
away by erosion and overgrown with weeds. It was not, as Ripley
believed, the Great Wall, which also can't be seen from the moon.

A brief entry on the Long Wall might read as follows: Having ruthlessly put down his domestic rivals, the First Emperor
(r. 220–210 BC) turned to the problem of the steppe. Employing
barbarian mercenaries, he campaigned into the lands slightly north
of the preexisting Warring States walls. There, in those profitless
regions that had never been coveted by the Chinese but that made
strategic sense as a site for a defensible boundary, he established a
fortified border for the state of China.

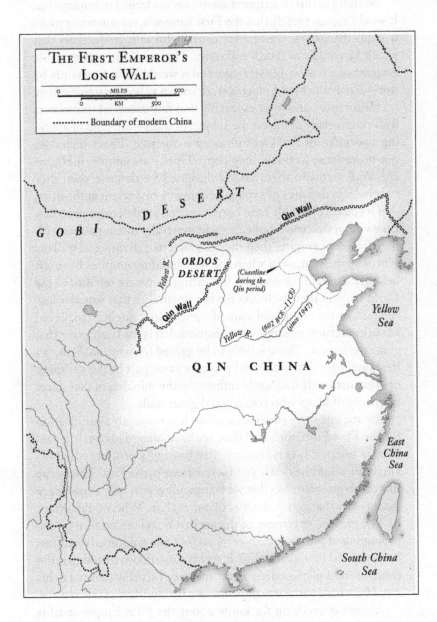

The First Emperor's
Long Wall

MILES   500

KM   500

-------- Boundary of modern China

G O B I   D E S E R T

Qin Wall

ORDOS
DESERT

Yellow R.

Qin Wall

(Coastline
during the
Qin period)

Yellow
Sea

Yellow R.   (602 BCE–11 CE)   (since 1947)

QIN   CHINA

East
China
Sea

South China
Sea

Nothing in this description seems, on the face of it, implausible. It would appear merely that the First Emperor, commanding more workers than soldiers, elected to overwhelm with productivity that which he could not defeat militarily. This would be a reasonable account of a reasonable strategy, and it would almost certainly be true—if only the First Emperor were known to be a reasonable man.

Historians—and most especially that tiny subset of researchers who occasionally opine on the subject of walls—are fond of applying a peculiar form of Occam's razor to the past. That which does not make sense to them, they deny. Thus, for example, if Hadrian's Wall seems to them poorly designed for defense, then they conclude, in defiance of explicit statements by ancient authorities, that it couldn't possibly have been intended for defensive purposes. Likewise, if defensive policies seem generally incompatible with their vision of empire, then they characterize all imperial walls as acts of aggression, even when the wall-building empires have left behind mountains of evidence indicating they were terrified of the world beyond their walls. As for the possibility that superstition, religion, or the emotional state of some despot might have played a role in decision making, this is dismissed. It is the latter error that concerns us now. There is little to be gained from rationalizing an irrational past. The irrational played a great part in the antiquity of every nation. It frequently influenced the thinking of that select fraternity of kings who constructed great walls.

An ancient story provides a much less reasonable justification for the First Emperor's wall than we have offered above. It is said that he ordered it constructed after hearing a prophecy that his kingdom would be destroyed by northern barbarians. This is the sort of inconvenient fact that we commonly report only in passing, a quaint story that gets in the way of our analysis. Who would believe it? The greatest enterprise of the ancient world undertaken on the prompting of some soothsayer? A project that consumed countless lives inspired by superstition? It seems superfluous to add that the emperor misunderstood his oracle and that it actually referred to his son, Hu, whose name was the same as a Chinese term for *barbarian*.

Almost everything we know about the First Emperor adds credence to the possibility that an entire nation was once put to work on an irrational whim. Like Nebuchadnezzar a lavish builder, the First Emperor had fantastic ambitions and a transparent contempt for those laborers who enabled him to realize them. At his Chinese Babylon, he had bells and statues made from the melted-down weapons of the armies he had defeated. Outside his palace, he constructed a sort of Disneyland of the Damned, where his legions of workers reproduced the palaces of vanquished kings. Each palace featured entertainments provided by captured musicians and dancers.

Megalomania gave rise to a consuming interest in the supernatural. The First Emperor surrounded himself with wizards and soothsayers. When a court magician suggested to him that he separate himself from his subjects, he resolved that none of them should ever see him again or even know where he was sleeping. He constructed 270 palaces near the capital, all connected by walled roadways that allowed him to move secretly from one palace to another, keeping one step ahead of assassins. Immortality became his obsession.

The First Emperor waged a private war against that same impermanence that the builders of his palaces and walls took for granted. He consulted prophets and alchemists and sponsored overseas expeditions in search of an elixir of life. To extend his life he drank poisonous concoctions of wine, honey, and mercury. Eventually, he took solace in the hope of a life after death. He ordered the construction of a massive, booby-trapped tomb, stocked with armies of terra-cotta soldiers and concubines. Rivers of mercury circulated around his tomb, which even today shows high concentrations of the element in the soil. He was not, the founder of China, a rational man.

The First Emperor brooded also on the immortality of his kingdom, and toward that end, rationally or irrationally, he built the Long Wall. These fortifications, the first built for the defense of all of China, would gradually come to define the nation. Built by soldiers, prisoners, vagabonds, and anyone else who could be pressed into service, the Long Wall stretched some 1,775 kilometers (1,100 miles) by conservative estimate, 3,100 kilometers (1,900 miles), or even 10,000 kilometers (6,200 miles) by more generous measures. Reputedly tireless, the First Emperor expected similar endurance from his builders. The workers shoveled and pounded earth across mountains and plains. In some areas, they toted tons of yellow loess up the mountainsides; in others, they bullied stone into place or made bricks. Where there was bedrock, they carved trenches and laid deep foundations. All the while, they were lucky to receive any supplies. According to one report, out of 182 loads of rice sent to the workers, only one finally arrived, such being the danger of their forward position.

Meng Tian, the general who supervised the construction of the Long Wall, later grieved that, in carrying out the project, he had "cut the veins of the earth." The thought made him suicidal. As for those who had followed his orders to exhaustion, they were relocated to one of the forty-four newly built walled cities, whose job of guarding the borders amounted to, in the words of China's Grand Historian, a life sentence. Many workers were force to toil away in the arid Ordos, a desolate loop in the Yellow River where the First Emperor established cities that were inevitably buried by sand dunes. A million or more hands participated in the construction of the Long Wall, and a million colonists were required to maintain it and supply the soldiers stationed there. Thus began a near two-thousand-year obligation to support China's massive defenses against the steppes.

When it was all done, the First Emperor memorialized his achievement with a monument that reads much like the commemoration of Shulgi's Wall of the Land in Mesopotamia. The people, he wrote, "enjoy calm and repose; arms are no longer necessary and each is tranquil in his dwelling. The Sovereign Emperor has pacified in turns the four ends of the earth." By then, Shulgi's wall was nearly two thousand years old, and tranquillity had settled permanently on the uninhabited ruins of Ur.

Chinese tradition turned more and more negative toward the First Emperor after his death. Each succeeding generation embroidered his legend with new myths to illustrate his tyrannical character. Historians ridiculed his appearance and his birth. They described him as stingy, cringing, and without grace. Perhaps their attacks amounted to nothing more than revenge for the First Emperor's having burned the books of history and buried alive any scholars who continued to discuss them. But as if this were not enough, they were also convinced that the Long Wall had been for nothing.

The Long Wall did not solve the problem of the Huns. Perhaps it was simply not long enough. If anything, the attacks worsened. Struggling to maintain their way of life in the face of implacable Hun aggression, the Chinese soon fell prey to pessimism and concluded that all offensive operations against steppe peoples would end in futility. A second-century BC scholar criticized his emperor for attacking the Huns. A nation too fond of fighting, he insisted, will perish, as all military endeavors are ultimately regretted. He reminded the emperor of earlier campaigns where untold numbers of soldiers fought in wastes and wildernesses while the rest of China toiled to exhaustion to supply them. The roads were filled with the dying.

One imperial adviser after another preached the hopelessness of retaliating against the horsemen of the steppe. "If we send parties of lightly equipped soldiers deep into their territory," wrote one imperial adviser, "our men will soon run out of food, and if we try to send provisions after them, the baggage train will never reach them in time." Like other civilized peoples, the Chinese glumly concluded that the barbarians were simply superior to their own soldiers. "They can withstand the wind and rain, fatigue, hunger, and thirst," wrote one official in 169 BC. "Chinese soldiers are not so good." The Huns, he added, could even shoot arrows while riding over dangerous, sloping terrain. Another adviser wrote that the Huns swarmed like beasts and dispersed like birds: "Trying to catch them is like grabbing at a shadow."

Emperors occasionally attempted to fight back against the raiders, but such efforts generally bore out the pessimistic predictions of the Cassandras in their cabinets. As often as not these campaigns ended in disaster. In 200 BC, an emperor's troops blundered into the steppe during winter, and a quarter of his soldiers lost fingers to frostbite—no small loss for an army of crossbowmen. Similarly, a late second-century BC campaign provoked the Huns to launch raids of such severity that the cost of sending Chinese armies to chase them back all but exhausted the empire.

Eventually, the emperors settled on two strategies for defending the people within the country's borders. Neither came particularly cheap, but such were the costs of trying to establish civilization in full view of the steppe. The first strategy was to buy off the barbarians. This became known as the "peace and friendship" policy and consisted of appeasing the Huns with annual gifts of silk, wine, grain, and food. Occasionally, the Chinese would rebrand this scheme to preserve the myth of imperial dominance. They insisted that neighboring barbarians become tributary states—an odd way of describing a situation in which the Chinese themselves forked over the tribute.

A human face is attached to China's appeasement of the Huns. Alongside the vast bribes of money and commodities were added Chinese princesses, packed up and shipped off to barbarian chieftains, their freedom sacrificed for the security of their country. They became the tragic figures of Chinese poetry, whose verses depicted them leaving never to return:

> Full in her face, the desert sand;
> Full in her hair the wind
> Her penciled brows have lost their black,
> The rouge has melted from her cheek.

The princess Wang Zhaojun, bartered to the Huns in 33 BC, became a beloved character in Chinese folklore. In second-century songs, she is the symbol of Chinese civilization itself; she commits suicide after her son informs her he would rather be Hun than Chinese. Hundreds of poems and plays eventually centered on her apocryphal stand against barbarism.

The emperors never fully abandoned their strategy of appeasement. Generations of Chinese silk workers, farmers, tailors, and goldsmiths toiled away only to see the fruits of their labor handed over to bullies. Money that might otherwise have been used to patronize art, literature, theater, or architecture was siphoned away and melted down for the crude bling of the barbarians.

The alternative to outright bribery—border walls—came no less cheaply. It was, like appeasement, the strategy of a people who would rather work than fight, continuously forced on them by those who would rather fight than work. Since at least 10,000 BC, the world had been gradually sorting itself into two camps: those who lived behind walls and those who roamed freely outside them. The builders and the barbarians were implacably opposed, representing not just two sides of every wall but two sides of a revolution in human society. It was, in many ways, the seminal moment in the history of civilization, but we can only understand it by examining the lives of those who had no part of it. We turn next to the world of those who built no walls at all.

Wallers and Warriors:
Life outside the Walls

EURASIA, 2000 BC–AD 1800

The great border walls had set an inharmonious world into stark relief, casting it into regions of light and shadow, like some dramatic chiaroscuro painting by Caravaggio. On one side of the walls were the builders, their history illuminated by every sort of literature. On the other were the people without any history. They fortified neither their borders nor their settlements, and appearing out of the darkness, they terrified the builders.

In the early sixth century AD, a Chinese general spoke on the topic of walls. Living in an era when borders were being fortified almost around the world, he was convinced of their necessity. Walls, he felt, were the only way to separate "those who eat grain, live in towns and houses, wear silk and walk like scholars from those of wild appearance, who wear wool and drink blood, who live with birds and beasts." This segregation was all well and good except when the Chinese found themselves in need of troops. Then they hired as many of the wild-looking, wool-wearing barbarians as they could.

Roman attitudes toward the peoples beyond their borders were equally ambivalent. By far, the bulk of Roman authors, safely ensconced in a walled capital deep in the heartland of a civilized empire, admired the unwalled outsider. They viewed peoples such as the Scythians and Germans as virtuous exemplars of the natural life—chaste, moral, and generally uncorrupted by the vices of civilization. Rarely, an author such as Ovid would be given a closer view of these outsiders, and this would prompt him to sing a rather different tune. Either way, the Romans agreed with the Chinese: the barbarians were best kept out—unless they could be recruited into the army.

The Chinese and the Romans were not the first to distinguish between those who built walls and those who lived outside them. Bronze Age writers had reduced the differences to symbols. To represent urban communities, they might draw a cross inside a circle, signifying streets intersecting within city walls. Those who lived outside city walls were generally designated in a more pejorative fashion—perhaps by images of the weapons they carried or the mountains from whence they came. In time, virtually every language spoken in the ancient Near East had developed a vocabulary to describe the unwalled outsider. A strange pattern presented itself: namely, if the original meaning of a word referred to nomadism—a way of life manifestly antithetical to walls—then the term inevitably became associated with raiding, robbery, and other criminal activity. If the original meaning denoted criminality, then it quickly acquired an association with nomadism.

Across Europe, Asia, and North Africa, authors described the people outside the walls in much the same terms: crude, tough, hardy, warlike, and aggressive, useful as allies but terrible as enemies. Even the contrarian Spartans, ruminating on walls, concluded, not too differently from the Chinese general, that walls bred scholars who were accustomed to soft clothes and fine buildings. The Spartans had, of course, taken up the other side of the debate. They regarded the cultured inhabitants of walled cities as weaklings and romanticized the primitive lifestyle of their unwalled ancestors. Otherwise, consensus prevailed.

It may seem incredible that the presence or absence of walls should render some men more warlike than others, yet support for this omnipresent ancient thesis is not lacking. We need only observe what happens when a people make the transition from unwalled to walled. We might consider, for example, the curious case of the Gauls.

When the Romans first encountered the Gauls in the fourth century BC, they considered the warlike northerners more like beasts than men. Polybius wrote that the Gauls slept on leaves and lived in unwalled villages where they knew nothing of art or science but much of war. A reputation for truculence and physical prowess—and an abundance of men with no skills other than fighting—made the Gauls attractive mercenaries, drawing them ever deeper into Italy, but this caused more problems than it solved, as the Gallic warriors inevitably looked with contempt upon their employers, who huddled behind city walls, unwilling to fight their own battles. When Roman ambassadors inquired of the Gauls by what right they had dispossessed Italian peoples of their lands, the Gauls replied that they carried their right at the tip of their swords.

In the early fourth century, the Gauls marched on Rome. Peasants fled their arrival, and nearby towns retreated behind their walls, but the Gauls ignored all targets of opportunity en route to the city. Roman leaders hastily levied troops and marched out to confront the Gauls at the river Allia, eight miles from the city. There they suffered one of the worst defeats in Roman history. No sooner had the Gauls attacked than the main body of the Roman army began to dissolve. Scores of Roman soldiers fled to the walls of nearby Veii. Others were cut down fleeing or drowned trying to swim across the Tiber.

The news from Allia generated hysteria in Rome. Most of the commoners fled the city altogether. The remaining able-bodied men and their families sought refuge in the citadel. Only the older folk, many dressed in ancient robes once worn by some ancestral magistrate, stayed in their homes, awaiting death. The Gauls, entering the city unopposed, rooted about for booty, a bit spooked by the spectacle of the elderly in their finery, until finally an old Roman broke the spell by striking a Gaul with a mace. The quiet plundering of the city then turned into a massacre. The Gauls looted and burned Rome for several days, during which time the Gallic leader Brennus reportedly uttered his famous dictum, "Woe to the conquered."

The defeat at Allia and the sack of Rome traumatized the Romans. The Gauls became a whisper on their lips, memorialized forever after in the Latin language by a phrase symbolizing the panic brought on by barbarian invasion: *metus Gallicus*, "dread of the Gauls." The survivors of the horror responded in the usual manner of civilized people recovering from barbarian invasion: they built walls. Rome's new fortifications took full advantage of the region's hilly terrain, stretching some seven miles around the city and reaching a height of over thirty feet. Aside from building walls, the Romans also took measures to ensure that they would never again be vulnerable to attacks by northern barbarians and that, above all, complacency never take root. Toward that end, they established an annual remembrance of Allia, a somber holiday during which no sacrifices could occur. Any subsequent appearances of Gauls resulted in a declaration of *tumultus Gallicus*, which required cessation of all regular business and a general mobilization of able-bodied men.

Three hundred years later, the Romans and Gauls met again, but on starkly different terms. By the time of Caesar's Gallic campaign in the mid-first century BC, the Gauls no longer even resembled the wandering cattlemen and warriors who'd once laid Rome low. The first-century Gauls lived in walled towns, called *oppida*, and had even developed a national technique for wall building. In every way, they had become more like the Romans: settled, agricultural, and urban. They lived in states that minted coins, maintained written documents, took censuses, collected taxes, held elections, and conducted trials. They built roads and bridges. The strongest evidence of their transformation can be seen in their attitudes toward foreigners: in the manner of wall builders everywhere, the Gauls of the first century lived in fear of their more primitive German neighbors. They competed for the services of German mercenaries who boasted of never sleeping under a roof. It comes as no great surprise, then, when we read accounts of Gallic men forming a civilized phalanx in the forum of their city, and even less surprise that the Romans should prevail over such foes. Caesar reduced the Gauls city by city, standard work for a Mediterranean army. Who's afraid of Gauls with walls?

The transformation of the Gauls was not unique. It may have been the common course for every ancient culture that developed civilization. Certainly, the Spartans believed that people became less warlike as they became more dependent on fortifications. Practically every Spartan wit employed some form of the quip in which one pointed at a walled city and asked, "What sort of women live there?" Only recently, however, have modern researchers started to get the joke.

The past twenty years have seen a revolution in our understanding of prehistoric and primitive peoples. A deeply entrenched dogma has been overturned, upsetting careers, touching nerves, and rendering obsolete decades of tainted research. The revolution commenced in the 1990s, when anthropologists such as Lawrence Keeley first openly attacked the commonly held and seemingly innocuous belief that warfare began with the walled cities of civilization. Keeley demonstrated that, for decades, scholars had ignored, explained away, or actively suppressed any evidence of war before or outside civilization. The belief in primitive pacifism had become, like all academic orthodoxies, an article of faith, fiercely defended by its high priests, who controlled hiring and publishing decisions. The paradigm shift did not come easily—Napoleon Chagnon was once physically attacked at a conference for daring to present firsthand observations of primitive tribesmen at war—but, in the end, all but the most die-hard proponents of the former dogma had been forced to concede to the voluminous evidence arrayed against them. Archaeologists everywhere, it seems, had been collecting piles of arrowheads, spear tips, mace heads, cracked skulls, burned settlements, and mutilated skeletons. It was only a matter of compiling it all. Yet Keeley, Chagnon, LeBlanc, and the other revolutionaries were concerned chiefly with anthropological rather than historical data, and even their evidence may have underestimated the centrality of warfare in the unwalled world.

The voice of the unwalled is perhaps first heard directly in Irish poems that originated as oral compositions around the time of Christ and were eventually transcribed by Christian monks. With these works we can finally glimpse something of that barbarian world that so terrified the civilized, causing them to live "like birds in a cage," behind walls guarded mostly by other barbarians. The Irish bards make no apologies for cattle raids and killings. They celebrate them. Their tales divulge a chaotic world of armies and herds, where kings and queens boast of their wealth in soldiers, cattle, and chariots, and wars are incited by cattle raids. The bards describe every manner of maiming and death in frank and sometimes scatological detail. In sharp contrast to the bloodless battle accounts of the Greeks, Romans, and Chinese, the lurid verse of the Irish tells of bloody sinews, smashed skulls, broken bones, and geysers of dung.

For the ancient Irish, who had neither cities nor walls, war was a way of life. Irish boys, much like Spartan youth, left their families to learn to fight. Even before puberty, they were organized into troops. The Irish hero Cúchulainn studied the warrior's arts as a child, when he mastered a long list of "warrior's feats," all with comically descriptive titles: the thunder feat, the feats of the sword edge and the sloped shield, the spurt of speed, the stroke of precision, the heroic salmon-leap, and so forth. These were the only things the young Irishman needed to know.

Socialized to think of themselves only as warriors, young Irish spoiled for battle. Their petty kings and queens provided them with ample combat opportunities. They were routinely roused to war by minor insults, lust, or simply greed for a fine cow that belonged to another man's herd. It wasn't that the Irish didn't seek peace. They never even considered the concept. Life for them was a series of raids and counterraids, and if a young warrior was lucky, he might return home from one enriched by cattle, gold, or, even better, some skull or other trophy proving that he'd fought well.

The Old English poetry of the early Middle Ages reflected a world not too far removed from that of the ancient Irish. Who can forget the death of Beowulf? The grasping old bastard had but one dying wish: to see for a final time the treasure he'd acquired by killing a dragon. His death would leave his loyal Geats in a terrible position, weakened and in possession of a pile of loot that would draw enemies like flies, but none of this concerned him. He thought only of the silver and precious gems.

Beowulf's values were the values of unwalled peoples across Eurasia. Raiding and warfare were viewed with amoral complacency, devoid of any ideological preference for peace or nonviolence. "Born in a tent, die in a battle," goes a Qashqai saying. The Bedouins of the Arabian desert—another unwalled people who inspired their share of walls built by others—spoke with similar matter-of-factness: "Raids are our agriculture" went a common dictum. The bulk of Bedouin culture consisted of poetry that boasted of their raids:

> We came upon the host in the morning, and they were like a
>   flock of sheep on whom falls the ravening wolf. . . .
> We fall on them with white steel ground to keenness;
> We cut them to pieces until they were destroyed
> And we carried off their women on the saddles behind us, with
>   their cheeks bleeding, torn in anguish by their nails.

Warfare did not merely exist in the unwalled world; it defined it. To a degree entirely alien to the Mesopotamians, Greeks, or Chinese, the preparation of young men for war was the dominant concern. Among the ancient Germans, for example, naked youths learned to dance while swords and lances were thrust at them. Once a boy had attained the age of manhood, he was rewarded with weapons of his own. He then went about armed as a matter of routine. German men transacted business armed and even used their weapons to signal their support of proposals at public assemblies.

The pressure on younger men to prove themselves in battle was tremendous. If a young German male found his tribe too long at peace with its neighbors, he sought opportunities to fight for other tribes. He might also seek his fortune as a mercenary in service of a civilized state. In one Germanic tribe, the males allowed their hair and beard to grow uncut until they had killed a man in battle. Shaving over the slain, the young warrior finally revealed his true face to his victim, only then having proven himself worthy of birth. Some German youth took the custom further, committing themselves to wearing a symbol of servility until they had killed a man.

The male of an unwalled society, training always for war, learned no other skills. "A German," noted one Roman author, "is not so easily prevailed upon to plough the land and wait patiently for harvest as to challenge a foe and earn wounds for his reward. He thinks it tame and spiritless to accumulate slowly by the sweat of his brow what can be got quickly by the loss of a little blood." All real work was left to women and the elderly.

Germans weren't alone in their expectation that all young males become warriors. Huns reputedly slashed the faces of newborn babies, teaching them to endure pain before they were even allowed to eat. Scythian men celebrated their first kill by drinking some of the victim's blood. Lusitanian youths without other prospects would take up their arms and form into large robber bands.

A Chinese author lived for a while among the Huns. He was astonished to learn that warfare was their only occupation. He observed that the best food and drink were reserved for those still young and strong enough to fight and that the Huns regularly practiced their riding and shooting. Other Chinese descriptions of the Huns could be curt: The Huns have no trade but battle and courage, wrote one author. They live not by plowing but by killing, wrote another. They take robbing and stealing as their business, wrote a third. There is no reason to question the accuracy of these statements. Of the two great steppe nations who succeeded the Huns, neither the Turks nor the Mongols even possessed a word for "soldier." The word for "man" sufficed.

Material possessions were few in the world beyond the walls, and weapons were prized above all things. Scythians swore oaths by dipping an array of arms into a blood-infused bowl of wine. Other possessions advertised success in battle. The Gauls, for example, collected heads. They returned home from battle with skulls dangling from the necks of their horses, then nailed the dreadful trophies over the doors of their homes. In the case of a particularly impressive kill, a Gaul might embalm the victim's head in cedar oil so that he could pull it out from time to time and show it off to dinner guests. The Irish shared this head-hunting habit. Scythians did, too. They presented the heads of the men they'd killed to the king, who checked their contributions before granting them a share of the loot. Some warriors preserved the skulls, cleaned them out, and used them as drinking cups. Those with gold might gild the skull. Chinese accounts of the Huns parallel Greek descriptions of Scythians almost exactly.

The desire for walls is not innate to the species; the need for security is. Reading the accounts that the ancient Mesopotamians, Greeks, Romans, and Chinese wrote about those outsiders they considered barbarians, it is evident that a great revolution had already split human societies. That divergence first appeared late in prehistory, just before the development of writing, when a small subset of peoples responded strategically to their insecurity by surrounding themselves with ditches, palisades, or mounds, then finally walls. To follow only their story and speak of the "birth of civilization" is to ignore, for most of history, the rest of the planet. Outside the clusters of walled cities—and, eventually, outside the great border walls that contained those clusters—other peoples continued to live in unfortified settlements, if they settled at all. The outsiders dwelled in an open and therefore dangerous world. Survival, in their eyes, depended solely on the skill, fitness, and courage of their "walls of men."

Unlike the wall builders, the outsiders didn't have the luxury of distinguishing between soldier and civilian. Every male was born to the warrior's life, and the measure of a man was his skill in battle. The relative impoverishment of the warrior societies—that dearth of cultural productivity that has generally struck civilized societies as "primitive"—stemmed directly from this limitation of men's roles. The warrior's disdain for what he perceived as "women's work" exacerbated this cultural impoverishment by forcing women to concentrate solely on domestic and agricultural chores.

The wallers were altogether different. If the building of walls turned men into women, as the Spartans alleged, then it was only because the women had previously done all the work and now the men pitched in, too. The more the men took up the life of labor, the less they wanted of war. They resigned themselves to long days of stacking bricks or tamping dirt because it kept war at a distance. They became like the Chinese, who, as a matter of philosophy, preferred civil and literary virtues (*wen*) to martial ones (*wu*).

If the barbarians could have read the books of the wallers, they might have noticed that even the finest military minds, such as China's celebrated Sun Tzu, valued clever strategizing over heroism, attaching little importance to warrior qualities such as courage and skill. Whereas warrior cultures celebrated deeds of valor in their songs, the histories of the wallers recoiled from providing detailed descriptions of military encounters, frustrating modern researchers with a studied silence, the "ellipsis of battle." Of the ancient honor of soldiering, little remained. The Chinese pressed vagabonds and criminals into service, drawing soldiers from the dregs of society—that is, from those who had no proper civilian vocation. As one Chinese proverb went, "One doesn't use the best metal to make nails, nor the best men to make soldiers." Other communities of wallers relied on citizen-soldiers—individuals such as Socrates or Aeschylus, who fought for Athens—but these weren't warriors, either. Socrates was, after all, principally a philosopher and Aeschylus a playwright. As soldiers, they were part-timers, for whom war was a temporary distraction from their true callings. That their callings had little to do with either warfare or agriculture only demonstrates how quickly the labor of the wallers had diversified. Freed from the expectation of lifelong soldiering, the male inhabitants of walled communities had learned to dabble in other pursuits. They had become scribes, authors, architects, mathematicians, playwrights, poets, philosophers, actors, athletes, and archivists. To the extent that they participated in necessary chores, they potentially freed up women for other occupations as well.

Societies of wall builders arose independently around the world, leaving behind concrete symbols of this revolution in human society. Yet the walls also stigmatized the builders in the eyes of the warriors, who questioned the courage and manliness of those who chose to live in cages. Over time, the gulf between those who would build walls and those who would roam freely across a world without boundaries only grew wider. The coexistence of workers and warriors was never peaceful. Soon that conflict spawned the great border walls that would give form to much of the modern world.

PART TWO

THE GREAT
AGE OF WALLS

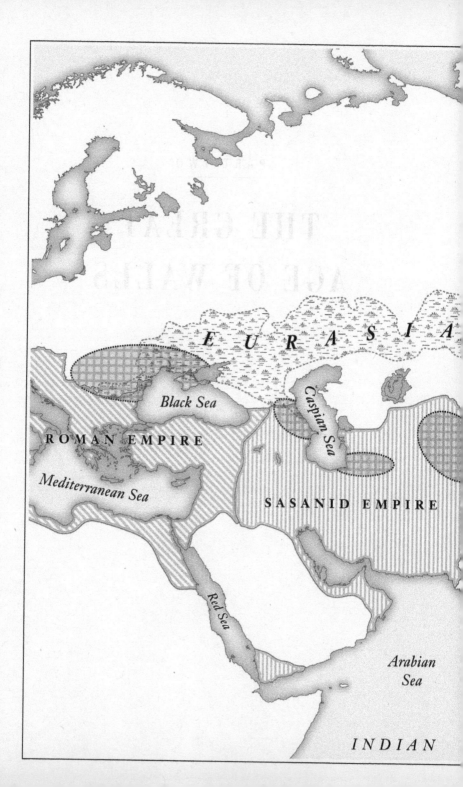

EURASIA

Black Sea

Caspian Sea

ROMAN EMPIRE

Mediterranean Sea

SASANID EMPIRE

Red Sea

Arabian
Sea

INDIAN

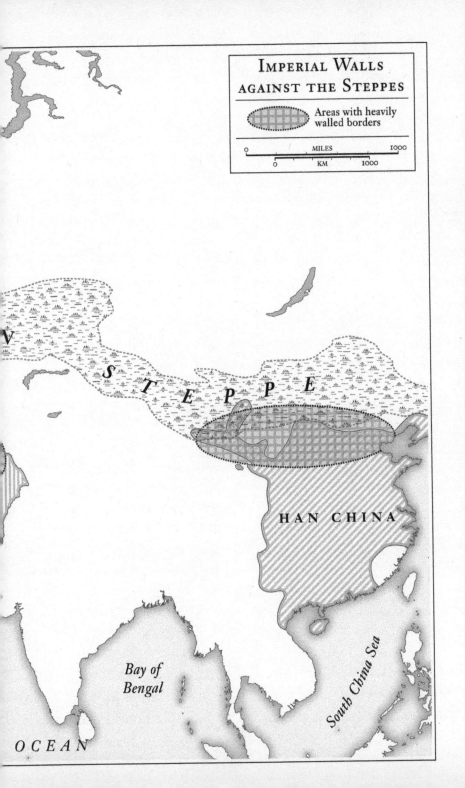

Areas with heavily
walled borders

MILES 1000

KM 1000

STEPPE

HAN CHINA

Bay of
Bengal

South China Sea

OCEAN

Prologue to the Great Age of Walls: Alexander's Gates

TIMELESS FOLKLORE

When the author of Genesis included a certain "Magog" among the descendants of Noah, he didn't choose to elaborate on that particular name. Magog appeared only as an entry on a list, no different from any of the other obscure individuals who typically populate biblical genealogies, tempting us to skip ahead to the more interesting sections. Was it Noah's fault that one of his grandsons hadn't amounted to much? However, scripture abhors a vacuum, and by the time the prophet Ezekiel introduced "Gog from Magog" in the early sixth century BC, Magog had expanded his reputation considerably, having apparently spawned a warrior who was destined to destroy Israel and do battle with God. According to Ezekiel, Gog would someday come from the north with a great horde of horsemen, like a cloud covering the earth. He would "go up against the land of unwalled villages . . . fall upon the quiet people who live in safety, all of them living without walls, and having no bars or gates . . . to seize spoil and carry off plunder."

Clearly, the Apocalypse was no time to live in an unwalled village.

As for the horsemen from the north, they had already arrived, although not yet in cloudlike numbers. A few decades before Ezekiel's birth, invaders from the steppe had ridden across the Assyrian Empire all the way to Egypt. The prophet was still a child when the horsemen culminated their adventure by sacking the Assyrian capital of Nineveh in 612 BC. Years later, the historical shock of

77

that episode still reverberated in his text. Ezekiel translated the events of his childhood into disturbing visions that profoundly influenced later authors. Gog *from* Magog metamorphosed inexplicably into Gog *and* Magog, and the ominous pair subsequently began appearing variously as individuals, lands, or peoples in rabbinical literature and Jewish apocryphal works. The decisive moment for this growing legend occurred in the first century AD, when the Jewish historian Josephus equated *Magogites* with *Scythians*, the Greek term for the horsemen of the steppe. Josephus then made an assertion that has echoed throughout world literature ever since: the Scythians, he said, had raided and plundered the kingdom of the Medes after a king near the Caspian Sea had allowed them to pass through the iron gates that Alexander had built.

The legends of Alexander on the one hand and the Bible on the other had long fought over the same turf. The merger of the two traditions, now united by the notion that Alexander had constructed an iron barrier against the pseudobiblical Magogites, probably occurred before Josephus put it in writing. Civilized peoples had learned they needed a hero, and Alexander, in much-revised form barely resembling the actual man, fit the suit. But how could the mortal Alexander have hoped to defend civilization for all time? Only by building a wall, apparently.

The tale of Alexander's wall would expand dramatically after its first timid appearance in the writings of Josephus. In the 390s AD, Huns rode through the Caucasus Mountains and launched devastating raids into Mesopotamia and Syria. In the aftermath of this catastrophe—and the equally catastrophic appearance of Huns on the edges of the Roman Empire—Alexander's biographers began seriously embroidering their accounts. A messianic aura soon shone over the putative defender of civilization. In an anonymous Christian variation of the popular *Alexander Romance*, Alexander is depicted with divine horns. Gog and Magog, meanwhile, have become kings of the Huns, endowed with all the standard characteristics of steppe horsemen. Like most of the feared barbarians of antiquity, they are given blue eyes and red hair. Their armies arrive on horseback, Amazonian women at their side, towering over civilized folk. Their customs are abhorrent.

They are unclean and clad only in skin. They feast on corpses and blood. Upon receiving reports of the beastly duo, Alexander commands a great iron door be built in the Caucasus Mountains. Three thousand blacksmiths and three thousand brass workers toil on the gate. With its completion, Alexander has shut out the North Wind along with the Huns. On the gate, he inscribes a prophecy: In 826 years, his wall will fail and the Huns will conquer both Persia and Rome. After 940 years, the forces of God, civilization, and Alexander will finally triumph over the Huns in a great apocalyptic war.

The tale of Alexander's apocalyptic struggle against barbarian horsemen threatening to overwhelm civilization spread to every corner of the Old World, gradually becoming one of the most widely told stories in all of world literature. In the Quran, Alexander became Dhul-Qarnayn, "the two-horned one," who builds an iron barrier against Yajuj and Majuj (Gog and Magog) in the space between two mountains. Persian artists depicted genies assisting Alexander in the construction of the wall. So great was the fascination with Alexander's Gates that a ninth-century caliph once dispatched a scholar all the way to northern China on a quest for the mythical barrier. Sallam the Interpreter traveled three thousand miles before he reached China's walls, and when he saw them, he concluded that Alexander's work remained intact. The myth of Alexander's Gates also made its mark in medieval European literature. European geographers, relying primarily on imagination and rumor, hastened to locate the structure. Around 1300, the Hereford Map authoritatively described the land beyond the Gates, where "everything is horrible, more than believed," and the inhabitants, who will escape their confinement in the age of the Antichrist, are the cannibalistic sons of Cain. Today, a rousing interest in Dhul-Qarnayn, Gog and Magog, and Alexander's Gates still animates pockets of the internet.

The myths of Alexander's Gates arose out of a protracted period in the history of civilization when steppe horsemen seemed the very embodiment of the Apocalypse. No city, no matter how magnificent its ramparts, could fend off such a threat. Even the great empires shuddered. The world outside their borders had become, for them, a vast no-go zone. From roughly the time of China's First Emperor to that of the Kievan prince Vladimir I (r. 980–1015), a span of over a thousand years, the great Eurasian states from China to Rome focused mostly on defense. They repeatedly reined in their ambitions and retreated behind massive border walls.

How great was the fear of the nomadic horsemen of the Eurasian Steppe? Here it would be appropriate to cite an impressive fact: the total length of all the walls built to defend against the steppe peoples. This number cannot be known. Few ancient long walls have survived to any appreciable degree. Those that have endured are often unidentifiable or known only to locals who themselves misunderstand the ruins on their land. Archaeological work has been desultory, and interpretations are frequently distorted by feelings of national pride. Yet the sources we do possess permit us to make a rather astonishing statement about the scale of the defensive efforts: virtually every potential opening along the roughly five-thousand-mile border separating the Eurasian Steppe to the north and the zone of urban civilization to the south was, at one time or another, walled off. And even this statement fails to account for the twists and turns of geography that necessitated those walls extend for more than five thousand miles. Of course, we must make some exceptions. Where the coastlines of the Black Sea and the Caspian Sea bound the steppe, there was no need for walls. Likewise, the desolate highlands of Tibet and certain desert regions didn't require fortifications. Everywhere else, however, the traveling horseman would have found his way south blocked by high walls guarded by imperial soldiers. The Two-Horned One had done his work; Gog and Magog were shut out.

The barriers of the Great Age of Walls rank among the most important structures ever built. They fostered the development of those three vast regions that would one day become China, the Islamic world, and the West. They shaped interactions with steppe peoples, who would affect the historical trajectories of all three regions. They did *not*, however, divide the civilizations of Eurasia, which never built walls against one another. In fact, the story of the age begins, quite unexpectedly, with the construction of walls that were designed to encourage reaching out, rather than turning inward.

Walls Connect Eurasia

The greatest long walls in Central Asia were built and abandoned long ago, blasted away by wind and sand until they became nearly indiscernible. They protected a region so desolate and so dangerous that the wall builders finally moved on with hardly a backward look, leaving behind only garbage, abandoned homes, and the desiccated vestiges of farms and orchards deprived of life when the irrigation ditches filled with sand. In this forsaken land, where the settlements were hardly more than way stations for travelers moving swiftly on, there was little to defend except a route that passed through hell. But a route is something worth defending, or at least this one was, and so hell was provided with a wall, establishing a secure corridor between distant peoples, linking them rather than keeping them apart.

The Chinese, who thrust a wall west into Central Asia in the second century BC, were establishing an exclusive club. The new fortification connected China to clusters of walled cities that were connected to other clusters of walled cities that were connected to still other clusters of walled cities. The wall enabled trade and communication over unprecedented distances, but only by excluding the nomads of the steppe. Many years later, the withdrawal of the wall's defenders would be the first move in a retreat that would one day render China remote and inaccessible to the West. By time of Christopher Columbus, the corridor that the wall had made possible was already long forgotten, necessitating the search for a sea route to China. Of the wall itself, only the ruins remained, awaiting rediscovery by a different breed of explorer, searching for a China that no longer existed.

The Hungarian-turned-British archaeologist Aurel Stein undertook his journeys some four hundred years after Columbus. He was the product of a vigorous and optimistic age, born into that plucky generation of explorers who in the late-nineteenth and early-twentieth centuries famously scattered around the world's deserts, mountains, and polar regions in search of knowledge or adventure. That generation numbered among its members Livingstone, Burton, Peary, and Shackleton, along with many other celebrated names, and quite a few less familiar ones, too: there was Lady Richmond Brown, plunging into the jungles of Panama; P. T. Etherton bicycling toward the "Roof of the World"; Rosita Forbes preceding Lawrence of Arabia into a Sahara then deadly to outsiders. These were the enthusiastic founders, joiners, and heroes of the Royal Geographical Society, the Russian Geographical Society, and the somewhat more democratized National Geographic Society, all of them infected with a mania for the foreign and unexplored. They were, even the best of them, mostly unprepared for their missions, more interested in adventure than science, and better endowed with courage than training. Stein was exceptional, a gifted polyglot capable of carrying out groundbreaking historical research even in extreme conditions.

Stein spent some forty-five years exploring Asia, and when he died at the age of eighty-one, he was still looking forward to a fresh campaign. Perhaps no one before or after ever exposed more virgin territory—lands then uncharted, ruins undiscovered, and languages unread. Stein's expeditions took him all over Western and Central Asia, up and down mountains and across every sort of inhospitable terrain. Enchanted by the promise of revealing the Central Asian past, he ventured beyond the familiar world of the old walled cities into the wastelands beyond, and there he found the greatest of all walls, stretching for miles along a wasteland more forbidding even than the harsh steppe to its north. That anyone had ever established a route through such a place was testimony to the pluck and determination of a far earlier generation.

Stein discovered his wall in an abandoned region of the old Silk Road where it snaked around the fringes of the Taklamakan desert. It took more than a touch of mania to go there. The Taklamakan is, even today, a forbidding place, as untamed now as it was a hundred years ago. Here was a wasteland among wastelands, a great oval of dune and doom that the Indians knew as the Great Sand Ocean and the Chinese knew as the Sea of Death. Taklamakan, the Turkish name, is perhaps the most straightforward. It translates to "go in and you won't come out." Good enough advice for most of us, but for Aurel Stein, it was more like a dare.

In his memoirs—and Stein was as indefatigable a writer as he was an explorer—the archaeologist spared only a few words to testify that the harshness of the Taklamakan exceeded that of better-known deserts in Arabia, America, or biblical lands. Those others were mere pretenders, in Stein's estimation, "tame" deserts as opposed to a "true" one. Even the mountains around the Taklamakan were more or less hostile to life, except for a few months each year when some vegetation struggled to viability at high altitudes.

In 1906, Stein set off into the land then commonly known as Chinese Turkistan with a ragtag crew of men, mules, and eventually camels. He described his team as follows: Rai Ram Singh, a crack surveyor from India; Naik Ram Singh, soldier and handyman; Jasvant Singh ("so reliable and gentlemanly in manners"), who cooked for the others but whose high caste prevented his cooking for Stein; and Stein's own cook, unnamed, "a Mohammedan Indian about whose qualities, professional and personal, the less said the better." It wasn't a large force. Mostly there was Stein, a one-man geographical society, who spoke every modern language, read every ancient language, drew every map, searched every ruin, and recorded every find.

The Taklamakan made for harsh travel. Stein conducted his Central Asian campaigns in the heart of winter because he found it easier to transport water in blocks of ice. The frozen desert yielded no supplies, and rations were precious. Even the camels received only half a pint of foul-smelling rapeseed oil every other day.

The crew traveled by day. At night, Stein huddled by a lamp to record his daily finds. He suspended his note taking whenever the ink froze, the temperature having dropped six degrees below freezing, as it inevitably did on its way to much colder levels. Of this brutal cold, Stein once recalled there "was little to complain of," and he later remarked that these expeditions had been "the happiest memories of [his] life." At the very least they must have been better than the expedition in which he lost several fingers to frostbite, these things being relative.

The Silk Road of Stein's day was bereft of traffic. Civilized folk had long abandoned Chinese Turkistan, and for that matter, the barbarians had, too. But the ruins of ancient settlements remained, perched on what looked like tiny mesas, the product of violent winds that had blown away all the land except the dirt directly underneath the buildings. Around these strange formations, Stein discovered the frozen remains of a lost world. Tree-lined avenues survived only in the desiccated trunks of poplars and fruit trees that the former inhabitants had once coaxed to life through irrigation. In the ghostly residences themselves, Stein found ancient wooden writing tablets, tossed aside by treasure hunters who'd come before him. Sometimes he chanced upon documents in rubbish heaps, still reeking after two thousand years. Stein spent days sifting through the detritus with numb fingers. Every evening, he stayed up late, wrapped in furs, deciphering the ancient texts while the thermometer plunged below zero.

Stein's initial discoveries revealed a close connection with India, but as he progressed farther north, Chinese finds began to predominate. At one abandoned Chinese camp, the wind had produced an awesome effect—leaving intact the massive walls but scooping out everything inside them to a depth of twenty feet. There, Stein found the first of many mummies, freeze-dried for eternity. Soon afterward, he spotted a line of Chinese watchtowers, each spaced three miles apart. Between them lay the sometimes faint traces of a long wall.

This last discovery, more than the cold, gave Aurel Stein goose bumps. How do you lose something over a thousand miles long? Put it in the Taklamakan. Stein had discovered a wall so ancient and obscure that even the Chinese had lost track of it. Here in the Sea of Death, a world away from the rivers of the heartland, Chinese conscript laborers had been transported, and here, as elsewhere, they had worked themselves to the bone in a foreign and inhospitable land. They had established forts and frontier towns, but they hadn't been able to make a go of it, and they'd left.

Poking the edges of the Taklamakan, the westernmost of China's great walls is surely the strangest. The Chinese constructed the wall out of great bundles of reeds, placed horizontally in alternating layers with the ubiquitous tamped dirt. By the time of Stein's discovery, the reed bundles survived in the same dehydrated state as the poplars and the mummies. Wind-deposited salts and minerals had nearly petrified the remains. In some places, the wall still rose several meters, although in other spots Stein could hardly distinguish it from the ground beneath his feet. The watchtowers made for helpful guideposts. They had once been coated with layers of white plaster, frequently reapplied in a losing battle against the sandblasting of the wind.

Stein recognized that he had stumbled on a discovery too great for his tiny party. For the first time, he was forced to make a wide detour to the only surviving settlement near the region, the so-called Town of Sands (walled, of course, even in the twentieth century). There he hired a small corps of indolent opium addicts and, reinforced by this ragtag band, set out once more across the frozen Taklamakan.

The days spent tracing the path of the reed wall across the empty landscape were particularly evocative for Stein. "No life of the present was there to distract my thoughts of the past," he recalled. Tramping across the desert, he gave free rein to his imagination, conjuring visions of long-dead Chinese soldiers and their crafty foils, the Huns. He could see the line of the wall most clearly in the evening when the setting sun lay low in the sky, casting shadows that revealed structures that had been almost entirely flattened and smoothed away by the wind. It was also at that time of day when he could most clearly see the well-worn track that ran parallel to the wall, the footprints of endless patrols of soldiers who once guarded the border. Occasionally, Stein chanced upon mounds of reed bundles carefully laid aside for producing smoke signals. He uncovered trash dumps just beneath the surface gravel, and in these dumps, writing. The documents had been written on slips of wood or bamboo. They were records of a mundane sort: brief reports, orders, private letters, school exercises, and the like. But they firmly established what Stein had suspected from the start—that the great reed wall was the work of China's Han dynasty.

Stein's discoveries thrilled students of geography and history, but he was not the first explorer to brave the Taklamakan. A far earlier traveler, arriving from another direction and with very different aims, had preceded him. The earlier explorer had brought back knowledge, too, but his findings had done something more than titillate academics, Boy Scouts, and readers of *National Geographic*.

The sponsors of the ancient expedition, the Han, were, in many ways, the formative dynasty of China. Having risen to power in 206 BC, during the overthrow of the dynasty established by the First Emperor, they brought stability to a young and still-divided nation. Han emperors centralized the governance of the state and fixed Confucianism at the center of Chinese education and culture. Behind the crumbling walls of the First Emperor, they also oversaw China's first great era of innovation in science and technology.

The First Emperor's Long Wall had done little to discourage the aggressiveness of the Huns. It had, however, created a frontier zone that could absorb Hun raids, allowing the older cities of the south to study history, mathematics, or Confucianism in relative security. Had the Long Wall succeeded? It depended on where you lived—or whom you asked. In the histories that were produced under the new rulers, the First Emperor was reviled. Han historians belittled him for his tyrannical ways, his alleged barbarism, his antipathy to scholars, and his walls. But the Han themselves were not exactly beyond such criticisms. The founder of the new dynasty, Liu Bang, once urinated on a scholar's hat. He rebelled against the First Emperor only after having failed to prevent the escape of convicts drafted to work on the First Emperor's tomb. Subsequently, the new dynasty adopted the strategy of the First Emperor and become builders of walls.

The new dynasty's fortification program started with the cities. The Han rebuilt city walls all around their empire, establishing a model for Chinese urbanism that persisted for the next two thousand years. In 169 BC, they also began colonizing the old wall zone in earnest, relocating slaves and criminals to highly fortified frontier towns. The new homes seemed endlessly distant to the ancient Chinese, part of a region long regarded as inhospitable wasteland. The wall's peasant custodians, miserable lot, sang folk songs about their plight:

> If a son is born, mind you don't raise him!
> If a girl is born, feed her dried meat.
> Don't you just see below the Long Wall
> Dead men's skeletons prop each other up.

More than two centuries after its construction, one Chinese author observed that the songs of the Long Wall were still being sung. By then the Han had given the people new walls to sing about.

The new walls were largely the project of Emperor Wu—an active and long-reigning monarch (r. 141–87 BC) who, in many ways, resembled the First Emperor. Like his predecessor, he became tyrannical and, in the end, obsessed with immortality. He consulted magicians and made extravagant pilgrimages in the hopes of cheating death. He, too, fretted for the immortality of his kingdom, and this led him to repair the hated Long Wall. Wu ordered new lengths of tamped dirt to link and augment the surviving segments. Early in his reign, he also dispatched the mission that would inadvertently change the course of history and lead directly to the wall discovered by Stein.

Wu's ambassador, the diplomat-explorer Zhang Qian, would have fit in well with the gallant company of Stein and his fellow adventurers. Sent off to the wastelands to make an alliance with a barbarian tribe that Wu hoped could assist the Chinese against the Huns, Zhang pursued his mission with the single-minded determination of a man who knew well the fate of those who failed at tasks assigned them by the emperor. Venturing beyond the old Long Wall onto the turf of the Huns, he was captured and held captive for ten years, but when he escaped, he simply resumed his mission, Hun bride in tow. By the time Zhang finally made it back to China, having lost all but one member of his original ninety-nine-man entourage, Wu had probably written off the venture as a loss. The ambassador had been captured twice and had loitered in between, hanging around a bit long, satisfying his curiosity for foreign cultures. He didn't return with the hoped-for military alliance, but the news he did bring was far more valuable.

Zhang's travels hold a special place in Asian history, comparable to the voyages of Columbus in the annals of the West. Like Columbus, he eventually went on three missions, each time exponentially expanding what was then known about the outside world, but the most important discovery was the first. He had learned that the Chinese were not, after all, alone in a world of hostile barbarians. He had found civilization on the other side of the wasteland.

The newly discovered peoples had never read the works of Confucius. They didn't subsist primarily on rice-based agriculture. They resembled the Chinese neither in appearance nor in language. The freeze-dried mummies discovered later by Stein and others in the Tarim Basin reveal the Central Asians encountered by Zhang to have been a towering fair-haired race, more like the hated steppe barbarians than the Han Chinese. None of this mattered. Race, language, and even customs were insignificant. For in a far more essential way, the Central Asians were just like the Chinese: They were workers, not warriors. They built walls.

Zhang had discovered a civilization every bit as old as China itself, a world whose walls and writings dated back over two thousand years. In Central Asia, isolated outposts of civilization bloomed like flowers in the desert. Great rivers descended from the mountains and crossed the arid landscapes, making settled life possible. Those rivers permitted oasis cities to form, much as the Tigris, Euphrates, and Nile had spawned urban civilization in Mesopotamia and Egypt.

In time, the oasis cities would become stops along the fabled Silk Road—Tashkent, Bukhara, Samarkand—magical names evoking lost splendors, and it is easy to become seduced by visions of their splendid minarets and dazzling bazaars, yet behind the exotic veneer of Central Asian civilization lay another reality: a hardscrabble existence of raids, destruction, cities built upon the ruins of cities, and walls built upon the ruins of walls.

Situated directly south of the steppe, the Central Asian oasis cities occupied some of the most dangerous real estate on earth. They owed their survival to walls. Most cities featured multiple layers of fortifications, with high citadels and walled lower towns. Expansion was no easy thing. Rather than extending perimeters that were already too large to defend, cities exploited vertical spaces. One-story homes grew to two and then three stories. When the buildings could go no higher, the top floors were made to project over the streets. The inhabitants of the legendary Silk Road oasis towns, sited on the edge of limitless open land, had no view of the sky, much less the horizon.

Staggering efforts went into fortifying the oasis towns. At Ghardman, the townspeople dug a moat so wide that an arrow shot from the bank couldn't pass over the walls. Medieval Sawran had no fewer than seven lines of walls. Similar fortifications date back to the very origins of Central Asian civilization, as can be seen in the massive Bronze Age walls of Gonur Depe North, built when the invaders from the steppe still rode chariots.

Outside the city walls, nowhere was safe. At Bayhaq, steppe raiders once made it impossible for farmers to tend to their fields for seven consecutive years. The suburbs, such as they were, contained only castles and fortified manor houses. Even villages were walled. In the ancient region of Bactria, centered on the Balkh oasis, one of the greatest cities of the ancient world lay in the plain between the Amu Darya River and the Hindu Kush Mountains. Bactria was wiped out by steppe invaders in the early second millennium BC, and this marked the first of twenty-three times Balkh would be destroyed by the nomadic tribes who made camp along the banks of the river. Twenty-three times brought to ruin!—such was the rhythm of Central Asian civilization. Occasionally, nomads camped in the remains of the cities.

Alexander campaigned into Central Asia. Did he provide the cities with an iron wall against Gog and Magog? The hyperactive young king rarely remained in one spot long enough to build anything. However, after his death, Alexander's successors provided Central Asia with its first long wall against the steppe. The Greek wall formed an impressive obstacle, heavily buttressed with forts, turrets, and bastions. As old as the First Emperor's Long Wall, and perhaps a bit older, it traversed valleys and mountain ridges and included the so-called Iron Gates (dozens of passes are so named) at Darband (another common name) in the region of modern Uzbekistan.

Zhang had seen it all—Samarkand, Bukhara, Balkh—the entire walled world of Central Asia. His reports galvanized Han China. The emperor listened intently to Zhang's tales of exotic plants and animals, including horses that sweated blood. Most intriguing were the reports of nations that dwelled in fortified cities. They were said to be adept at commerce but "poor in the use of arms and afraid of battle"—standard characteristics of the walled and civilized. Zhang described "large countries, full of rare things, with populations living in fixed abodes and given to occupations somewhat identical to those of the Chinese people."

People who lived like the Chinese? Now that was welcome news. In a flash, China's alleged isolation was swept away. The Chinese had retreated behind walls only because they knew the world to be hostile and barbarian. Now they knew otherwise. Wu sent great expeditionary forces to open a lifeline to the newly discovered brethren in the fraternity of wall builders. At the time, only massive armies dared cross the terrain of the Huns, so Wu endeavored to make the route safe for travelers. He ordered the construction of a new wall—the reed-and-dirt wall discovered by Stein—to defend China's thin link to the civilizations of Central Asia and beyond.

* * *

There had never been anything like Wu's wall. It extended the old Chinese Long Wall into a desolate region, far from China, in which no one actually lived. But Wu understood that the edge of the Taklamakan was critical. If he could shield that region by walling off the Huns to the north, he could establish a safe route to China's newly discovered Central Asian brethren in the fraternity of wall builders. The Silk Road was born.

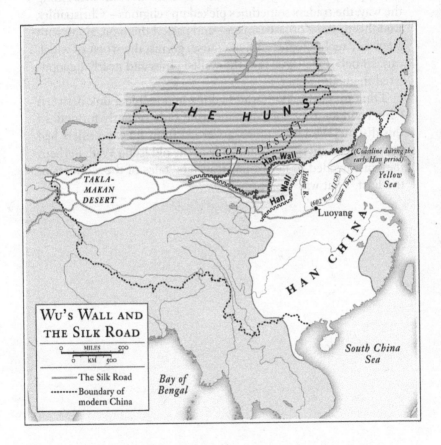

Wu's wall marked the first large-scale attempt to solve a problem as old as civilization itself: how to bridge the gaps between the clusters of walled cities. For more than two thousand years, those gaps had been deadly and terrifying, the impetus for many a panicked flight, such as that described by our skittish Egyptian in the first chapter. Now travelers could pass safely by the edges of Hun territory, taking a route that for the first time connected the wall builders of the ancient world. The impact of the new wall was immediate. Traders and ambassadors from as far as Rome could reach the Chinese court, exchanging drugs, dyes, jewels, coins, perfumes, and glassware for China's coveted silks. Along the way, the traders sometimes picked up religions—Christianity, Buddhism, and Zoroastrianism—and passed them on, along with a few key technologies and, of course, germs, the worst of which carried bubonic plague into the walled cities and nearly depopulated them altogether.

Diplomatically, Wu's wall had made possible a link between China and another ancient state, itself only recently formed. In this distant, Western empire, governed from Italy, no rulers had yet produced anything comparable to the old Long Wall. Perhaps they just needed to hear a few travelers' tales of the wonders of the East. That was soon coming.

Hadrian's Walls

THE ROMAN EMPIRE, AD 117–38

The Roman Empire was the first Western state to emulate the model of ancient China and surround itself with barricades, even though, prior to the second century AD, border walls were curiously unprecedented in Roman history. Could China have influenced Rome's decision to fortify its borders? The notion is not entirely far-fetched. Wu's wall had established a secure land route between China and the West, and straightaway Roman authors started making references to a Far Eastern, silk-producing land, which they called Serica. The Romans developed an insatiable appetite for silk. Before long, the satirist Juvenal was openly fretting about the feminization of Roman men who sashayed about town in transparent silk gowns. Amid this robust transcontinental trade, it would seem near impossible that accounts of Wu's wondrous wall had not yet reached Roman ears. Josephus's initial references to Alexander's Gates date to the first century AD and probably draw on tales of China already common in the Roman world.

If the question of outside influence is uncertain, the outline of Roman history is not. In the second century AD, Rome abruptly curtailed its sallies into barbarian territory and began constructing border walls on a massive scale. The new strategy marked a sudden and radical change in policy. The second century had actually opened on a decidedly expansionist note, with the reign of Rome's last great adventurer, Trajan. Trajan was no wall builder. His aggressive drive into Dacia (now part of Romania) violated all the wise counsel Rome's first emperor, Augustus, had bequeathed to his successors, when he advised them to live within the Empire's borders. As for Trajan's character, we have depressingly scant information. He was the sort of individual who frustrates historians. We have the nagging suspicion he is getting away with something, but we can't prove it. All his press was positive. In Rome, the people joked that Trajan's name appeared on so many buildings that it must have spread on them like a vine. When Trajan first entered the city, the people poured out en masse, old and young, sick as well as healthy, crowding the streets and rooftops to cheer him, and not just because he was giving out money (or at least that was what they said). The Senate, not to be left out of the general orgy of sycophancy, officially ordained him the Best. Ancient biographers struggled to say anything critical of him. One observed that, whereas Trajan was a pedophile, at least the boys didn't mind. Everyone loved Trajan, except perhaps the Mesopotamians, who rebelled against him, and the Jews, who rebelled against him. The Dacians also rebelled against him—twice—and they might have done it a third time, but by then most of them were already dead.

Trajan preferred bridges to walls because bridges made wars possible, whereas walls were intended to prevent them. He constructed the first bridge across the Danube to enable Roman legions to campaign into Dacia. Defensive strategies held little appeal to Trajan. He protected a few areas with forts, but only because he was too preoccupied with launching invasions elsewhere. In northern England, he established the line of forts later dubbed the Stanegate Frontier, and he created similar hedges of forts in Germany.

In AD 117, a man believed by some historians to be one of Trajan's former lovers succeeded him. The new emperor cut off any discussion of invasions or expansion. In fact, he repudiated Trajan's aggressive foreign policy with such thoroughness as to call into question whether he and the boys had really enjoyed sleeping with the Best quite as much as the old man's apologists had let on. It was this new emperor, Hadrian, who finally enlisted Rome in the ranks of the great wall builders.

In his own lifetime, when Hadrian (r. 117–38) was known for more than just his namesake wall, his reputation was decidedly mixed. The fact that he essentially started his reign by having four high-ranking politicians put to death tended to get things off on the wrong foot. Neither was he especially esteemed for relinquishing the recently won provinces of Armenia, Assyria, and Mesopotamia, all of which he deemed indefensible. The decision was typical of Hadrian. Defense, materialized in walls that stretched across horizons, would be the principal legacy of his reign.

In his own way, Hadrian was among the most civilized of the protectors of civilization—certainly more refined than the rambunctious Alexander. As a youth, Hadrian had developed such an obsession with Greek studies that he was teasingly referred to as a "Greekling." Eventually, he grew into a notorious know-it-all who held forth authoritatively on every subject from astrology to architecture, poetry, comedy, and tragedy. Experts in nearly every field conceded Hadrian's superiority, although as the rhetorician Favorinus observed, this was probably the prudent way to deal with a man who commanded thirty legions. The one expert who held his ground was the proud architect Apollodorus, who brusquely responded to one of Hadrian's questions with the ill-conceived riposte "Oh, go away and draw your pumpkins!" Hadrian eventually had Apollodorus put to death, proving that Favorinus probably had the right idea all along.

Hadrian's natural inclination was to build, and that impulse alone placed him in the same company as Shulgi, Nebuchadnezzar, and the First Emperor. Hadrian bestowed new monuments on almost every city he visited, and where there were no cities to embellish, he established new ones, including Hadrianotherae, which he built to commemorate the time he killed a bear. Everywhere, the goal seems to have been to overturn or exceed Trajan. Where Trajan had constructed a bridge to enable Roman troops to campaign across the Danube, Hadrian had it destroyed, lest the barbarians use it for the same purpose. Where Trajan had adorned a city, Hadrian adorned an empire. Where the Best had established lines of forts, Hadrian built walls.

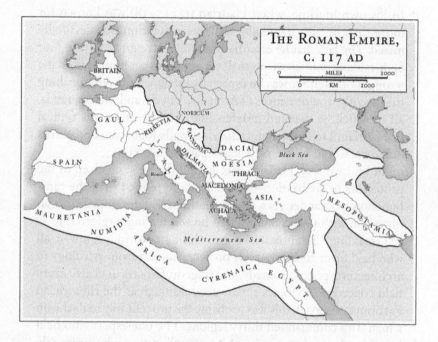

Early in his reign, Hadrian embarked on a tour of the provinces to assess and shore up their defenses. In Germany, where the threat to security was most keenly felt, he commenced whipping his soldiers into readiness by denying them all material comforts. To make camp life tougher for them, he eliminated dining rooms, covered walkways, and ornamental gardens—not bad work for a man whose own villa had two towering libraries, an astronomical observatory, three massive swimming pools, and a fourth doughnut-shaped pool that appears to have been an ancient version of a lazy river.

The wall that Hadrian built in the north of England—"to separate the Romans and barbarians"—is, along with the Great Wall of China, one of only two long walls widely known to the general public. Nowadays, the beguiling ruins meander through sheep pastures, drawing small clusters of hikers and tourists, but these are mere fragments of the monument that once guarded Roman Britain. In its original state, the Wall ran over seventy miles across the neck of Britain, standing more than fifteen feet high and augmented by ditches, mile castles, and forts. Here in northern England, where wind and climate were powerless against the Wall's stone, medieval peasants did the work of tearing it down. Locals carted away stones for fences, churches, and castles. At some buildings, still-visible Roman inscriptions testify to the origins of the reused blocks.

The modern study of Hadrian's Wall was transformed in the twentieth century by Robin Birley's discovery of the Vindolanda writing tablets. Birley is not as prominent in the history of archaeology as Heinrich Schliemann or Aurel Stein, but he is living proof that sometimes the best discoveries are those made in one's own backyard—as long as your backyard happens to include an old Roman fort. Birley belongs to the second generation of a still-thriving line of excavators founded by his father, Eric, who acquired the grounds of Vindolanda immediately after graduating from Oxford with a degree in classics. Like all Birleys, Robin took up his trowel as a teenager and had already accumulated decades of experience by March 1973, when, expanding a drainage ditch, he first started turning up slivers of wood. Two of the slivers were stuck together, and when Birley peeled them apart, he was astonished to find writing. Neither breeding nor experience had prepared him for this discovery. The slender tablets, written in a script that the excavators didn't recognize, were perplexing enough, but soon the faint ink letters began to fade, like ghost writing. Within fifteen minutes, the writing had disappeared altogether.

Birley acted quickly to preserve the find, packing the wood in damp moss and rushing it to a nearby specialist in paleography—the study of ancient writing. Richard Wright, who had literally written the book on Roman inscriptions in Britain, examined the blank slivers, swallowed any incredulity he might have felt, and suggested that infrared photography might recapture the phantom text. It was a fortuitous hunch. The photographs, taken by a specialist in medical imagery, revealed letters and other documents that hadn't been read in over two thousand years—all written in Latin cursive, a script so thoroughly forgotten that Birley had initially mistaken it for Arabic.

The Vindolanda tablets lifted the veil on the experience of Roman border guards, barbarians who'd been assimilated into the Roman army, taught Latin, and shipped off to a rainy frontier where they periodically had to tear down a rotting wooden fort and rebuild. Guarding such a frontier, even in peacetime, wasn't easy. Neither was it cheap. The manpower demands alone strained imperial resources. Forts were placed close together—those at Vindolanda and Housesteads, for example, were just three miles apart—and when the Wall was complete, smaller fortlets filled even those gaps. Every unit housed a substantial number of soldiers. One of the tablets—the only document of its kind ever recovered from the Roman Empire—put the strength of Vindolanda's cohort at 752 men, although 456 had been variously redeployed, and 31 were sick, wounded, or suffering from an apparent epidemic of pinkeye. Vindolanda was a mere auxiliary fort. A legionary fort would have housed thousands of troops.

Vindolanda's border guards came from outside the Empire, natives of those unwalled barbarian societies that provided Rome with a perennial supply of young men eager for military action. In the years during which the tablets were being written, around AD 100, most of the guards were either Batavians or Tungrians, fierce fighters whose fathers had once thrown a scare into the Empire by revolting from Roman service and forcing the surrender of two legions. Pacified and redeployed to Britain, they'd fought hard in battles such as Mons Graupius, where "the open plain presented an awful and hideous spectacle . . . and the earth reeked with blood." They were rough men—at least at first.

Border service slowly transformed the hardened barbarian auxiliaries. The Spartans had always insisted that walls softened those who lived behind them, and reading the Vindolanda tablets, one cannot help but wonder if they were onto something. On Rome's northernmost frontier, men raised to be warriors gradually acclimated to work and bureaucracy. One of the Vindolanda duty rosters recorded 343 soldiers "in the workshops." Of those, some were assigned to repair tents, others to build a bathhouse, still others to make shoes, dig clay, work at kilns, collect rubble, assist in plastering, or load wagons—everything, it seems, but fight. Other duty rosters have soldiers building a house, burning stone to make lime, or preparing wattle for fences. Vindolanda's guards spent their lives in menial labor, doing the sort of things that barbarians generally considered the responsibility of slaves and women. They stood in lines and had chores assigned to them.

Living in their walled forts, the warriors of Vindolanda were themselves becoming wallers, and they eventually lived in the shadow
of a great wall that they themselves had built.

Had the experience of doing routine work actually made the
Wall's defenders less warlike? Again, the evidence supports the
Spartan perspective: some fifty years after Hadrian's visit, northern
British barbarians poured over the Wall and slaughtered a Roman
army.

In northern England, Hadrian's most famous wall was constructed
of masonry blocks. Elsewhere, his designs generally made use of the
materials at hand, always with a nod toward economy. According to
one ancient biographer, the second-century emperor implemented
a flexible strategy that occasionally called for less grandiose visions,
such as relying on the defensive advantages of rivers or driving
large stakes into the ground to form palisades. That description
accurately portrays Hadrian's efforts in Germany, where his timber
palisades extended for some three hundred miles, a forest-devouring
effort, each kilometer of which required the felling of approximately
seven hundred old-growth oaks.

In North Africa, the chief threat to Roman farms and cities came
from the nomads of the mountains. Hadrian visited the region in
AD 128 as part of his grand inspection of imperial defenses. There,
in that perilous zone, where even the farmhouses were heavily fortified, Hadrian ordered the construction of ditches and walls that
hemmed in the Aures and Hodna Mountains, deterring the rough
mountain men from attacking the precious fields. In other parts
of North Africa, where desert nomads posed the principal threat,
Hadrian placed six-meter-high masonry walls in the transitional
zone between desert and farmland.

In southeastern Europe, the Empire touched upon the western
tip of the Eurasian Steppe. The various Gogs and Magogs had
yet to appear so far west in Hadrian's day, yet there were some
troublesome local tribes, mostly on the coastline of the Black
Sea, where Ovid once suffered in miserable exile. Determined
invaders could also enter the Empire through the Carpathians,

and the impact of any such movement could be magnified if the newcomers drove other barbarians off their lands. Consequently, Hadrian laid out yet another barrier immediately south of the Carpathians, an earth-and-timber construction that ran parallel to the Olt River for more than one hundred miles. Like most Hadrianic ramparts, it was supported by numerous forts. Later, after the frontier's destruction by fire, the line was withdrawn to the river's more easily defended west bank.

Not far away, the region of Tomis finally received a fortified barrier against the barbarians. Of its date, we can only state with certainty that it arrived far too late to help Ovid. The first of three barriers in what was clearly a hot zone was a large earthen wall constructed in a style similar to that of other second-century barriers. It faced the steppe to its north and was supported by forts, fortlets, and ditches. Evidently the wall failed at its task, as a later Roman stone wall is made up of materials from the abandoned or ruined buildings of Tomis. A final, small earthen barrier cuts through both earlier ones and may have been hastily constructed in a later time when even barbarians were erecting desperate barriers against the Huns. Together the series of three barriers traditionally carry the name Trajan's Walls, although few scholars believe they had any actual connection with the Best, and it would seem a rather improbable oversight if Hadrian had somehow left this region untouched.

In Jordan and Palestine, where the external threat to Roman settlements came from the Arab nomads known to Roman and Byzantine authors as Saracens, Hadrian completed a Trajanic initiative for fortifying the border. Lacking the resources to build a proper wall along the four-hundred-mile boundary, he hedged the edge of the desert with lines of fortresses and watchtowers.

In all, it took less than two decades for Hadrian to extend barriers across parts of three continents. He reigned for twenty-one years, dying at the age of sixty-two. When the end came, he was no Chinese emperor, swilling elixirs to extend his life. The old drama queen staged several abortive suicide attempts, seemingly careful that each one be discovered and stopped. For his immortality, he produced only some autobiographies, parceling them out to trusted freedmen who then published the books under their own names to create the impression that Hadrian had been widely admired. He finally died of sickness, having fooled no one, although Machiavelli belatedly anointed him one of the Five Good Emperors, a reputation he has carried ever since.

Posterity's treatment of Hadrian provides ample reason to be mindful of how reputation and legacy sometimes diverge. Roman authors invariably praised the aggressive Trajan, while criticizing the more defense-minded Hadrian. But it was the latter who proved more influential in both the long run and the short. Subsequent emperors showed little interest in emulating the Best. Instead, they understood their job exactly as Hadrian had handed it down to them: to defend civilization, not extend it. Sometimes this meant walls. Sometimes it meant bolstering other types of frontier defense. Here and there, rivers obviated the need for man-made barriers, but Hadrian's successors did not ignore them completely. A late second-century inscription, for example, describes how Commodus (r. 180–92) fortified the entire length of the Danube with towers and garrisons. Commodus was that notoriously cruel man-child whose reign, it was said, reduced Rome to rust. In other regions, he devoted little attention to Hadrian's crumbling frontier defenses, preferring to booze it up with his cronies and strut in the arena, where he reputedly killed a hundred lions.

The eventual collapse of Hadrian's border walls proved devastating to the unwalled towns of the provinces. Nearly every city in the Empire was subsequently challenged by the necessity of shoring up its defenses. In the third century, those cities received a makeover so thorough as to render them unrecognizable under any name.

Paradise Lost

THE ROMAN EMPIRE, C. AD 300

The Greek orator Aelius Aristides, writing shortly after Hadrian had girded the entire Roman Empire with walls, credited Rome with a rather extraordinary achievement: the Empire, he declared, had brought an end to war. Accustomed only to peace, most Romans had come to doubt that wars had ever really happened. Reports of battle were dismissed as fairy tales. Civilians no longer worried that they might be called to arms. The entire population of the Empire had given up its weapons, entrusting its security to garrisons stationed on distant frontiers. Inside the walls, the Empire had become a sort of civilian paradise: the whole inhabited world, Aristides wrote, had turned to pleasures of every sort. Gymnasiums, fountains, temples, monumental arches, artists, and schools filled the cities. Absolute security, "universal and clear to all," prevailed.

Aristides routinely tailored his opinions to please his audience—in this case, Hadrian's successor, Antoninus Pius—but his glowing portrayal of the state of things in the mid-second century AD wasn't entirely fiction. Most of the provinces had developed at least the rudiments of urban life prior to assimilation into the Empire, but only Rome, the improbable defender of civilization on three continents, had made such conditions universal: literacy, scholarship, monumental architecture, fine art, science—the accomplishments, in short, of a people who didn't realize they were doomed. Rome temporarily freed the Western world from its fear of the warriors outside, and the result was a culture so prosperous that even those who most enjoyed it sometimes worried they had grown decadent.

The source of Rome's security, and the key to its prosperity, was, to Aristides, obvious: walls, "unbreakable and indissoluble," manned by countless ranks of soldiers, defended the state. The emperors had put up fortifications around "the entire world," ranging from Ethiopia in the south to the Euphrates in the east and Britain in the north. Back in Italy, the capital city lay open because it had nothing to fear. Border walls—made of immense masonry blocks, according to Aristides—extended the same protection to all the cities of the Empire. Rome's walls surrounded the Empire like a trench encircled an army camp.

Of course, we know that Aristides has gotten a few things wrong, and few of Rome's frontiers were fortified by masonry walls, although perhaps the emperors preferred that their subjects believed they were. Most Romans never saw the vast array of towers, mounds, palisades, ditches, and forts that defended the frontiers, still less the soldiers who patrolled them. The borders were far away, and that distance added to the myth of invulnerability. Moreover, for those provincials who'd learned to accept Roman rule, the idea of enclosed borders wasn't at all uncomfortable. Rome was too large to feel like a garrison state. If only it hadn't all cost so much, if only there had been enough soldiers to man the walls, if only the walls could have held, Aristides's walled paradise might have lasted indefinitely. As it was, Rome's total security, "universal and clear," didn't even last until the end of Aristides's life.

In 2012, workers expanding a highway in Romania unexpectedly revealed the remains of a previously unknown Roman settlement, dating from the time of Aristides. Such discoveries, which can hold up projects for months, are a recognized construction hazard in Europe. They regularly frustrate contractors and developers, who can only hope the archaeologists will find little to extend the initial delay. The Romanian discovery, however, was extensive: a small town and its associated necropolis. All work was forced to a halt; bulldozers, graders, spreaders, and pavers were idled until archaeologists could excavate the site, officially dubbed Sibot-3.

From the start, the archaeologists had to work quickly, knowing that the road crew was anxious to resume work in good weather. In a perfect world, where archaeology is practiced only painstakingly and with infinite patience, the site deserved better. Sibot-3 was impressive in both its size and refinement. Here was one of those "border cities supplied with useful crafts and other adornments," described by Aristides, the sort that flourished fearlessly in the shadow of the Empire's fiercest enemies. Sibot-3 lay deep in Roman Dacia, a restive borderland that Hadrian's aggressive predecessor, Trajan, had conquered. Yet even in this dangerous neighborhood, Roman life apparently prospered in the second century. Elegant buildings featured ornamental tiles. No fewer than seven workshops manufactured ceramics on a nearly industrial scale.

As a member of the team that excavated Sibot-3, I vividly recall my first view of the site. When our crew initially learned of the discovery, we were still domiciled well over an hour away, and the unexpected assignment required a long trip to the work site. For the first of several such commutes made before our relocation, we rumbled to the excavation in a dangerously overcrowded minibus, unair-conditioned in the hundred-degree heat, with windows closed in accord with Romanian custom. Puttering along local roads dotted with horse manure, on our way to the highways, we entertained ourselves with chatter that at least occasionally diverted our thoughts from the likelihood that we would arrive at the site as a busload of suffocated corpses. When we reached Sibot-3, still alive except for some brain cells that had starved for lack of oxygen, we unpacked our legs, sucked in great gulps of fresh air, and scattered across the grounds for a first look. By then, a few preliminary test pits had already been dug, and in all of them a thick black line formed a distinct horizontal stratum. This was unmistakably a burn layer, ashes from the destruction of Sibot-3 during the Marcomannic Wars of Marcus Aurelius.

* * *

Marcus Aurelius (r. 161–80) assumed the throne just a few years after Aristides delivered his rosy account of the Roman Empire. The new emperor is generally said to have embodied much of what is best in civilization. A model philosopher-king, his stoic *Meditations* are still admired today. But Marcus was not fated for a life of peaceful contemplation. He was dragged into war by enemies from beyond the walls, and in the end his celebrated philosophical and scholarly pursuits never provided more than a temporary escape from a duty that pressed down hard on him. In AD 166, the Empire was invaded by barbarian Langobardi and Obii. The campaigns that followed saw Marcus defeated by Marcomanni and Quadi. Costoboci swept into Marcus's beloved Greece, homeland of the philosophers who so inspired him, and sacked the ancient shrine of Eleusis. Who were these dangerous, unknown peoples? It didn't matter. After Marcus, there would be no more philosopher-kings. Virtually all his successors were soldiers.

An epidemic ravaged Marcus's Rome. It arrived courtesy of that distant Chinese wall that had linked together the far-flung empires of Eurasia. As it turns out, Wu's wall had enabled more than just trade to pass between China and Rome. Chinese documents record Roman visitors to the imperial court during the time of Marcus. By then, China had already suffered its initial outbreak of that mysterious epidemic known to classicists as the Antonine Plague. Traders had apparently carried the disease to Mesopotamia, where it was contracted by Roman soldiers. Within a few years, an estimated 5 million people had died of plague in the Roman Empire, including a disproportionate number of soldiers on the frontiers. Aristides had once boasted that there were so many soldiers on Rome's border walls that an arrow couldn't pass through their ranks, but the plague now turned hyperbole into lie. Marcus Aurelius died in AD 180, leaving the borders more vulnerable than they'd ever been. His last words concerned the plague.

Marcus's reign marked a turning point in the history of the Empire; the Hadrianic frontiers, with their walls, palisades, and ditches, had at last been overwhelmed. Throughout the provinces, a crisis of confidence threatened the very foundations of civilization. Signs of destruction, defeat, and decline mark the archaeological remains of second-century Roman cities, and not just the frontier settlements, such as Sibot-3. Deep in the heartland of Aristides's walled Eden can be found whole towns entirely abandoned after violent demolition. Others suffered brutal destruction but survived. In Roman Lyons, the heavily settled hill of Fourvière was deserted. At Orange, one of the busiest neighborhoods—crowded with houses since the first century BC and honored with a grand public building in the first century AD—was abandoned, too. A shrinking Paris withdrew from its most far-flung neighborhoods. Second-century Tours suffered a contraction so severe that only two streets survived from the original plan.

Art historians have observed the changed mood that resulted from this first great failure of the Roman walls. Rome was the natural heir to the serene beauty of classical Greek art, but in the late second century that aesthetic skipped town altogether. A grim, violent sensibility replaced it. Many a Roman aristocrat went to his eternal rest in a stone coffin embellished by twisting, crowded, graphic scenes of war. Even Marcus Aurelius—he of the lofty ideals and philosophic spirit—inspired a massive column featuring sculpted images of barbarians being speared and beheaded. In several scenes, women are stabbed or dragged away. The Roman soldiers on the column resemble grinning ghouls as they go about their murderous work. It was an art to turn the stomach and sicken the soul, but an artist can only reflect the age in which he lives, and in this age the border wars had taken precedence over all that was elegant or beautiful.

To students of Roman history, the third century is notorious: a numbing catalog of raids, border wars, and invasions that shocked and devastated the Empire. In AD 238, for example, barbarians destroyed the ancient Greek colony of Histria. Thirteen years later the Emperor Decius launched a campaign to halt Gothic raids across the Danube. Lured into swamps and annihilated, he was the first Roman emperor to fall in battle against a foreign enemy. Subsequently, the Goths acquired boats, sailed through the Bosporus into the Aegean, and raided the magnificent Greco-Roman cities on the coast of Asia Minor. They even destroyed the Temple of Artemis at Ephesus—a larger version of the original structure once deemed one of the Seven Wonders of the World.

Panic swept through Greece. The Peloponnesian Greeks attempted to insulate themselves from the horror by building a wall at the narrow isthmus that connected them to the mainland. They ransacked every public building within reach for stone. To their north, the Athenians, who had for so long put all their faith in Rome, repaired their city walls for the first time in over three hundred years. Their efforts came too late. Athens was sacked by the Goths, and even the buildings around the great central marketplace were burned and destroyed. Subsequently, the Athenians used blocks from the ruined Agora to build a protective wall around a small area north of the Acropolis. Broken segments of columns and sculptures were stacked unceremoniously in the new rampart. Glorious Athens, the home of tragedians, mathematicians, and philosophers, the city that had twice fought off the mighty Persian Empire, had lost its nerve. The city's retreat into insignificance had begun.

To the barbarian invaders, all this frantic fortifying was unthinkable. Having been raised to esteem only those men who could achieve feats in arms, they watched with contempt as Romans hid behind walls. They taunted civilians whose hands had never held weapons and who wanted to avoid combat at all costs. The Romans, they declared, had more confidence in objects than in themselves. And in an insult that echoed the ancient letters of the doomed Bronze Age king Rib-Hadda, they ridiculed the Romans for living *like birds in a cage*.

Virtually no part of the Empire escaped destruction during this awful time. The Goths continued on to Italy. According to some of the more hyperbolic sources, they sacked five hundred cities along the way. Britain suffered heavily from barbarian raids. The provinces that sprawled from the Danube to the Balkans fared even worse. Three of the Empire's most heavily defended regions were abandoned altogether, given up to barbarian occupiers. Gaul survived the turbulence of the third century, but just barely.

A forlorn practice testified to the sheer panic of civilized folk: in province after province, anxious civilians buried their money in pots under the ground, hoping to retrieve their fortunes in more secure times. Most never did. Countless such hoards remained exactly where they'd been buried, unretrieved and undisturbed, for nearly two thousand years until discovered by archaeologists or amateurs with metal detectors.

Rome itself wasn't immune from the panic of the third century. The Eternal City hadn't really, as Aristides claimed, eschewed ramparts, but it had theoretically been vulnerable since the fourth century BC, the last time it had updated its aging, inadequate defenses. Since then, the city had sprawled far beyond the circuit of its walls. In the early 270s, the Emperor Aurelian finally bowed to reality—reality, in this case, being the memory of a recent Alemannic invasion of Italy—and constructed new walls.

As Rome went, so went the provinces. For nearly three hundred years, Roman cities had given little thought to protecting their citizens, relying, just as Aristides said, on faraway troops and eventually border walls to hold the frontier against the warlike peoples massed outside. Some cities, mostly the older ones, had outgrown their ancient walls. Others had never had any walls at all.

In the whole of world history, there had never been an experiment as grand as that of an empire composed mostly of unwalled cities. By leaving so many towns undefended, the Romans had adopted a comprehensive approach to local security—hundreds of miles of border walls and other barriers designed to create a massive, impenetrable shield over all Western civilization. In the aftermath of the third-century invasions, that all changed: the emperor Diocletian (r. 284–305) implemented a program to fortify the suddenly insecure cities of the western provinces. It was the last great construction boom of a city-building empire, and it was an act that repudiated every Roman belief in what a city should be.

With due deliberation, the wall builders dismantled those splendid, open cities that their fathers had created in earlier, more confident days. Buildings in the paths of the new walls were razed. Some were torn down simply to provide stone. In the rush to fortify the cities, the relentless chisels of the laborers broke apart tombs, temples, columns, baths, theaters, and amphitheaters. They tore friezes, relief sculptures, and capitals from their settings, using the bigger blocks for masonry and crushing the rest for rubble. Many an inscription, once intended to ensure immortal glory, was wrenched from its proper place to rest ingloriously among the bricks, masonry, and concrete of a rampart.

Late Roman construction possessed none of the exuberant confidence of earlier Roman urbanization. In the new work, luxury made way for pragmatism and toughness. The fourth-century townspeople of Bordeaux would have watched workers shoring up the banks of the Devèze River with fragments of ancient architecture, marble capitals, and columns. This was no time for sentimentality. Strong men were burying Bordeaux's last urban monuments in the muck.

In cities everywhere, townspeople did what had to be done, making choices that would have seemed unthinkable during the early imperial period. In Paris, for example, miners cleared a densely inhabited area near the forum and dug shafts there for the extraction of gravel. In Fréjus, citizens succumbed to the pressure for space by sacrificing their public baths; they tore down the marbles and mosaics and reused the remaining structure for rough habitations. At Arles, excavators have discovered the fire-gutted ruins of houses, shops, and baths outside the walls. That area was reborn to a cruder existence in the fourth century, but few chose to live there. Late-Roman Arles could scarcely contain the timid masses who preferred a squalid but secure life within the walls to the more sumptuous suburban living of days gone by. The circus was transformed into a sort of apartment complex, and in the fifth century, the portico of the forum was leveled to provide material and space for housing. Townsfolk moved into mausoleums in the once-prestigious cemetery outside the amphitheater, a building that must have seemed far less imposing surrounded as it now was by lean-tos.

The wallers rebuilt their cities with a remorseless sense of purpose. Sprawling cities full of open spaces and beautiful monuments were reduced pitifully in size. Metropolises withered and shriveled up. The transformation is stunning—and even more so when we consider how it must have affected individuals sacrificing lifestyle for security. In Clermont-Ferrand, for example, a third-century aristocrat constructed a huge and impressive town house. We don't know how long his family occupied their new home. Yet when the town retreated five hundred meters up the hill to a more defensible location, the house was carefully cleaned out, vacated, and left in the hands of workers who destroyed it. Likewise, in southern France, one family after another quietly evacuated five grand houses in the periphery of Aix-en-Provence. One by one, the families resigned themselves to the decline of their city. The stubbornness of the last inhabitants broke down only slowly, until at last a single household remained, alone, surrounded by empty buildings, in a curmudgeonly refusal to concede a diminished future. Eventually, that family, too, gave up.

Late Roman cities quickly acquired the look of fortresses, typically high, invariably walled, often surrounded by water. There is a strange déjà vu in seeing so many of the rebuilt towns conform to the same plan and surface area as their Iron Age predecessors. It was as if the squat fortress-towns of the Gallic world had simply fallen asleep for a while, dreaming of baths and amphitheaters, only to awaken some three hundred years later looking much the same as they had in the days before Caesar.

It seems incredible, perhaps, but the shrinking cities of Spain, Gaul, Greece, and Asia Minor were luckier than many. They had, at least, survived. In the region once known as the Agri Decumates, only ghost towns remained. According to one Roman author, the Germans who moved into the area after Rome's withdrawal avoided the abandoned towns as if they were tombs. On occasion, the triumphant barbarians would settle in the vacant country home of a departed Roman squire, but as if to underscore the defeat of civilization, many preferred to occupy prehistoric hill forts instead.

Roman civilization was in full retreat: provinces abandoned, fields deserted, art, literature, and science put on hold. The once gorgeous towns with their gleaming triumphal arches had shrunk into toughened little nuts, but even these soon became targets of raids. In province after province, the barbarians found their way around the border walls, probing imperial defenses much in the way that water, spilled on a floor, flows to the lowest level and finds its way through cracks. Often, the Hadrianic defenses forced the barbarians to detour through unwalled provinces that had previously been considered safe. As early as Marcus Aurelius's time, the establishment of barriers near the mouth of the Danube had redirected steppe raiders through the Carpathians, spelling doom for settlements such as Sibot-3. Later emperors paid greater attention to these detours. Walls begat more walls, but it was already too late.

In AD 284, a Roman embassy arrived at the Chinese court. Ordinarily, transcontinental business was conducted by middlemen, and these ambassadors may have been the first Romans to pass through the old Han walls since the days of Marcus Aurelius. When the embassy returned home, it reported to a new emperor. We may never know if Diocletian was influenced by tales of the Chinese wonders, only that he apparently ordered yet another round of border walls.

New border walls soon crisscrossed the map of southeastern Europe. Viewed from a distance, it is almost as if one can see a giant hand at work, placing lines here and there to plug up holes in the old Hadrianic frontiers. In northwest Dacia, the Romans blocked gaps in the Carpathians with earthen and stone barriers. South of the Carpathians, they established vast earthworks—the so-called Devil's Dykes—stretching well over four hundred miles. Taken in combination with another early-fourth-century earthwork, the nearly three-hundred-mile-long Brazda lui Novac, Roman barriers completely encircled the lower Carpathian Mountains.

Diocletian may have built more than he could defend, and as the fourth century progressed, his successors abandoned the long lines of southeastern Europe and concentrated on shorter lines closer to the two capitals. Constantinople was given protection by a new twenty-seven-mile wall that bisected the gateway of the steppe in a region of modern Bulgaria well south of the ruins of Tomis. Italy, meanwhile, was fortified by a system of walls blocking the various passes through the Julian Alps. All told, the latter fortifications totaled around forty miles of walls, guarded by soldiers occupying some seven hundred towers. These closed off key choke points in the routes through Slovenia, Croatia, Austria, and Italy.

In the Rhineland, which had never been walled owing to the defensive properties of the flowing river, the collapse of the frontier came so quickly that the Roman soldiers never had an opportunity to construct new walls, if any were ever contemplated. By one count, some forty Rhineland towns were ravaged by Germans during the reign of Constantius II (r. 337–61), even while steppe peoples overran the Danube. This was some two hundred years after the great projects of Hadrian. The wooden palisades that had once stretched for hundreds of miles had all rotted away.

By the late fourth century, the great prosperity once celebrated by Aristides existed only in memory. Hadrian's walls had failed. Civilization was under siege. Fear had returned, and with it came all the ugly transformations of a society placed perpetually on a war footing. The Empire devolved into little more than a totalitarian state. In earlier times, happier, brimming with humor, and vibrant with opportunity, Roman satirists had lampooned a lively capital filled with quack priests, queer foreigners, flamboyant fashionistas, and slaves-turned-millionaires. By contrast, the later Empire regulated religion, dictated which nationalities could intermarry, and required people to remain in the occupations held by their fathers. Imperial edicts forbade long hair and even specified the sort of clothes Romans could wear. Onerous taxes left citizens destitute. Some fled to the barbarians to escape collection. Those who remained were at the mercy of tax men who seized not just money but also women's jewelry and even clothing, right down to the underwear.

What drove Rome to these extreme measures was the sheer cost of walling off its civilian population and defending it against the barbarians. It was a cost that threatened to destroy the economy of the Roman world. By the mid-third century, the cash-starved emperors had so debased the currency that Rome's "silver" coin, the denarius, contained no more than 5 percent of the precious metal. Emperors complained that the army could no longer be fed or clothed. Taxpayers complained that the cost of the army was crushing them.

How do we assess the impact of Rome's participation in the Great Age of Walls? It would be easy enough to manufacture a cost-benefit analysis slanted to prove whatever thesis we like. Hadrian's walls do seem to have temporarily secured the Empire, making possible an age of productivity, creativity, and prosperity, during which civilians did not have to fear for their lives. But those same walls required tens of thousands of border guards, perhaps *hundreds* of thousands, necessitating that Rome rely heavily on foreign mercenaries, whose leaders would eventually turn against the Empire. And perhaps Rome would have required even more mercenaries if the emperors had never built any walls at all.

A thousand questions still beg to be answered: Did Rome's walls deter barbarian aggression or provoke more of it? Would the Hadrianic fortifications have held out if only the Antonine Plague hadn't denuded the walls of their defenders? Were the ancients correct in believing that warriors living behind walls eventually lost their edge? History has a maddening habit of raising more questions than can be answered. As the Great Age of Walls reached its climax in the West, the questions only multiply.

Defenseless behind Walls

———

Sometimes when a civilization dies, it doesn't happen in a cataclysm. The cities survive—after a fashion. So, too, do the people. The end itself is anticlimactic. Fire comes, as it invariably does, but finds little to consume. A spiritual destruction has preceded it, leaving behind little of value—diminished art, narrowing intellectual interests, a rotting infrastructure long neglected by engineers. The survivors, too weary to put up an apocalyptic struggle, offer little resistance. Some welcome the end. Others live in extravagant denial.

There had been a time, back in the second century, when it must have seemed like a good idea to surround the Empire with walls, so that the people, relieved of insecurity, could concentrate on music, art, philosophy, and fine buildings. Hadrian, the architect of the policy, loved all those things. But the Greek-loving emperor had picked and chosen from the lessons of history. He was always more enamored with Athens than with Sparta; otherwise, he might have heeded the ancient Spartan warnings about walls. He might have worried that the walls would change the people they were protecting.

Aristides had also missed the warning signs. When the orator celebrated the peaceful, prosperous conditions that prevailed behind Hadrian's walls, he embraced the demise of the citizen-soldier. Rome, he declared, would never stoop to asking its own citizens to fight. He never considered the possibility that a people who'd forgotten what war was like would be utterly unprepared for it when it came.

The later Roman emperors, who so frequently endured the ver-
bose, unctuous flattery of professional sycophants like Aristides, didn't
have the luxury of being oblivious. They were increasingly tasked
with defending a population that could not defend itself. Frequently
they came to doubt the toughness even of the soldiers themselves.
They tried to stiffen up the troops by denying them the luxuries
that had become the raison d'être of Roman life—*do as I say, not as
I do*—but this rarely accomplished much. Eventually, the emperors
doubled down on the Hadrianic strategies that had briefly succeeded
in the second century. They built more border walls and more city
walls, while recruiting ever more soldiers from the ranks of the
unwalled warrior societies beyond the borders. None of this would
have mattered had Rome's enemies been the sort who believed wars
were fought between states and that civilian populations should be
spared from violence. But the warriors from the unwalled regions
didn't even recognize the *concept* of civilians. In the civilized Romans,
living behind walls, they saw only wealthy weaklings—the sort of
people who would give up everything they had just to be left alone.

By the late fourth century, the Roman Empire, civilization's
longtime bulwark against the forces of the forests and steppes, was
a spent force. The vast energies that had once propelled classical
civilization from the shores of the Mediterranean to the edge of the
Atlantic were exhausted. From Greece to Britain every monument,
every achievement, had been founded on the essential belief that
what one built would not soon be destroyed, and that cities were
more than mere castles in the sand. Now it seemed as if nothing
could withstand the tide. If there was a way to resist it, the people
didn't remember how.

In AD 376, a large body of Goths arrived at the Danube River,
pleading to be allowed into the Empire as refugees. These were
the same barbarians whose forefathers had slain an emperor, sacked
Athens and Ephesus, and taunted the walled-in Romans for living
like birds in a cage. They had recently received their comeuppance
from the Huns and Alans—two nations then widely identified with
Gog and Magog. The Goths had no answer to the tactics of the

steppe men, and after a desultory attempt at building their own great wall, they decided that perhaps the Empire knew a thing or two about security after all.

The Romans would have been amply justified in turning away their old foes. The Goths certainly had it coming, and schadenfreude, after all, is a dish best served while watching one's archenemies scramble haplessly to construct a proper wall. But thousands of men, socialized from birth to be warriors, were seeking entrance into an Empire whose greatest problem remained how to recruit soldiers from a walled and unwarlike populace, and from a certain perspective the arrival of the Goths could be viewed as an opportunity. A bold and unfortunate idea presented itself. The Romans, eyeing the crowd of barbarians as just so many potential recruits, agreed to the Goths' request. Roman officers supplied vessels to transfer the Goths into the Empire, ferrying them across the Danube on boats, rafts, and canoes for several days and nights. At the time, it must have seemed like a clever and perhaps even generous move—good for both the Goths and the Romans—but this Gothic Dunkirk soon turned sour. For in the memorable phrase of the Roman historian Ammianus, Rome had just admitted its own ruin.

The refugees, unhappy in their new conditions, had hardly entered the Empire before they turned on their hosts, ambushed a Roman garrison, and began raiding cities and villas. According to Ammianus, the land was set on fire. Women watched while their husbands were murdered. The Goths tore babies from their mothers' breasts and dragged children over the dead bodies of their parents. They drew ever closer to Constantinople, the city that had only recently emerged as one of the dual capitals of a state that in those days typically had two emperors. The refugees had become invaders, and this at last roused the attentions of the eastern emperor, Valens.

Valens was an unmemorable leader, the latest of dozens who spent their careers in ceaseless, desultory combat against barbarians. He briefly earned praise for repairing the border walls and ending the practice of paying out vast tribute to barbarians. But posterity recalls him for another reason: the horrific defeat of his army by the Goths.

The Battle of Adrianople (AD 378) figures prominently in nearly every account of the fall of the Roman Empire. In the centuries leading up to the great defeat, the emperors had all but extinguished the warrior element within their own subjects and, in their search for hired killers, had badly miscalculated in allowing the Goths to immigrate. When night fell over that terrible battle in which Gothic axmen hacked through the ranks of the Roman soldiers, the survivors scattered or fled to the protection of the nearest walls. There, the townspeople of Adrianople—in Latin, Hadrianopolis, fittingly "the city of Hadrian"—closed the gates before their protectors could even get inside. The next day, when the Goths attacked the city, searching for an alleged cache of imperial treasure, the cornered survivors fought with their backs to the walls. When the Goths finally relented from their attacks, the townspeople rolled huge boulders behind the gates.

Adrianople lay just one hundred miles west of Constantinople, which was now vulnerable after the defeat of the emperor's troops. When the barbarians marched on the great eastern capital, it had no Roman troops left to defend it. Only a band of Saracen warriors that the Empire had imported from the deserts of Arabia rallied to the city's defense. In the fields outside Constantinople, a bizarre spectacle ensued. Barbarian fought barbarian, one band a Rome ally, the other its sworn enemy, neither side gaining the upper hand until a lone Saracen, wearing only a loincloth, raced into the meat of the Gothic host, stabbed a soldier, and sucked the blood from his throat, terrifying even the Goths. This is what the battle for civilization had become: Constantinople—the "new Rome"—saved by the most feral feat of barbarism, while the citizens watched from the walls.

Had the Spartans gotten it right all along? Had the Romans authored their own demise by constructing walls that turned their men into hapless softies? The brash future bishop Synesius, who arrived in Constantinople to deliver his opinions some twenty years after Adrianople, certainly thought so. For Synesius, who fancied himself of Spartan descent, the triumph of the civilian element in Roman society had gone too far. He insisted that the Empire had pampered its citizens by importing barbarian mercenaries to defend the state while excusing native Romans from service. In the course of a long oration in which he repeatedly decried the effects of luxuries on the martial spirit, Synesius naturally came around to the topic of walls. After declaring that the early Romans had never walled their city—a patently false remark, as everyone in his audience, being familiar with the myth of Romulus, very well knew—Synesius prescribed nothing less than the complete dismantling of the civilian society so praised by Aristides. Rome, he said, should be drafting its farmers, philosophers, craftsmen, salesmen, even the ne'er-do-wells who loitered incessantly around the theater. Until then, the only real men in the Empire were the barbarians. Native Roman men had been reduced to playing the woman's part, and the barbarians would soon take over.

Synesius's prescription never stood any realistic chance of adoption. It went against every impulse that civilized people had shown for at least three thousand years. Not just the Romans, but, before them, the Mesopotamians, Egyptians, Chinese, and essentially every civilized nation in Europe or Asia had concluded it was better to allow walls and foreigners to do their fighting for them rather than devote their own lives to constant preparation for war. They opted for baths, theaters, games, and schools over tests of endurance, beatings, periods of deliberate deprivation, and other toughening exercises. It all seems obvious in retrospect, but Synesius couldn't quite see it.

What Synesius *could* envision—the demise of Rome—played out exactly as he had expected. A new breed of ambitious foreigners arose to exploit the weaknesses that Synesius described. Bred from the Empire's desperate gambit of hiring barbarian mercenaries to defend unarmed Romans, they were sophisticated enough to play at imperial politics while at the same time still savvy to the desires of their violent, crude men. They straddled two worlds and very nearly mastered both. The late Roman world teemed with such creatures. Gainas, a Goth, briefly took control of Constantinople. Another Goth, Alaric, shook the world.

In the autumn of 408, Alaric besieged Rome for the first time. The city's vast Aurelian walls were enough to keep out the barbarians, but they simultaneously imprisoned the hapless civilian populace. Corpses filled the streets of the starving capital. After a while, the Romans tried to bluff Alaric, sending envoys to inform him that they had taken up arms and were prepared to fight. Alaric only laughed at the threat. His famous reply—"Thick grass is more easily cut than thin"—is a bit of a puzzler, perhaps because the cutting of grass was just another civilian activity about which the warrior Goths apparently knew nothing. But clearly, any notion that a community of poets and politicians could intimidate the Goths, most of whom had never spent a day behind walls and had lived all their lives in camps, seemed ludicrous to Alaric. He demanded all the gold and silver in the city.

"What will be left to us?" the Romans asked.

"Your lives," came Alaric's reply. He refused to allow any Roman to leave the city for food until they began melting statues to provide him with gold.

The Romans temporarily satisfied Alaric's demands, but he returned again the next year, and then again the year after that. Finally, in August 410, when Alaric's negotiations with the emperor were interrupted by a surprise attack—made, naturally, by barbarians in the service of Rome—the Goth led his troops into Rome and pillaged the Eternal City.

The aura of Rome failed to endow the city with any special protection. Women were raped, and corpses left unburied. In some quarters, the burned shells of buildings stood unrepaired for decades. Refugees streamed out of the city and took boats to distant cities such as Jerusalem, where Saint Jerome helped take them in. Leaving behind the smoking capital, Alaric and his Goths passed into southern Italy, where an observer writing more than a century later could still see the rubble of cities left in his wake. *Rome* had been brought low by a band of barbarians, and, worse still, by barbarians who were supposed to be defending the Empire. "The brightest light of the whole world is extinguished," wrote Saint Jerome. ". . . The whole world has died with one city."

And yet the Roman Empire did survive the brutal sack of its capital. The emperors continued to sit in Ravenna or Milan or Rome and

Constantinople for some decades, weaving their little webs, cutting deals with barbarians, imagining they still ruled the world. They possessed few options beyond hiring barbarians to defend their provinces, and that was no real option at all. The barbarians, by and large, did as they pleased, accepting the emperor's expensive bribes, then taking what they wanted from the cities they held hostage.

The century after the sack of Rome sorely tested the late-Roman strategy of using city walls as a last-ditch defense. As rural folk fled to the walled cities, agriculture was neglected, causing a famine so severe that many were driven to cannibalism. One wretched woman was stoned to death for eating all four of her children.

The old border walls had become obsolete. They required the sort of support a fading Empire could no longer afford. Many of the Roman troops formerly stationed on the frontiers gave up and left when they realized that no pay was forthcoming. In the region of Austria, a single garrison of border guards held out in isolation. Desperate for money, the troops sent some men to Italy for pay, but the expedition was ambushed by barbarians. The bodies of the slain washed ashore by a river. In Britain, Roman troops finally abandoned Hadrian's Wall, allowing the area to return to forest. A hundred years later, a Greek author recalled the Wall only as a mythic barrier erected by "men of old." Beyond the Wall, he wrote, lay an uninhabitable zone where the poisonous air would suffocate a man if the countless snakes hadn't gotten him first. He was referring to Scotland.

A British contemporary of the Greek author's also tried to make sense of the demise of Roman Britain. He reckoned it had happened something like this: a defenseless Britain, denuded of its imperial troops, had petitioned Rome for aid. The Romans subsequently sent an army and drove off the enemy, but then departed, leaving instructions that the British should construct a wall against future invasions. The provincials built this wall out of turf, but it did little good, as the enemy soon swarmed over it, slaughtering everyone they encountered. For a second time, the Romans dispatched an army to save the Britons, but this time their advice was sterner: stop being such lazy cowards, take some weapons, and learn to fight your own battles—oh, and build a better wall. Left to their own devices yet again, the provincials obediently constructed a towering wall of stone. Unfortunately, they were unable to defend it. The enemy dragged them off the wall with barbed weapons and dashed them to the ground.

Our British author was wrong in nearly every detail. He is aware of both Hadrian's Wall and the later Antonine Wall, which was made of turf, but he has confused their histories and reversed the timing of them. Only in his general theme has he gotten it right: the Romans of the provinces, long accustomed to peace inside their walled world, no longer stood a chance on their own.

Synesius had seen this coming all along. Just a few years after delivering his ranting jeremiad in Constantinople, he experienced the mixed fortune of seeing his dire prophecies borne out. In North Africa, where his brash leadership had been awarded with a bishopric, his home city of Ptolemais came under siege by barbarians. The meekness of the townspeople confirmed Synesius's darkest fears. Far from rallying in defense of their property and families, the Romans of North Africa had merely huddled behind their walls, praying for the intervention of the army and complaining when it didn't come. The barbarians seized women as slaves, took away livestock, killed any men they found outside, and left the rest imprisoned behind their own ramparts.

For Synesius, this was all too much. The self-proclaimed descendant of Spartans and apostle of self-help chafed for action. Against the advice of his own brother, the two-fisted bishop began organizing his fellow citizens. He oversaw the manufacture of weapons, including even a type of artillery for hurling heavy stones from the walls. What he could not manufacture, he purchased from traders. Although hindered significantly by the region's lack of iron production, Synesius amassed a patchwork arsenal: three hundred lances and single-edged swords, along with some hatchets and clubs. For soldiers, he attracted volunteers from among the young men. Some he placed as guards around the wells and rivers. The rest he led out on morning and evening patrols.

The raiders, for their part, were bemused by the philosopher's efforts. Having encountered some of Synesius's scouts, they sent word to the city to prepare for battle. They were curious, they admitted, as to what sort of sedentary people could possibly have the audacity to go out and fight warlike nomads such as themselves.

Synesius's militia succeeded only temporarily, holding back the deluge for a short while until a Roman army finally arrived to scatter the nomads. Fifteen years later, the North Africans would receive no help from Rome when the Vandals arrived in 429. The new invaders were far more destructive than their predecessors. The Vandals left large piles of bodies outside town walls to suffocate any holdouts with the stench of putrefaction. Using Africa as a base, the Vandals launched annual spring raids on Italy and Sicily, where they razed some cities and enslaved the populations of others. Bishops debated whether Matthew 10:23 ("When you are persecuted in one place, flee to another") licensed them to abandon their congregations. Talk of Gog and Magog was in the air. No civilian resistance materialized, however. In Roman Carthage, the townspeople ignored the calamities befalling the cities all around them and continued to attend games and circuses. More than one author observed with disgust that the oblivious Carthaginians went to the circus on the very day the city fell to the Vandals in 439. They'd put all their faith in the walls.

Occasionally, as the Empire collapsed around them, some Roman in this or that province would rally a few men, Synesius-style, to take up arms against the barbarians, but such heroics were rare. As a measure of how helpless and dependent the inhabitants of the walled cities had become, an edict issued by Valentinian III (r. 425–55) makes for a rather poignant memorial: it reminds the people of their obligation to defend their city walls. How could this not have gone without saying?

In the meanwhile, the countryside, suffering as long-term battlegrounds so often do, belatedly followed the lead of the cities. The great villas where aristocrats had long lived in pampered luxury, swimming, reading, exchanging chatty letters, and commissioning extravagant art, were gradually abandoned in favor of more secure hill forts. The transformation of the western Roman Empire was soon all but complete, its abandoned border walls gradually replaced by hundreds of smaller walls, most of them slapdash timber palisades.

Aristides wouldn't have recognized the place.

* * *

For some time after the fall of Rome, new earthen walls crisscrossed much of Europe, even when no great empires were left to build them. In England, the numbers of Devil's Dykes, Devil's Ditches, and Devil's Banks is exceeded only by the number of Grim's Dykes, Grim's Ditches, and Grim's Banks. Denmark is similarly replete with medieval earthworks. Even the Slavs, themselves only recently arrived from the steppe, constructed long barriers against their former homeland. The long walls of the Dark Ages are impossibly anonymous, and the tendency to reuse older Roman or even Iron Age defenses only muddles their histories more. None of these barriers played more than a passing role in providing local or national security.

The ancient model of empire, defended by walls and mercenaries, survived only in southeastern Europe, where the eastern half of the Roman Empire did not fall in the later fifth century. Benefiting from a securely walled capital, it carried the name of Rome for another thousand years, although we have retroactively dubbed it the "Byzantine" Empire.

The eastern emperors abandoned the Hadrianic strategy of placing a hard shell around the provinces in the early fifth century. From that point on, all efforts were concentrated on the defense of Constantinople. The construction of new walls for the capital gained particular urgency after the sack of Rome. Theodosius II receives credit for the project, although he wasn't yet ten years old when it commenced (he'd been made co-emperor as an infant, so in theory he wasn't without experience). Over time, he supplied Constantinople with fortifications worthy of Nebuchadnezzar's Babylon. Three progressively taller walls surrounded the city. The innermost wall stood an imposing twelve meters high and bristled with towers. The outermost wall overlooked a wide moat. Inside, Theodosius and his successors secured the water supply with wells, reservoirs, and spectacular underground cisterns. They also ensured that Constantinople wouldn't fall victim to the helplessness of its populace. Reigning over a city obsessively devoted to spectator sports, they established early on that every citizen had a responsibility to defend the walls when the city came under assault.

The decision to prioritize the walls of Constantinople over the old imperial border walls had immediate consequences. In the agonizing period from 422 to 502, when the western Roman Empire was crumbling, barbarians ravaged the region north of Constantinople eight times, an average of once every decade. There wasn't much that could be done about the invasions in those days. By the time an aging Anastasius (r. 491–518) came to power in the late fifth century, it was clear he'd been dealt a losing hand, although he put a brave face on it. To the kings of the Franks, Ostrogoths, and Vandals, who had taken control of France, Italy, and North Africa, respectively, he granted impressive-sounding Roman titles and "special friendships," as if he were still their emperor. The barbarians, so far as we can tell, thanked him for his kindness, patted his ambassadors on the head, and carried on as if he were some distant Constantinopolitan relic of a bygone era—which, in fact, he was. Back in the capital, Anastasius drew up plans for a new border wall closer to home.

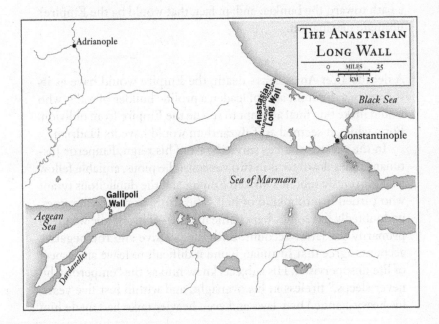

THE ANASTASIAN
LONG WALL

MILES 25
KM 25

Adrianople

Black Sea

Anastasian Long Wall

Constantinople

Sea of Marmara

Gallipoli Wall

Aegean Sea

Dardanelles

The Anastasian Long Wall ran well south of previous barriers, stretching approximately forty miles from the Black Sea to the Sea of Marmara. Anastasius thus despaired of protecting not just Ovid's former home of Tomis, but the earlier lines once created by the misnamed Trajan's Walls. Most of Roman Thrace (primarily modern Bulgaria) now lay well north of the new fortifications. This was all terrible for the inhabitants of Byzantium's most endangered province, but the wall's location did make sense, at least from the emperor's point of view: it was close enough to the capital to be defended by residents of the city. On numerous occasions, Constantinopolitan sports fans were called away from their games to defend the Anastasian Long Wall. The wall proved its defensive value repeatedly, stopping the Avars and Slavs six times in one ten-year period.

It was all a game effort, but Anastasius was no Hadrian. Already elderly by the time he took the throne, he simply didn't have the energy to fortify the entire Empire and probably never gave serious thought to the notion. Anastasius had reduced his ambitions to suit his reduced circumstances. He was putting Byzantium on a path toward the bunker, and, in fact, that would be the Empire's ultimate destination.

A decade after Anastasius's death, the Empire would have as its sovereign a different sort of leader, a prolific builder of walls, who would make one final attempt to rescue the Empire from oblivion. For a while, it seemed as if Byzantium would have its Hadrian.

In the various sources surviving from his reign, Emperor Justinian comes down to us in two versions: the pious, amiable fellow who gloriously rebuilt a broken Empire and the duplicitous tyrant who turned it into a kind of hell. The truth, as the saying goes, undoubtedly lies somewhere in the middle—if by middle we mean primarily the latter account. Both the positive and the negative accounts agree that Justinian found it difficult to leave any aspect of life unsupervised. His subjects knew him as the "emperor who never sleeps," tireless in his oversight, and within just five years, his heavy-handed new laws and even heavier taxes had made him so universally loathed that he had seemingly done the impossible and united every sports hooligan in Constantinople in opposition to his reign.

The riotous union of rival chariot-racing factions in AD 532 shook the palace so thoroughly that Justinian nearly abdicated, but the empress, Theodora, was made of somewhat sterner stuff. She declared that she would rather die than not be empress. Theodora is herself notorious in the annals of the Empire. Justinian's court historian, unleashing some pent-up venom in a scandalous tell-all, insisted that the empress, in her former career as a prostitute, had routinely worn out ten clients in a single evening before wearing out their thirty servants for her own amusement. She's also reported to have performed a rather infamous stage act in which she sprinkled seeds on her private parts, then allowed geese to pick them out. As empress, she frequently played bad cop to Justinian's good. In this capacity, she spared no cruelty—being the sort who would accuse a man of homosexuality and then have him tossed into a dungeon and tortured.

The imperial couple's innate tendencies to despotism would soon be channeled in a familiar direction. In the 540s, various barbarians arrived from the steppe and fell upon the Byzantine Empire. Here and there, they encountered old walls. On the Gallipoli peninsula, they took to the surf to slip around and attack the wall's defenders from both sides. Similarly, at Thermopylae, the barbarians skirted the old wall that had saved Greece from invasion just two decades earlier. All of Greece north of the Peloponnesus was overrun. The invaders massacred any Romans they captured. Some they impaled, others they tied to stakes and beat to death, and still others they burned to death in their huts. Many country dwellers fled to the walled cities, which quickly filled up with slapdash stone-and-clay houses. Others fled into mountains and forests, their country reduced to a "Scythian desert." When the invaders plundered even the suburbs of Constantinople, Justinian barricaded himself in the palace. The invaders returned home flush with booty and over one hundred thousand prisoners.

The experience of being trapped in the palace was quite enough for Justinian. Like a host of other monarchs before him, he calculated that he had more workers than warriors and then put them to work. The emperor had always fancied himself a great builder. Earlier in his reign, he'd constructed lavish churches and elegant cities; even his cisterns resembled cathedrals. Upon completing the reconstruction of the great domed church, Hagia Sophia, he boasted that he had outdone Solomon. However, the extravagant quality of Justinian's early work vanished in his later efforts. Now, as he sought to outdo not Solomon but Hadrian, he repented of his earlier emphasis on aesthetics and concentrated on stouter, more formidable things.

Justinian erected fortifications across southeastern Europe. He rebuilt cities that had been destroyed, constructed new walled cities in strategic locations, established new forts along the rivers, and even fortified rural farmsteads. At the storied pass of Thermopylae, he erected new walls not only at the traditional gates where the three hundred Spartans had once fought the Persians, but at every nearby route through the mountains as well. He restored an isthmus wall of the Kassandra peninsula in northern Greece and even provided long walls to a community of Christian Goths in the Crimea. At Corinth, he continued a tradition dating back to Mycenaean times when he rebuilt the old wall that had formerly blocked off the Peloponnesus. Meanwhile, he bolstered the Anastasian Long Wall above Constantinople and, at Gallipoli, demolished the eroded ruins of an old wall and erected in its place a far more formidable structure, vastly higher, with a roof over the fighting platform and with bastions extending well into the water on either end. Justinian's building program was so vast that the task of describing it finally overwhelmed even Procopius, his generally indefatigable court historian. After dutifully writing a few volumes on the emperor's fortifications, the muse deserted Procopius altogether, and he could do no better than list the new works. As it turned out, he wasn't terribly impressed by all the frantic wall building anyway; he was more interested in dishing on the empress's sexual history.

Justinian's walls had not come cheap, and as Procopius reveals in his *Secret History*, the cost of guarding them all but drained the Byzantine treasury. When Justinian's notorious subordinate,

Alexander the Scissors, eliminated the venerable tradition of having local farmers man the famous wall at Thermopylae and replaced them with two thousand regular troops, the expense nearly bank-rupted Greece. Making matters worse, the emperor had started paying his longtime enemies, the Persians, to construct walls. In 562, Justinian purchased from the Persians an expensive peace treaty. The agreement stipulated that Persia should never allow Huns or Alans to cross through a walled pass in the Caucasus. Byzantium—itself only a fading, overtaxed rump of the Roman Empire—was now subsidizing the participation of two empires in the Great Age of Walls.

To pay for both his walls and Persia's, Justinian ransacked the Empire as thoroughly as any barbarian horde. The new tax required to support the garrison at Thermopylae nearly crippled the imperial economy. Justinian was forced to stop all salaries paid to physicians and teachers. He also confiscated the municipal funds of every city in Greece, leaving the towns in such woeful straits that they could no longer keep their streetlamps burning. Without public support, theaters, hippodromes, and circuses shut down. The Hadrianic dream of a civilized people living securely and comfortably behind walls was no longer even a goal. Laughter, wrote Procopius, was no more; the people knew only sorrow and dejection.

None of this sacrifice impressed the Empire's enemies. In the late 550s, another round of Huns arrived, seeking women as much as loot. They encountered little resistance from the exhausted Empire. One division targeted the region north of Constantino-ple, where it found the Anastasian Long Wall undefended and in disrepair. The barbarians stopped to pull down a part of the wall, "setting about their task with the nonchalant air of men demol-ishing their own property." Not even the sound of a barking dog disturbed them.

Increasingly unable to build or maintain walls, the Byzantine Empire gradually shifted toward other strategies—careful intel-ligence gathering, diplomacy, the buying of allies, and, above all, the bribing of enemies. But the legacy of Justinian lingered. The autocracy and higher taxes required by his walls and wars became fixtures of Byzantine life. "I am told I am free, yet I am not allowed to use my freedom," a citizen once complained to him. Another fifty generations of Byzantine citizens would make the same complaint.

In the end, the only Byzantine walls that mattered were the walls of Constantinople itself. They were the one constant in a state whose borders routinely collapsed upon the capital. If the walls of Constantinople fostered a bunker mentality, they at least did their job, and at times what was at stake was much more than the preservation of a doddering empire. Twice between 674 and 718, Arab armies laid siege to Constantinople, and both times the city withstood the assault. The second of the two sieges, when the caliphate dedicated as many as two hundred thousand troops to defeating the Christian capital, is widely regarded as one of the greatest turning points in history. The Empire, such as it was, still played a crucial role in organizing the defense of the West. As long as the walls of Constantinople held out, they halted the Western advance of Islam and allowed Western civilization to continue to develop upon its Christian and classical roots. By contrast, the Persian Empire—defended by long walls facing the wrong direction—had already fallen to Arab armies. The consequences of those simultaneous wars reshaped the cultural and political map of Eurasia. Even faraway Chinese chroniclers took note—not that they didn't have troubles of their own.

Cycles of Walls and Despots

In the thousand years after the construction of the First Emperor's Long Wall, the spread of border walls transformed societies across Eurasia. With the ages-old duty of citizens to perform occasional military service largely commuted into an obligation to support distant border walls through taxes and labor, civilians were relieved of any direct military role, and as the ancient world drew to a close, bristling with Gogs and Magogs of ever-increasing menace, the security of virtually all of Eurasian civilization depended upon just three states. The emperors of China, Persia, and Rome inspired little love for their efforts. They were widely despised for their taxes, their forced labor, their unruly barbarian mercenaries, their arrogance, and their caprice. Citizens across all three empires sometimes imagined they might be better off under the barbarians or at least escaping to some otherworldly realm offered by religion.

Of the three, China lasted longest and had the most complicated relationship with walls. In the churn of dynasties and emperors that makes up most of Chinese history, the great border walls rise and fall to their own rhythm. They are in turns ignored, defended, skirted, breached, debated, extended, and repaired. Great lengths of ancient walls survived from one era into another, tacitly goading new generations of emperors to compete with emperors past. Rulers, drunk on unchecked power, repeatedly envisioned the impossible.

They conscripted ten thousand men to labor on their walls, then a hundred thousand, a million, 2 million.

For most of Chinese history, the question is not whether the walls worked but whether they were worth the trouble. Was the threat of invasion greater than the horrors of despotism, which ruined so many men on work crews on distant frontiers?

The walls alone have seen the truth, and they are mute.

The long history of the Chinese long walls was nearly cut short in the second century. Across China an oppressed peasantry finally vented its hatred for the dynasty that had taxed and conscripted them to support the building of walls and paying of bribes to barbarians. The targets of their rage were not the barbarians, who seemed, for many at least, a distant and rather abstract source for their troubles, but the emperors, who were for them the face of oppression. In the late second century, around the time that Marcus Aurelius was struggling against the first major collapse of the Roman frontiers, rebel leaders rallied peasants against the Han. A mostly barbarian force, composed of soldiers who'd formerly been tasked with defending China, drove the young emperor and his court from the capital at Lo-yang in AD 189–90. Thousands of hungry refugees followed in the wake of the displaced monarch, scrounging for food. When the walled frontier collapsed, there was little that the northern settlers could do but stream south in enormous numbers hoping to find refuge in safer territories.

Ninety years later, in AD 280, the founder of the short-lived Western Jin dynasty, Sima Yan, reunified China. Sima Yan was a contemporary of the Roman emperor Diocletian's, and like Diocletian, he embarked on the construction of new border walls. A Confucian scholar apparently didn't see the point. "Trust in virtue, not in walls," he counseled. As for the emperor, he celebrated his victories with such a large collection of concubines—over ten thousand reputedly—that the task of selecting a nightly lover finally exhausted him. Leaving the matter to fate, he resorted to riding around the palace in a goat-drawn cart, allowing the goats to choose his lovers. Virtue was not Sima Yan's strongest suit.

The emperor's walls only created a facade of national unity. Within a few years of Sima Yan's death, internal squabbling had resumed under the weak hand of his eldest son—the one widely regarded as a moron. The titles that Chinese historians posthumously awarded the Western Jin emperors attest to the ruling family's rapidly declining fortunes: the "Martial Emperor" was succeeded by the "Benevolent Emperor," who was followed by the "Missing Emperor," and finally the "Suffering Emperor." The latter ended his days waiting tables at a barbarian feast.

In the troubled half-century of their rule, Sima Yan and his descendants learned a familiar lesson, only destined to become more familiar over time—that a wall is only as good as its defenders, many of whom tended to be warlike foreigners of dubious loyalty. In AD 304, a Hun chieftain in Chinese service had the serendipitous recollection that one of his ancestors was a Chinese princess who'd been bartered off to the barbarians in hopes of buying peace. Via this slender claim to the Chinese throne, he declared himself emperor. The great walls could offer little protection when their defenders had turned against the state. Hun warriors overwhelmed Chinese defenses and in AD 311 sacked the capital. Thirty thousand townspeople died. The grand city itself was burned. The survivors scattered and took to the roads or to crime. In areas that had been overrun by the Huns, agriculture ground to a halt. Some refugees fled to the mountains. Most streamed south to where ethnic Chinese maintained traditional culture in a more secure environment.

For the common man, Buddhist monasticism now offered a radical alternative to a chaotic world, but the appeal of the religion, still relatively new to China, was not strictly spiritual. Monks alone escaped the heavy burdens placed on the Chinese by the need to fortify long borders. While new emperors conscripted yet another round of hapless peasants to build new walls, monks enjoyed an exemption from all physical labor. Buddhism spread rapidly in those northern regions that were home to the border walls.

For those who eschewed escape into a monastery, there was always work, overseen by the emperors from their position of absolute despotism. Whenever the old walls sank into obsolescence, new walls were ordered to replace them. One dynasty after another tried their hand at civilization's oldest strategy—using their building prowess to construct a durable defense. The Northern Wei emperors (AD 386–534) mobilized some one hundred thousand workers toward that end, following the advice of those urging them to construct walls to alleviate "anxiety about border defense." Not to be outdone, their successors, the Northern Qi, put even larger crews to work on walls. The new dynasty's mad founder, Wenxuan, who kept a crowd of prisoners close at hand for those moments when he would fly into a drunken rage and feel the need to torture or kill someone, mobilized his peasants to construct another 133 miles of barriers. These walls—the pride of an emperor who once beat his son silly for being too squeamish to carry out an execution—were but a prelude to the 300 miles of walls built in 552, and those were but a prelude to the walls that, by 556, extended China's fortified frontier all the way to the sea. Nearly 2 million men wrestled stones into place or heaped and tamped dirt while their emperor streaked naked, caroused both day and night, and dismembered anyone who offended him. By the time Wenxuan died in 559, his walls traversed over a thousand miles. His mourners, such as they were, strained to demonstrate sadness, and only one was able to force a tear.

The new walls spread across the border like a fast-growing vine—a hundred miles here, another hundred there—yet distance alone understates their impact. Measured in men, they loom even larger. Emperor Wen dispatched 30,000 men to build a wall in AD 585, then 150,000 the next year, and another 100,000 again in the year after that. Wen's son Yang outdid him, sending a million men on a wall-building campaign in 607, followed by another 200,000 in 608.

Of the great wall builders, Wen was unusual in almost every respect. Frugal and sympathetic, he reduced taxes and banned luxuries from the palace. In 595, he forbade the production of weapons and confiscated any that already existed. The edict exempted only his home province. Wen's policies set China on a starkly different course from that taken by the contemporary, post-Roman West. While Europe was militarizing during its Dark Ages, as aristocratic families that had once prided themselves on their libraries, luxuries, and civil service constructed timber castles and assembled private armies, China was pushed ever deeper into the civilized world of workers and wallers.

Wen's strategy had its benefits. It enabled a walled and predominantly civilian China to advance during a time when Europe largely stagnated. However, it also solidified the subjugation of the Chinese to their despotic rulers. Wen's benevolent paternalism was rare, at least among emperors. More common was the attitude of his son Yang, who viewed his defenseless subjects as commodities, easily replaceable and in endless supply. Like Hadrian, Yang was something of a know-it-all, who tried his hand at many things and found it annoying when other people showed more talent. A determined poet, he once produced the following quatrain:

> I wish to return but cannot do so
> Alas, to have encountered such a spring!
> Songs of birds compete to urge more wine,
> Blossoms of plums smile to kill people.

When two poets created superior works, Yang had them put to death. In retrospect, they never stood a chance. How could they have written anything worse?

The casual student of history too easily forgets that the great advantage of democracy is not that it guarantees the will of the people—such a thing hardly exists—but that it prevents the madness of despots. Scholars estimated that half a million workers died on the despotic Yang's walls, and that wasn't the end of it. The walled frontiers, positioned far from China's agricultural heartland, required a constant flow of supplies, and in the early seventh century Yang undertook construction of the Grand Canal to support the wall's defenders. Five million workers labored along its eleven-hundred-mile course. When it was done, the Grand Canal connected the Yangtze and Yellow Rivers to some thirty thousand miles of local waterways, allowing China to achieve a unity unprecedented among the Old World empires. The canal was a wonder, but it didn't come cheap. To the number of workers who died in its construction must be added those who died in the famines caused when Yang's conscriptions carried off so many peasants that there weren't enough field workers to tend the crops. Chinese historians logged numerous complaints about the project: the construction never ceased, the people were exhausted, and, worse, Yang used his troops to control the people. Could building the wall and the canal that supplied its defenders have cost more lives than the wars it prevented? This didn't square with Yang's calculations. He celebrated his new wall in characteristically artless verse:

> Building the wall is a stratagem that will benefit a myriad generations
> Bringing peace to a hundred million people.

Peace, of course, is a worthy goal, but it is possible the wall worked too well, at least from Yang's point of view. The Chinese, uninterested in vilifying foreign enemies who could not penetrate the frontier wall, united instead against the emperor who made them build it. Tales of Yang's tyranny took on a new life after his death. A hundred years after his court spent its final night in oblivious partying, while rebellion closed in on them, Yang became a figure of legend. Storytellers wrote of how the emperor had buried fifty thousand workers alive, headfirst, for the crime of having dug parts of the Grand Canal too shallow, how he'd employed a million workers to build a vast pleasure garden and tens of thousands more to construct a labyrinthine pavilion where he could privately pursue his aphrodisiac-driven sexual desires. All this is to say nothing of the women he forced to haul his enormous barges up the canal, their punishment for not making the cut for his harem.

The next dynasty repudiated Yang's walls. "Emperor Yang exhausted the country in building long walls," announced a Tang emperor. He preferred to defend the Empire with Turkish steppe warriors. The Empire itself continued to unite and divide as it always had. New dynasties brought new despots, and new despots typically brought new walls.

It wasn't until the thirteenth century that a genuine existential threat arrived at China's borders, unexpectedly vindicating all those infamous emperors who'd been convinced that there were worse fates than conscript labor. The shock of the Mongol conquest reweighted the balance sheet of Chinese strategy. Will half a million die in construction of a new wall? Small price compared to whole cities burned, their inhabitants put to the sword. Will the people suffer from exhaustion and overtaxation? At least they'll have their lives. Could a wall protect China for "a myriad generations"? Maybe this time. A dozen dead despots, reviled for the crimes they'd committed to fortify China's borders, smiled in hell.

The nation that would have such a profound impact on China emerged somewhat belatedly out of the swarm of tribes occupying the steppe to China's north. Prior to the twelfth century, the Mongols were generally indistinguishable from other sheep-herding steppe warriors whose confederations rose and fell over time. They moved about with their animals, forever squabbling with their neighbors, such as the Tatars, with whom they were later confused. To the Armenians, they were the "nation of archers." To the West, they were the Tartars, a nation sprung straight from hell ("Tartarus"). Like nearly all unwalled peoples of the premodern world, they dedicated their men to war. A modern historian has observed that for the Mongols "the whole of life was a process of military training." Every Mongol male learned fighting skills. Boys learned to ride and shoot as toddlers, and with that training came a brutal toughening process that taught them to endure hunger, thirst, and cold. Even the annual hunts, during which the entire army formed a vast ring that slowly encircled its prey, served as exercises in discipline.

Genghis Khan once remarked that man's greatest joy lay in cutting his enemy to pieces, seizing his possessions, making his loved ones cry, and raping his women. Whether any of this is true, I lack the experience to say. At the very least, Genghis's pronouncement captures the spirit of the nomadic warriors he collected into his war machine. Genghis knew that the strength of his host lay in its rough-and-tumble lifestyle, and in his Great Yasa he forbade any of his men from moving into a town and adopting a sedentary life.

As if to bolster this decree, he insisted that his Mongols should not show favor to any particular faith, religion being the stuff of cities, temples, mosques, and books—all things of no value to the Mongol soldier. Urban life was entirely distasteful and alien to him, and he intended it to remain so for his men as well. To Genghis, the Mongols would always be "the people whose tents are protected by skirts of felt," men whose loyalty he rewarded "with things he takes from earthen-walled cities."

Ah, those earthen-walled cities! How it disgusted Genghis to contemplate men living in such fashion. Like most barbarians, he never quite understood that the treasures he coveted were only produced by people living behind the walls he disdained. In the early-thirteenth century, he passed bloodlessly through China's border walls, the gates having been opened to him by Chinese subjects who could not imagine anything worse than their tyrannical emperors. To put it charitably, their decision ranks as one of the greatest miscalculations in history. Genghis initially demanded a heavy tribute of gold, silver, satins, and other luxuries, but this tribute stayed his hand for only a year, after which he impatiently manufactured an insult and broke the peace. He also declared himself insulted by the Tanghut people who occupied northwestern China. "The Tanghut are people who build city walls," observed one of his advisers. "They're people whose camps don't move from year to year. They won't run away from us carrying off the walls of their cities." This was in summary the nomad's view of the civilized wall builders: sitting ducks whose occasional slowness in forking over their wealth offended the natural order in which civilized folk paid craven tribute to superior barbarian warriors.

The Mongols possessed a ruthlessness rarely found even among warrior peoples. When assaulting city walls, Mongol generals mercilessly placed Chinese captives at the vanguard of their assault forces, knowing that the city's defenders, recognizing their relatives in the firing line, would hesitate or even refuse to unleash their arrows upon them. Mongol rank and file unflinchingly obeyed commands to commit genocide and seemingly thought nothing of meeting quotas for numbers of civilians slaughtered. In one town, a general might order his men to slaughter five townspeople apiece. In another, he might command them to slaughter forty. The soldiers carried out these commands and moved on to the next town.

Two decades of civilian massacres all but depopulated northern China. When Beijing surrendered to the Mongols after a long siege had left starved inhabitants resorting to cannibalism, the Mongols turned the city into a slaughterhouse. Fires burned for a month, while bones lay in heaps, unburied, the ground all around still oily from human fat.

At one point, the Mongols considered destroying all of China, with an eye toward razing the earthen-walled cities and using the land for pasture. A Chinese adviser convinced them they'd be better off with millions of cowed tribute-payers. In retrospect, they seem to have split the difference. The population of China fell from around 120 million in 1207 to less than 60 million in 1290, with most of those losses occurring in the battle-scarred north, a region that included not just the walled frontier along the steppe but the Yellow River itself, ancestral homeland to Chinese culture. The Mongols could boast that they could ride over the sites of many former cities without encountering any ruins high enough to make their horses stumble. To Genghis, who regarded the fact that he still ate simply and wore rags as proof of his righteousness, the destruction of China had been foreordained. "Heaven is weary of the inordinate luxury of China," he said.

China's new Mongol rulers lacked any appetite for great walls. Not even Genghis's cosmopolitan grandson, Kublai Khan, for all his public appreciation of Chinese culture, could be bothered with such a traditional use of resources. For a hundred years, the Chinese people—what few were left—were finally allowed to rest from their monumental labors. Five generations were born never knowing the experience of shoveling windblown loess for a madman. They had only the folk stories to weigh against the tales of Genghis Khan. And when they had lived under the Mongols until they could stand it no longer, they finally produced a new dynasty and resumed work on their walls.

The Ming era (AD 1368–1644) took root in long-simmering Chinese resentment toward Mongol overlords. Zhu Yuanzhang, the founder of the dynasty, believed himself on a divine mission to restore a true China. He attempted to remake China as he imagined it had once been: ethnically and culturally homogenous, uninterested in universal empire, and resolutely focused on the defense of its limited borders. He also envisioned the Chinese state as a nation enclosed. In the instructions he left to his successors, Zhu warned future emperors against seeking conquests, instructing them instead to maintain a strong defense. The early Ming, obedient to these principles, rebuilt the city walls destroyed by the Mongols. Thousands of walled cities again populated the map of China.

Some later Ming emperors, temporarily enjoying a respite from Mongol raids, chose to ignore Zhu's advice and even flirted with naval policies that might have made China master of the seas and colonizers of the New World. Chinese fleets reached the coast of Africa. However, it would not be China's destiny to beat the Portuguese in the race to establish a sea link between Europe and Asia. In 1433, the revival of Mongol power revived old fears. The emperors abruptly reined in their maritime ambitions. Isolationist-minded advisers, never fans of overseas adventuring, won the day, pointing to a loss suffered by China's great fleet off Vietnam, and more important, the need to retrench in the face of a resurgent Mongol threat. The Empire scuttled the largest navy in the world and turned its back on exploration. In that same decade, though China's engineers had overcome the technical obstacles to providing year-round water to the north, the country's officials chose to withdraw from garrisons that couldn't be easily resupplied by sending materials up the Grand Canal. The frontier lines were brought in by nearly two hundred miles.

A military disaster precipitated the country's final retreat behind walls. In 1449, the Mongols invaded yet again. Taking personal command of his troops, the young emperor, Yingzong, set out to find and punish the invaders. When the Mongols attacked his camp at Tumu, they destroyed most of the army and captured the emperor. The Tumu Crisis ended any lingering possibility that the Chinese would look outward like those Western nations already dispatching traders and explorers to new lands. From that time on, the Ming would follow the advice of their founder. They would shut themselves in, eschew cosmopolitanism, cling to tradition, and concentrate on defense. The emperors would redirect the nation's energies to building walls. The Mongols had left them no choice.

In the Ming era, the familiar role of the ruthless despot is conspicuously missing. While court officials exchanged theories of national security, the emperors allowed local officials to construct new walls, improve old ones, or fill important gaps, utterly unaware that they were overseeing, in this patchwork fashion, the construction of a Wonder of the World.

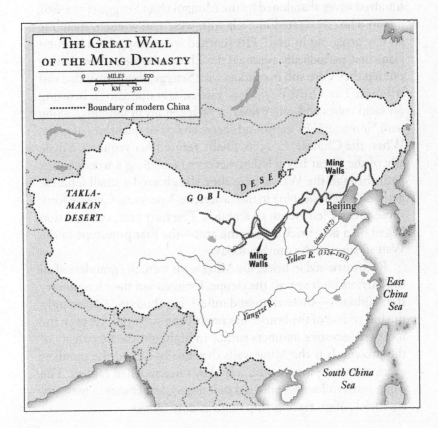

The Great Wall now took form in fits and starts, in unconnected stretches in often remote regions. New lengths were added whenever the Mongols found an existing gap and exploited it. During the Ming era, the Chinese were forced to fight nearly two hundred wars against the Mongols. As the gaps in the Wall gradually filled, knitting together the Ming defenses, the Mongols found it harder and harder to break through. The Wall was, for all its modern detractors, effective at its task. It fended off attacks by Mongol raiding parties numbering in the thousands.

In 1576, a minor Mongol raid precipitated the Wall's final significant redesign. The proximate cause of the raid was, according to one leading wall researcher, the fury of a woman scorned. The woman, known only as the Great Beyiji, was one of at least one hundred wives abandoned by the Mongol chief Sengge (1522–86), a man who "dissipated himself with wine and women, spending all day groaning in bed." His scorned wives, supported by their clansmen, periodically swarmed the Chinese border, where, letting on that they were still in cahoots with Sengge, they demanded vast tributes. The Great Beyiji was particularly obnoxious, insisting on satin robes and other fineries "stacked up in mounds," along with "innumerable" cattle and sheep, and great quantities of grain. When the Chinese, in 1576, finally refused her requests, a male ally of the Great Beyiji led his seventy men along a woodcutters' path through the Wall, where they slaughtered a small Chinese garrison caught sleeping in their barracks. A pursuing Chinese force subsequently fell victim to ambush. The next year, construction began on a new brick wall in the area—the first prototype of the Wall so admired by tourists today.

Reconstructed in brick, the Ming walls were the grandest of all the barriers built against the steppe. Estimates of their length vary tremendously—three thousand miles? Ten thousand? Amazingly, the full course of the border has never been surveyed, yet even the most conservative numbers suffice to highlight the immensity of the project. It is the Ming walls that finally earned the moniker *great*, attracting tourists the way they once repelled raiders. The Ming walls roll across hills and mountains, sometimes in masonry and brick, often resting atop huge granite blocks.

In the twenty-first century, historians continue to discover other Ming defenses, long overshadowed by the Great Wall. Far from the steppe, for example, the Chinese had walled off their southern border. In the sixteenth and seventeenth centuries, the emperors deemed the highland Miao of Vietnam a threat great enough to merit hundreds of miles of walls, and perhaps they were right: the Miao destroyed one border wall in the seventeenth century, and the Chinese were still building stone barriers in the region as late as 1805.

The Ming emperors were no more successful than their ancient predecessors in selling the idea of the Wall to the people they drafted to build it. Nearly two thousand years had passed since the time of the First Emperor's Long Wall, and public opinion in the Ming era was so hostile to the memory of it that the emperors were careful not to use the term *Long Wall* at all. The usual poetry of resentment circulated: folk tales of a nation crushed by the work of it all. How could mere humans have produced such a prodigious monument? Mostly through supernatural assistance, apparently: a supervisor is assisted by an old man who knits the wall out of brambles; workers see a length of silk falling from the sky and use it as the inspiration for moving granite blocks down a giant ice slide. Apparently, the supernatural did not extend its assistance to the Chinese at war. In the seventeenth century, the barbarian Manchu were let through by a disloyal Chinese general.

The Manchu were as foreign to Chinese civilization as any nation from the steppe. At first, the conquerors could hardly tolerate walls of any type. If they occupied a building, they'd sometimes knock down the walls, leaving only pillars to support the roof. They also refused to play the traditional role of barbarians assimilating into Chinese society. Like the ancient Spartans, the Manchu preferred their homeland not be contaminated with too much civilization. They clung to their traditional ways and even forced Chinese men to adopt Manchu hairstyles. They ridiculed the Chinese, but especially their walls: "The men of Qin built the Long Wall as a defense against the barbarians," wrote one historian for the Manchu. "Up went the Long Wall and down came the empire.

People are still laughing about it today." As for the Great Wall, the Manchu wrote an epitaph:

> Endlessly they built walls, without ever pausing for breath.
> The builders worked from dawn till dusk, and what was the use?

A Chinese author once reflected on the history of his nation with a resigned fatalism: "The empire, long divided, must unite: long united, must divide. Thus it has ever been." The author who added these words as an introduction to the bloated fourteenth-century epic *Three Kingdoms* can be forgiven his cyclical view of history. Time and again, the Chinese had succumbed to the cyclicality he so succinctly described. Time and again, barbarians had crashed down upon the Chinese and seized control of the northern regions. Sometimes the invaders were mercenaries who turned on the people they'd been hired to defend. Either way, China's unity would be broken. Millions would flee south, leaving the defense of the north in the hands of upstart, barbarian dynasties. The new defenders would learn to build walls. China, wherever or whatever that was, would go on. The walls, like China itself, outlasted the Empire, but not because they stood forever. Once built, the walls had to fall; once fallen, they had to rise again. Thus it was for the walls, just as it was for China.

For the author of the introduction to *Three Kingdoms*, it was enough to observe the cycles of Chinese history. Historians, however, must view those cycles in their broader context, and some cycles are more important than others. The Ming-era retreat behind the Great Wall wasn't just another turn of the wheel. The rise of the West owed much to the timing of those Ming walls, which prevented newly walled Chinese from competing with a burst of expansion by the West. The rise owed perhaps even more to the failure of walls in another vast and important region.

Walls and the Apocalypse

WESTERN AND CENTRAL ASIA, AD 500–1300

In the early-nineteenth century, some four thousand years after kings and pharaohs first began inscribing bricks and tablets with bombastic announcements of their great walls, a British poet penned a sonnet about a statue that had once squatted in the sands of Egypt. The poem contrasted the boastful inscription of a long-dead king with the desolation of his former domain. Its fourteen lines are among the most famous in the English language, and more than a few of us gratefully acknowledged their admirable brevity in selecting a work to memorize for our high school literature class. Even the trauma of declaiming the poem before an audience of bored gum-chewing classmates couldn't entirely diminish the power of the last stanza:

> And on the pedestal these words appear:
> "My name is Ozymandias, king of kings:
> Look on my works, ye Mighty, and despair!"
> Nothing beside remains. Round the decay
> Of that colossal wreck, boundless and bare
> The lone and level sands stretch far away.

At the time Shelley wrote "Ozymandias" as a belated epitaph for a dead civilization that had long ago fallen into ruin, the contrast between the poet's home—a rapidly industrializing Britain, swarm-

145

ing with inventors, engineers, scientists, philosophers, writers, and artists—and the ancient cradles of civilization was nearly total. At least Egypt still had its statues. In Western and Central Asia, the magnificent Bronze Age cities had been reduced to piles of dirt. So thorough was their oblivion that almost no one seemed to have given any thought to what lay beneath the great mounds until an amateur antiquarian and employee of the East India Company took an interest in the remains of Babylon in 1811. Real excavations wouldn't commence for another three decades. Over the nineteenth century, archaeologists and antiquarians trickled over in greater numbers, steadily unearthing a world long disrupted—ancient canals filled with silt, tablets inscribed in obscure, forgotten scripts. All about them as they worked, the excavators saw nomadic herdsmen with their flocks. Lions and other predators still roamed. While railroads and telegraph lines crisscrossed the Western European homelands of the archaeologists, the territories of Mesopotamia and neighboring regions were less urban and more pastoral than they'd been in the days of Gilgamesh, four thousand years earlier. Bedouins still raided traveling parties, and mountain nomads still menaced the cities.

The ancient founders of the civilizations that once flourished in these ancient lands had originally defended themselves from the nomads with city walls. In time, the Ozymandias-like kings of Ur had mobilized their basket carriers to erect the first border walls, and more than a thousand years after that, the kings of Babylon had ordered the construction of even grander walls. It wasn't until the Great Age of Walls, however, when China and Rome were erecting fortifications that ran for hundreds of miles, that an empire finally dedicated its resources to a more comprehensive defense system in the heartland of civilization, strategically placing barriers intended to seal off all of Western and Central Asia.

The Persian fortifications, like the Roman, have only a short history. It is a dark comedy of sorts, a tale of walls intended to resist an old enemy from a familiar direction, completed just before the arrival of a new enemy from another direction. Later, when those walls might still have been pressed into service to save the ancient cities from a second, more devastating invasion, there were no longer any guards in the towers or patrolling the walkways. Send in the soldiers? Too late for that. Send in the clowns.

Despite its twists, the story of the border walls of Western and Central Asia occupies a special place in history, partly because it illustrates the great stakes that were always at play with ancient border walls, but mostly because the consequences of abandoning the walls has influenced the world geopolitically and culturally ever since. It was the beginning of a great turn in world history, an unexpected pivot that saw an enormously important part of the world begin its descent into obscurity. In the later Middle Ages, a vast and populous region that had radiated art, culture, and political power long before either Rome or China fell strangely silent. It has never fully recovered. Today, the map of Western and Central Asia is populated by an array of struggling nations, each characterized by varying degrees of violence, repression, poverty, and closed-mindedness. The descendants of the old Persian Empire include Afghanistan, Uzbekistan, Tajikistan, Turkmenistan, Iran, Iraq, Azerbaijan, and Syria. In all of them lie the remains of forgotten walls, like colossal wrecks, boundless and bare, where lone and level sands still stretch far away.

The Persians, who built most of the Western and Central Asian border walls, had little hand in the creation of the ancient civilizations of Asia. Much like the barbarian dynasties of northern China, they inherited most of their walled cities through conquest, having overcome the Babylonian border walls in the sixth century BC. The Persians only gradually adapted to the settled habits of the countries they ruled. In their early years, they perfected little more than the art of unleashing arrows from the back of a horse. Herodotus, writing in the fifth century BC, reported that the Persians taught their young just three things: riding, archery, and truth telling. Having become the possessors of palaces and cities, they eventually fulfilled the prophecies of those Western and Chinese thinkers who argued that civilization dulls the warrior's edge. In the fourth century BC, the Empire fell to Alexander the Great.

Alexander transformed the landscape of Western and Central Asia, replacing the age-old temple towns with Greek cities.

Although popular tradition credited Alexander with supernatural powers in the defense of civilization, his Greco-Asian world was in reality short-lived, falling to various steppe peoples, some of whom reestablished a smaller version of the old Persian Empire, under the Parthian dynasty. For a second time, a nation of horsemen reigned over a civilization they had initially intended only to raid, and like their predecessors, the Parthians gradually learned to think of defense in the manner of civilized folk. Just as the Romans had built colonies fashioned after their rectangular military camps, the Parthians eventually rebuilt the ruined rectangles of Alexander's Greek cities to reflect the circular arrangement of their own camps. Towns such as Merv, once a proper Greek quadrilateral, were given ring walls. Meanwhile, Parthian art finally adopted new styles, as the rulers, gradually losing touch with the tastes of the steppe, began at last to "swallow the Greek poison." By the third century AD, the Persian state was sufficiently prepared to receive a dynasty wholly committed to urban civilization and wholly separated from the society of the steppe. That new dynasty—the Sasanid—developed the idea of an Iranian nation that had to be defended in the manner of other great empires. The Sasanid shahs brought elegance and sophistication to Persian culture. They also brought a quintessentially civilized view of the world, and a plan of protecting the entire Empire with walls.

The Sasanids were the first Persian rulers to erect colossal fortifications on the borders of their realm. As early as the mid-fourth century, Shah Shapur II (r. 309–79) revived the old idea of protecting Mesopotamia with a wall. The immediate threat to the Land between the Rivers came from the Arabs, against whom Shapur campaigned ruthlessly. For his policy of threading ropes through the shoulders of Arab prisoners, Shapur acquired the sobriquet "Lord of the Shoulders." He constructed the so-called Moat of Shapur west of the Euphrates to hold off these desert enemies and made the wall part of a broader defensive system.

Toward the end of Shapur's long reign (its longevity benefited from his having been crowned while still in his mother's womb) the Huns announced their presence in Western Asia, arriving through the Caucasus Mountains to "fill the world with panic and bloodshed." The rattling of Alexander's gates shook two empires. Both Rome and Persia were directly imperiled, and the rapprochement that followed was heartwarming, as long as you don't examine it too closely. The two ancient foes fell into each other's arms like star-crossed lovers in a romantic comedy and, in the grip of mutual goodwill, tempered by terror, agreed to collaborate on a joint effort to limit the Huns to the steppe. Emperor and shah signed treaties to the effect that Rome would bear half of the costs of Persia's defense of the Caucasus. That treaty would be confirmed repeatedly throughout the fifth century and, after a rather vicious spat, replaced by a new one in the sixth century.

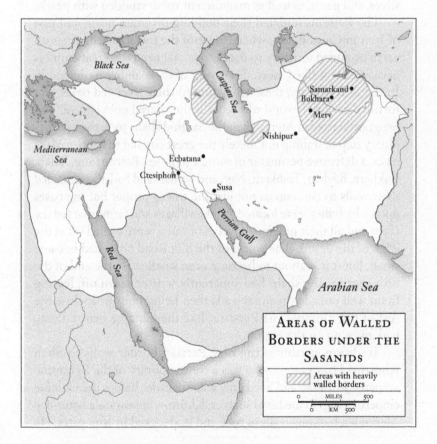

AREAS OF WALLED
BORDERS UNDER THE
SASANIDS

Areas with heavily
walled borders

0   MILES   500
0   KM   500

The Persians put the Roman funds to use as best they could—sometimes fighting the Huns, sometimes paying them just to go away. From time to time, the Persians sought additional capital, arguing that by fending off the barbarians they were defending both empires. Increasingly, Persian strategy had but one aim: walling off the steppe. The Arab frontier was thus ignored while Persian rulers constructed oasis walls in Central Asia, bottleneck walls in Caucasian mountain passes, and long border walls in the plains where the mountains entered the Caspian. The shahs pursued the new strategy at fantastic expense, "bleeding their country," according to one author. With what money remained after the building projects, they bought off the steppe barbarians with gold, silver, and gems, as well as magnificent robes studded with pearls.

The Persians initiated their building program north and east of Iran in Central Asia, where some of the most ancient cities on earth occupied territory so dangerous that even the great empires occasionally walked away, despairing of their ability to defend it. In the fifth century, these cities turned their river-fed oases into fortified prisons beyond whose walls they dared not venture. The program started at Merv, when the Sasanid shahs took the extraordinary step of walling not merely the great city but the entire Merv oasis, a defensive perimeter of some 150 miles. Before long, Balkh, Bukhara, Bayhaq, Tashkent, Nur, and Samarkand had also extended their walls to encompass not just the towns proper but the oases upon which they were located. All the villages and farms that fed the cities and all their precious sources of water were walled off at the edge of the desert. The world of the Silk Road cities had become small, but it was about to become even smaller. By the end of the fifth century, the shahs had apparently written them off, leaving them well outside the great walls then being built to enclose the rest of the Empire. The Persians, like the Chinese before them, had given up on the region.

Tradition attributes the new Persian border walls to Shah Khosrow I (r. 531–79), who was a contemporary of the Byzantine emperor Justinian and lived only a few decades before the Chinese emperor Yang. In medieval sources, Khosrow appears as a latter-day Alexander, building walls of rock and lead locked by iron gates. He is said to have constructed more than twenty new walls throughout the Caucasus and several more east of the Caspian. The longest, the Sadd-e Anushirvan, bears his name (Anushirvan being a kind of epithet for him). Scientific dating techniques, however, haven't definitively confirmed tradition. Archaeologists believe that the walls attributed to Khosrow could have been built in either the late fifth or sixth centuries, so it is likely that Khosrow's father, Kavadh I, initiated many of them, even if he didn't live to see them completed.

Kavadh and Khosrow were certainly cut from the same cloth. Like all good father-son teams, they worked well together, especially in their joint repression of the Mazdakites, a communistic religious cult that advocated the abolition of private property and the sharing of all wealth and women. Ironically, Kavadh had briefly flirted with Mazdakism as a youth. It was the usual story in which a teenager, nearing adulthood and fancying himself a heroic crusader for justice, falls for the seductions of some impractically radical group, subsequently outgrows the infatuation, and has the remaining members of the group put to a horrible death. The young Khosrow actually handled the purge for his father. Although only a despot-in-training at the time, Khosrow's final disposition of the Mazdakites was so horrific, so creative in its sadism, that generations of Persian artists seem to have specialized in lurid illustrations of it: the cult members are depicted buried upside down, their feet sticking up as if growing out of a human garden; their leader, Mazdak, must witness their executions before being hung upside down and riddled with arrows. Kavadh and Khosrow had a penchant for such deeds. The father once blinded his own uncle, either by pouring hot olive oil over his eyes or by pricking them with white-hot iron needles (no one could remember which). Upon succeeding to the throne, Khosrow had his brothers and nephews put to death.

It seems that the father was the first to take an interest in walls. In 502, Kavadh learned a firsthand lesson in the value of fortifications when he assaulted a Byzantine city in Mesopotamia. Without any assistance from the Byzantine army, the civilians of the city defended their walls for so long that the town prostitutes eventually took to mounting the ramparts and taunting the shah with displays of their private parts. This was the kind of thing a proud tyrant doesn't easily forget. However, another factor almost certainly played a part in intensifying his, and Khosrow's, interest in walls. Between 455 and 522, an unprecedented ten Persian diplomatic missions reached China, the first such travels ever recorded. At least one is known to have carried a letter from Kavadh. Subsequently, Khosrow dispatched several delegations to China as well. For the first time, Persian delegations would have passed through the outer walls of the Chinese Empire, eventually returning to their own land like tourists coming back from a trip to the Great Wall, breathless with tales that must have piqued the imaginations of the shahs.

Whenever or however they decided to wall off their realm, Kavadh and Khosrow already had laborers at hand for the work. The father constructed many new cities, while the son put his civilian labor force to work on any number of infrastructure projects: clearing roads, digging underground aqueducts, bringing new land under cultivation. Once, upon building a city designed to look like Antioch, Khosrow dubbed it "Khosrow's 'Better Than Antioch' "— a name that, mercifully, failed to stick. Khosrow spared no expense on his public works. To help fund them, he overhauled the tax system. Managing far-flung projects from his personal estate—which was also surrounded by high walls—Khosrow apparently resolved to fortify the Empire with barriers that would stand forever. At the Sadd-e Anushirvan, better known as the Red Snake, or Great Wall of Gorgan, his men had at their disposal only the same windblown loess as the ancient Chinese. Unwilling, however, to settle for a Chinese-style barrier of tamped earth, they dug long canals to supply water for brick making. Every fifty yards or so, they placed kilns. It was an extraordinary effort, but it had a purpose. The builders knew that whereas sun-dried bricks crumble easily, baking them creates a ceramic, like a modern bowl or dish, in which the high heat has chemically transformed the clay. Ceramic is as timeless as any substance on earth, a fact that can be easily demonstrated if you have enough patience and the right genes for longevity. Take a dish, bury it in your backyard, and if you're still alive in a thousand years, you can dig it up and you will find it hasn't changed. Eons hence, long after the sun has gone dark, that ceramic will remain unchanged. A thick, well-made ceramic brick is resistant even to hammering.

The Red Snake, which was guarded by at least thirty-six sizable forts and supported by a vast hydraulic system designed to provide water to approximately thirty thousand soldiers, formed only a part of the Sasanid state's defensive system. A similar barrier, the so-called Wall of Tammishe, ran perpendicular to it, and the two walls may once have intersected in an area now submerged under the Caspian Sea. The great border walls of northern Iran were matched by fortifications on the other side of the Caspian, where the shahs directed especially strenuous efforts toward shoring up the defenses of the Caucasus Mountains. To seal off the route between the eastern foothills of the Caucasus and the shore of the Caspian, the Sasanids constructed no fewer than five barriers, the most visually impressive of which blocked off the plain between the mountains and the sea at Derbent in what is now the Russian republic of Dagestan. Originally constructed in the mid-fifth century, the Derbent wall was funded by annual payments of 136.5 kilograms of gold from the Romans, who designated the money be used for defense against "Alans and other barbarians."

Posterity exaggerated the Derbent barrier. Succeeding generations, obviously impressed by the rampart, imagined it as a "Great Caucasian Wall" that had once extended the entire distance from the Caspian to the Black Sea. In time, it was attributed to Alexander. It was inevitable that Alexander should appear in the tangled folk histories of the Sasanid walls. By the time the poet Ferdowsi wrote Persia's national epic, the *Shahnameh*, around AD 1000, the great conqueror, who had destroyed the original Persian Empire and become a cursed name in Iran, had already been sufficiently rehabilitated to play the hero. And what had Alexander done to redeem himself in Persian eyes? Why, nothing less than build five-hundred-yard-high walls against those northern barbarians, now described as giants, Gog and Magog.

Horsemen from the steppe never did bring down the Persian Empire. When the men of the north finally arrived in force, the

Empire was already gone. Kavadh and Khosrow had walled the wrong borders. The Persian walls, which were built to defend against the Huns, were quiet when the Empire fell. Persia succumbed instead to a different sort of enemy, a new religion that had announced its birth by declaring war on the world. In the seventh century, the armies of Islam found little resistance from a war-weary and plague-ravaged Persia. The Empire, with its dozens of north-facing walls, was taken from the south.

Ironically, the caliphs and sultans who succeeded the Persian shahs quickly adopted the latter's views regarding the urgency of fortifying the northern frontier. In the early eighth century, Muslim rulers established a border wall far to the north of any of the old Persian barriers. They hoped to protect a vital region of Central Asia that is now part of Tajikistan and Uzbekistan. Later in that same century, the townspeople of Bukhara beseeched their governor for still more protection from steppe raiders. They complained that the Turks, who'd succeeded the Huns as the dominant menace from the steppe, frequently arrived without warning to plunder their villages and carry off slaves. They pointed to a lesson from their history: in days gone by, they said, a queen had constructed a long border wall and attained respite from the Turks. Who was this queen? We have no name, but she was clearly well-known, a sort of local Alexander, if Alexander is understood to be mostly a builder of walls. The name Divar-i-kanpirak, or Kempirak, which was given the wall subsequently built by the Muslim governor, translates as "old woman" and is not unique. A number of "old women" figure in the landscape from Uzbekistan to Afghanistan. This first wall, which stretched along the banks of the Zeravshan River to Samarkand, was soon supplemented by a second, built in the area northeast of Tashkent. As in China, the price of security created an unbearable burden on the locals, and the Bukharans soon regretted their earlier requests. They complained so much about the effort of maintaining the walls that, after some years, the governor at last "freed the people" and took the field against the Turks. He would have been better served defending the wall. By the tenth century, Turks had overrun most of the old Empire.

Turkish rule was the beginning of the decline for most of Asia.

The new rulers—being warriors accustomed to the open steppe—never quite understood how to manage the ancient, walled world they had inherited. In Mesopotamia, old waterworks that had been carefully repaired and expanded by earlier caliphs received little attention from nomadic Turkish horsemen, who simply ignored the necessity of regular maintenance. Wherever the locals abandoned their ages-old tasks, the canals filled with silt, and salty water gradually drenched the fields. In Central Asia, one of the great cities carried on—Merv (now in Turkmenistan) briefly became the largest city on earth—but the border walls were altogether forgotten. No guards were standing watch when the apocalypse finally arrived.

Gog and Magog were real, as it turns out, even if they appeared under another name. It was Genghis Khan and his sons, freshly arrived from the invasion of China, who reduced the cosmopolitan cultural capitals of Western and Central Asia into sand-blown ruins. Their impact, when they finally rode around the undefended border walls, was everything the prophets of doom had feared and then some. The Mongol conquest of the region from Uzbekistan to Syria nearly exterminated civilization there altogether. Millions died in the genocide, and for those who were left alive, it was difficult to attain even the essentials of life.

It would be anticlimactic, after having seen so many walls built against the steppe and so much mythology develop around the walls' legendary foils, not to give at least some account of what finally happened to the most ancient of the walled lands. A summary account would begin in 1219, when Genghis Khan turned his attentions to the Central Asian region of Transoxiana, where Tashkent, Ferghana, Balasaghun, and other cities thrived. This would be the end for a resourceful and resilient people. The Mongols returned the region north of the Syr Darya River to its natural state, its landscape marred only by ruins and empty buildings. The old border walls were covered with dust, fading into the deep obscurity that nowadays renders them all but unnoticed, a source of mystery even to the locals. The irrigated farmland that once supported the great cities was deliberately returned to steppe.

As the Mongols moved south, the great cities fell one by one, beginning with Bukhara, which had been a center of learning filled with doctors, jurists, and savants of every religion. The great city's final days passed swiftly, beginning on that day the inhabitants first looked out in panic and saw the countryside choked with horsemen. Great clouds of dust, kicked up by the horses, turned day into night. Most of the Bukharans fled to the citadel, while an army of twenty thousand Turkish soldiers and citizens met the Mongols and was wiped out. Upon entering the city, Genghis wondered quizzically if the mosque was the palace of a sultan. When told that it was the house of a god, he lost interest, dismounted his horse, climbed to the pulpit, and announced, "The countryside is empty of fodder; fill our horses' bellies." He then ordered the cases used for storing the Quran turned into mangers and commanded Muslim priests, teachers, and scholars to serve as grooms. Later, angered by the continuing resistance of the still-unconquered citadel, he ordered the entire town burned and slaughtered every male who "stood taller than the butt of a whip." As one survivor put it, "They came, they sapped, they burnt, they slew, they plundered, and they departed."

At Samarkand, the number of the slaughtered rose to fifty thousand. It could have been worse: At Tirmiz, Genghis had his soldiers rip open the townspeople's bellies in case they'd tried to hide their valuables by swallowing them. At Balkh, the Mongols left behind so many corpses that lions, vultures, and wolves mingled among the carrion without quarreling. The Mongols swept through the remaining towns of Central Asia with dispatch. Merv made the mistake of resisting a bit too strenuously. It took four days for the Mongols to march all the townspeople out onto a plain for their annihilation. The corpses lay in piles so high as to make mountains look like hills. Several people attempted to count the dead and came to a figure of 1.3 million. This had become the inevitable end for cities that resisted the Mongol onslaught. After a while, the numbers of the slaughtered—given as 1.6 million in the city of Herat alone (2.4 million according to another author)—seem to have overwhelmed the survivors' ability to count.

The Mongols reached the climax of their destructive energies at Baghdad. In the thirteenth century, Baghdad was the city of the caliphs, an intellectual center, home to hundreds of bookstores and libraries at a time when books were scarce in much of the world. When the Mongols arrived in huge numbers, well prepared with Chinese siege engines, civilians from all over Iraq took refuge behind Baghdad's walls, crowding the streets and stores. However, the defeat of the caliph's armies doomed the city, leaving too few soldiers to man the ramparts. The slaughter of Baghdad's citizens went on for a biblical forty days. When it was finally over, the traumatized survivors came out of hiding, their faces drained of all color. They looked, according to one contemporary, "like the dead emerging from their graves on the day of resurrection, fearful, hungry, and cold." Some eight hundred thousand had died, "not including children thrown in the mud, those who perished in the canals, wells, and basements, and those who died of hunger and fear." The dead lay in great mounds, exposed to the rain that fell on them, accelerating the putrefaction. Flies swarmed everywhere. A great stench pervaded the air, forcing the survivors to hold onions close to their noses to block the smell. In the meanwhile, floating corpses contaminated the canal water and caused an epidemic.

The fall of Baghdad extinguished the last embers of resistance in Iraq. Iraqi civilians, the descendants of the ancient Mesopotamians, having not even the deeds of warlike ancestors to inspire them, declined even to mount a fight. The contemporary Arab writer Ibn al-Athir of Mosul expressed his disgust at the sheeplike acquiescence of civilians to their fate, not realizing he was simply describing the most ancient of differences between wallers and warriors. He recounted several stories: how a single Mongol had slaughtered every member of a heavily populated village because not one of the villagers had defended himself; how a man patiently waited while his Mongol captor rode off and fetched a sword with which to kill him; how seventeen men were too frightened of a single Mongol not to follow his orders to tie one another up. A thousand things distinguished the civilized Iraqis from the Mongols. The Iraqis could read and write and create an array of products foreign to the Mongol economy, but when the two peoples met, all that mattered was that the Iraqis had lived behind city walls for at least fifty centuries and had little experience of violence.

The slaughter of the wallers was accompanied by the devastation of the infrastructure that had long made civilization possible in dry lands. In western Syria and northern Iraq, nomads drove farmers completely off the land, and this condition persisted well into the twentieth century. The Mongols delivered the coup de grâce to an agriculture in decline, destroying the old irrigation works. Thousands of miles of canals, channels, and ditches fell into ruin. By the twentieth century, only one of the ancient canals still functioned. The Tigris and Euphrates, no longer disciplined by the hand of man, changed courses, as rivers are occasionally inclined to do, bringing disaster. This was the end for many of the world's most ancient cities.

Similar destruction occurred throughout Central Asia. At Bukhara, Merv, and Gurganj, the Mongols destroyed damns and dikes crucial to the region's hydraulic infrastructure. Urban life there was largely exterminated. In the Persian heartland, which had no extensive sources of fresh groundwater, civilization depended on the maintenance of underground irrigation channels and access to aquifers. The Mongols destroyed that hidden infrastructure, too. Genghis himself, in a final, gratuitous parting shot, destroyed the granaries of Iran as he left the country.

The failure of the walls of Western and Central Asia marked one of the great turning points in world history. It was, along with China's withdrawal behind the Ming Great Wall, one of the key factors in Europe's sudden rise to global dominance. The West had simply outlasted its two chief competitors.

The survivors, with what energies they had left, rebuilt, minus the bookstores, schools, and other nonessentials. Gone, too, were the old walls, which the inhabitants of Western and Central Asia had been building and rebuilding for longer than any other people on earth. They had once constructed the world's first city walls and, within those walls, the first civilizations. Of their ancient civilized ways, they now retained mostly the meekness. They put up no resistance while warrior peoples steadily trickled in from the steppe, establishing nomadism where cities had once flourished. In time, the ancient heartland of civilization was reduced to little more than a place for cavalry maneuvers. By the seventeenth century, the population of Baghdad had fallen to just fifteen thousand, a paltry fragment of its former peak. By contrast, the number of wandering tribes in the country was said by one eighteenth-century traveler to be "infinite." As late as the nineteenth century powerful new tribes of nomads were still filtering into Syria. The nomadic Fid'an, for example, encircled the city of Aleppo in 1811, destroyed forty of the city's villages, and ate up the entire harvest. Camel-riding Bedouins crossed the Euphrates around the same time, resisted only by the sheep-herding tribes that were already there. Villagers, beset by raids, deserted their homes and gave up their fields. The "desert line" in Syria moved steadily west as abandoned villages came to outnumber inhabited ones.

The last walls in either Western or Central Asia were anything but great. They were proof, reduced to the absurd, of the thesis that where there are no border walls, there will be city walls, and where there are no city walls, there will be neighborhood walls, and where there are no neighborhood walls, there will be walls of an even smaller sort. In the nineteenth century, Turkish tribesmen still hunted Persians to be captured and sold as slaves. The whole of Iran was soon dotted with "Turkoman towers," into whose tiny openings Persian villagers crawled to escape Turkish slave raiders. The great walls had been reduced to the pathetic. But the Persians can hardly be faulted for the small scale of their efforts. There was, by then, little point in attempting to re-create a lost world of securely walled cities. That world was gone forever, not simply in Persia but everywhere, ruined by a new type of military technology that rendered almost every sort of wall obsolete.

PART THREE

THE WORLD
IN TRANSITION

The Horrible Bombard

Constantine Palaeologus sleeps now. He has joined that select company of heroic monarchs who, like Arthur or Alexander, are supposed to return someday to revive and defend their nations. He is the Marble King, rescued by an angel, turned to stone, and placed beneath the Golden Gate of the walls of Constantinople, where he waits, sleeping, until that day he will awake, take up his sword, and chase the Turks from the city.

The historical Constantine—who ruled as the eleventh Roman or Byzantine emperor by that name—did not have the honor of reviving a nation. He was fated for a very different role, that of doomed hero, in the final defense of Constantinople. Constantine exited the stage only shortly after his entrance, at that moment when the civilized world was finally stripped of the security that had been, for ten thousand years, provided by city walls. For his part in that drama, Constantine was uniquely qualified. Prior to assuming the throne, he had served the Empire as Despot of the Morea, the title then given governors of the Peloponnesus. In that capacity, he had reconstructed the old wall that formerly sealed off the peninsula at the isthmus of Corinth. Despite its unimpressive dimensions, the Corinthian barrier was the grandfather of all European border walls, originally constructed during the Mycenaean era and later rebuilt several times by the Greeks or Romans. Justinian had added towers to it in the sixth century.

More recently, Constantine's own father, the theologically minded Manuel II, had personally overseen repairs. None of these earlier builders had ever faced anything like what came crashing down on Constantine and the wall in 1446: fifty thousand Turkish troops, armed with cannons and catapults. Within weeks, the Turks had broken through, ravaged the Peloponnesus, and forced the future emperor to pay tribute to the Ottoman sultan.

In 1449, Constantine assumed the Byzantine throne, just in time to defend another set of walls against a far larger force. He was forty-three at the time of his coronation, middle-aged and seasoned, stoically prepared to assume his life's work as defender of a lost cause. He would soon prove himself worthy of ranking with the likes of Leonidas at Thermopylae or Travis at the Alamo, although the empire Constantine was defending was hardly worth the effort. Fifteenth-century Byzantium was a shriveled thing, imperial in name only, having already surrendered most of its territory. The Holy Lands, along with North Africa, had fallen to the initial surge of Islamic armies out of Arabia and been traded back and forth by crusaders, Mongols, and Turks ever since. Asia Minor had held out somewhat longer. It was not lost until the eleventh century, when it fell to the Muslimized former steppe peoples who gave their name to Turkey. The Eastern European provinces, meanwhile, had fallen under the sway of various minor powers. By Constantine's day, all that remained of the old Empire were some islands, a few Greek cities on the Black Sea coastline, the ravaged Peloponnesus, and Constantinople.

The capital, like the state it governed, retained little more than a historical claim on its former grandeur. Early fifteenth-century visitors invariably commented on the city's vacant and dilapidated condition. Nearly all the magnificent buildings of Justinian, save the massive domed Church of Hagia Sophia, had gone to ruin. Only the great Theodosian Walls, which had been repaired and augmented after the siege of 1432, recalled the glorious past of the city once called the New Rome.

Inside its thousand-year-old walls, Constantinople had functioned for fully seven hundred years as a strategic command center in a great clash of civilizations. During the Dark Ages, the Byzantines had, along with the Franks, been one of only two Western powers capable of arresting the onslaught of Islam. Time and again, the emperors had rallied their financially depleted and plague-ravaged state to stave off disaster. Time and again, the caliphs and sultans had made Constantinople their chief goal, driving huge armies to the very gates of the city, where the walls would always stymie them, foiling their dreams of achieving a conquest prophesied in Muslim lore.

The ambition of conquering Constantinople was passed down from caliph to sultan, Arab to Turk. The twelve-year-old Mehmed II, already a sultan, experienced an early disappointment when his impetuous plan to take the Byzantine capital was rejected by his elders. The desire for Constantinople turned to obsession for the young monarch. A few years later, when a nervous adviser sought to soothe the sultan with a plateful of gold coins, Mehmed spurned the offering. "Only one thing I want," he said. "Give me Constantinople."

In late summer 1452, Mehmed took his army to the very walls of Constantinople, where Constantine Palaeologus could only watch helplessly while the sultan and his engineers spent three days studying the fortifications. At least the walls remained formidable. Fourteen miles in circumference, they still enclosed every side of the triangular city. The two longer sections faced water: the Sea of Marmara to the south and the inlet known as the Golden Horn to the north. Both of these sides were essentially impregnable. Attacking the southern Sea Walls would have required an enemy to make an amphibious landing in full view of the defenders. Meanwhile, the walls facing the Golden Horn had been made even more secure by a massive chain that could be dragged across the opening of the inlet, closing it to Turkish ships. The Land Walls, roughly facing west, were also forbidding. They retained all the elements of their original Theodosian design: a massive dry moat, which could be flooded, a stout initial barricade, and, inside them, two sets of successively higher walls, dubbed the Outer and the Inner.

In the ten thousand years since city walls had first made their appearance in prehistory, the techniques for attacking them had advanced only glacially. Late medieval armies had at their disposal essentially the same tactics and tools that were employed by the ancients. They could attempt to take a wall by direct assault, but this was no easy task. The defenders had to be driven from their positions, usually with arrows and slingstones, and then the walls scaled on rickety ladders that had been hastily set up on the uneven ground around the base of the fortifications. Alternatively, an attacking army might attempt to smash the gates with battering rams, or it might employ one of several stone-throwing devices of dubious accuracy, the onager, mangonel, catapult, ballista, and trebuchet. Undermining was another common tactic: tunneling beneath a city's walls, then filling the mine with flammable materials and setting a fire that burned away the tunnel's wooden props, causing the mine to collapse and caving in the walls above. Finally, an attacker might employ a siege tower, a sort of clumsy forerunner to the tank—wooden, three stories high, shielded with hides, and mounted on wheels that allowed it to be rolled directly against a wall, where it could provide a protected platform for weapons crews, miners, or climbers.

All these siege techniques were fraught with danger. Mines collapsed on the sappers. Ladders slipped, broke, or could be pushed away. Battering-ram crews were exposed to enemy fire. Stone-throwing onagers received their name (which means "wild ass") because they kicked like mules and could kill or injure an unwary attendant as easily as a foe. Siege towers were often set on fire, could be undermined, and generally required soldiers to work in exposed conditions while preparing a lane for the tower or constructing a causeway across a moat. The walls of Constantinople had defeated all these tactics many times in its history.

In the fifteenth century, Mehmed had all the traditional tools of siegecraft at his disposal and another one, besides. A Hungarian foundryman had defected to the Turks. Initially, this expert in bronze manufacturing, whose name is given only as Orban, had offered his services to Constantine, but the money-strapped emperor couldn't meet his salary demands. The Hungarian promptly shopped his services to the sultan. There the mercenary foundryman faced some initial skepticism. Some hard questions were asked at the job interview. But when Orban boasted he could manufacture a cannon capable of shattering Constantinople's walls to dust, that was good enough for Mehmed. The sultan furnished his brash new employee with a lavish salary and provided him with men and materials to set up his foundry in a city just over one hundred miles northwest of Constantinople: Adrianople. The City of Hadrian.

In all the folklore of sleeping kings, there are no myths of a risen Hadrian. The great Roman wall builder was too unpopular. Now out of the city that bore his name would arise not a ghost or a resurrected emperor but a monster, a war machine unlike any other the world had ever seen: a pulverizer of walls.

Cannons had debuted on the battlefield only a short while earlier, if one discounts the steam-powered version invented by Archimedes during the Second Punic War. The Chinese first applied gunpowder as a propellant, and in the thirteenth century that technology had spread quickly from China into the Islamic world and eventually into Europe. The early gunpowder cannons were mostly ineffective against walls and were more often put to use defending them than destroying them. In fact, in 1396, the Byzantines had used the newfangled weapons to drive away an earlier army of Turks from Constantinople. A half-century later, the boastful Orban, loyal only to the gold in his purse, set himself to building cannons capable of destroying the walls of Constantinople. When he was done, he had revolutionized cannons, warfare, and the manner in which civilized people had lived for ten thousand years.

The first step for Orban and his workers was to form an enormous mold, twenty-seven feet long, out of clay, hemp, and linen. The finished mold was laid in a pit and packed tightly all around so that it could withstand the strain of being filled with tons of molten metal. Once casting started, the foundrymen toiled under hellish conditions. The air stank from noxious fumes. Workers resorted to prayers and superstitions to ward off explosions. The great furnaces radiated heat, the great bellies rising to over a thousand degrees Celsius. They were maintained at that infernal temperature for three days as workers pumped ceaselessly on bellows to feed oxygen to the fire. For fuel, they used charcoal, stoking the fire with shovelful after shovelful from a mountainous pile, taller than the foundry itself. The great cauldron they fed with hundreds of pieces of bronze scrap. Where had they acquired such an enormous quantity of expensive scrap metal? Old church bells? The weapons of long-dead soldiers? Two thousand years before Orban, the great walled cities of the classical world had produced countless magnificent bronze statues. They have nearly all vanished now, a misfortune of having been made of a useful, reusable metal, which, unlike iron, doesn't rust. How many of those old statues, having been melted down and recast many times, were now tossed into Orban's bubbling cauldron?

It took Orban and his crew three months to cast the great bronze cannon, and when it was complete, Mehmed ordered a test. The cannon shot an enormous stone ball, more than seven feet in circumference, a distance of over a mile. A team of sixty oxen and two hundred men subsequently began dragging the cannon to Constantinople. Ahead of them, Mehmed had another 250 men making the usual preparations for war: building bridges—in this case, structures sturdy enough to allow the massive bombard to be transported to its position outside the city, where it could roar and thunder and throw its mighty stones.

In Constantinople, the anxious residents worked diligently on their walls, making last-minute additions and repairs. There was no surplus of labor for the task, or for the defense of the city. The great capital's population had dwindled to perhaps fifty thousand souls. Much like the Empire itself, the city was hardly more than a paltry vestige of its former self. Constantine had his secretary conduct a census. He counted just under five thousand able-bodied men and two hundred foreigners. The numbers were sobering: placed evenly around the wall's entire fourteen-mile circuit, a force of five thousand men would have left undefended gaps of sixteen feet between every two soldiers.

Hadrian had already made his cameo; now it was Justinian's turn. In January 1453, a company of seven hundred Genoese mercenaries arrived by boat, led by their young captain, Giustiniani (the Italian form of Justinian). The thirty-four-year-old had personally organized and paid for the mission, the only Western aid that the Christian capital would receive. Constantine put great stock in Justinian's reputation. The two would work in concert to orchestrate the defense of the city. Upon assessing the defensive potential of the various fortifications, they elected to place all their men on the Outer Wall—technically, the middle section of the triple-layered Theodosian fortifications. The defenders would have few guns and would be unable to make much use of their own cannons, for fear the recoils might damage the fortifications on which they were mounted. Stationed outside the Inner Wall, they would be fighting with their backs to the gates.

The great city was defended by a motley array of forces. All around the fourteen miles of walls, some guarding sea, some land, Constantine stationed in small companies the pitiful numbers he had at his disposal. A cardinal commanded two hundred men in one sector; an archbishop headed the defense of another. One stretch of wall was guarded by Greek Orthodox monks, another by the entourage of a pretender to the Turkish throne. Venetian traders and Genoese mercenaries took responsibility for the most critical areas. Greek troops and townspeople covered the rest, but their pitifully small numbers meant that any real hope of surviving the siege depended on the bricks and cement of the walls holding out until relief finally arrived from the West.

A force reportedly numbering three hundred thousand or even four hundred thousand men was bearing down on the city. When it arrived, Constantine sent out his Venetian troops in their colorful uniforms to parade in front of the walls in a pathetic attempt to intimidate the sultan.

On April 2, 1453, the battle for Constantinople commenced. The emperor drew first blood by launching a small sortie against the Turkish vanguard. Although the mission inflicted many casualties, the futility of the heroic charge gradually became evident when great numbers of Turks began to arrive. Constantine subsequently recalled his troops and ordered them to destroy any bridges over the moats. With the gates of the Inner Wall now locked behind them, the defenders were isolated, as if on an island. Everything depended on the Outer Walls.

Four days later, the sultan had finally put his artillery batteries in place. An unearthly bombardment began. Even at a great distance, the Orban cannon left the defenders dumbstruck. Those who went on to write accounts of the battle struggled to find a word for the awesome new weapon. They searched their classical vocabularies for terms meaning "city taker" or "missile thrower." Some coined new terms, which translate roughly as "long-range engine" or "stone-throwing engine." To one, it was simply a "terrible, unprecedented monster." To the archbishop Leonardo, who fought on the walls, it was *bombarda horribilis*.

With Mehmed watching intently from his red-and-gold pavilion, the Horrible Bombard crushed whatever it hit, spraying deadly fragments of ball and wall in every direction. After each firing, the Turkish gunners poured gallons of olive oil down the cannon's mighty gullet to keep the overheated barrel from exploding. It had to cool for more than two hours before being fired again, limiting it to just a few uses each day. Even with these limitations, the great cannon's impact was breathtaking. Within twenty-four hours an entire section of wall had collapsed. Attacker and defender quickly fell into rhythm. Every day, the Turkish cannoneers would blast away at the walls. Every night, the gates of the Inner Wall would open, allowing townspeople, including women and children, to pour out and assist their husbands, brothers, and fathers in the repair of the walls.

In the area where Orban's cannon concentrated its fire, the wall was quickly crushed beyond repair. To fill its place, the defenders erected a wooden stockade, resembling the primitive fortifications that prehistoric villagers once placed around their homes. It was all they could do under the circumstances, and the Turks immediately recognized it as the weak spot in the city's defense. On April 18, the Sultan sent his elite troops, the Janissaries, in a direct attack on the stockade. The Janissaries came mostly from Christian, Eastern European families. Taken from their parents as children, they were raised to be fanatical Muslim warriors and formed the infantry wing of Mehmed's army. But Giustiniani's Genoese repelled them, inflicting heavy casualties on the attackers without suffering any losses of their own.

Two days later, the Sea Wall defenders had a bird's-eye view of an extraordinary event. Three Genoese ships sailed into view, along with a Byzantine vessel, making a dash for the city's harbor. All carried food, arms, or provisions. At first, it appeared the tiny fleet would race past the blockade, but when the wind died, the current pushed the four ships away from the city and into the teeth of the Turkish navy. Turkish warships, too numerous to count and armed with cannons and soldiers, swarmed the tiny Christian fleet. In the vicious battle that followed, the Christian ships had only the advantage of height, unless pluckiness can be counted in the balance. Under heavy attack, Genoese and Byzantine sailors climbed their masts to hurl projectiles down on their enemies. Thirty and even forty Turkish ships surrounded every Christian vessel, attempting to hook and board them after their cannons had failed to do their job. The Westerners, helpless to escape as long as the wind left them becalmed, used axes to chop at anyone climbing aboard. Onshore, the sultan watched the spectacle, becoming so engrossed that more than once he charged with his horse into the water, as if he might somehow ride to the aid of his armada. To his dismay, all four of the Christian ships survived the onslaught and finally caught a wind that carried them to the safety of Constantinople's harbor.

The arrival of the emergency supplies provided the beleaguered defenders with a glimmer of hope. Perhaps, they reasoned, flotillas of Western troops were soon to follow. Two days later, even that hope was extinguished. The Turks had found their way around the great chain: they'd placed part of their navy on rollers and dragged the boats over land from the Sea of Marmara to the Golden Horn. With the loss of the Golden Horn, Constantinople no longer possessed a safe harbor that could receive reinforcements. While Venetians and Genoese squabbled over how to address this newest catastrophe, the Horrible Bombard pounded the walls relentlessly. To Italian eyewitness Nicolò Barbaro, it sounded as if the sky would split in two.

On May 7, the sultan launched a new land assault on the city. Thirty thousand troops, including crews with battering rams, stormed the city amid a chorus of cries so loud that it could be heard dozens of miles away. As before, the attackers were driven off.

Five days later, the same hideous sound was raised—augmented by a cacophonous array of drums, cymbals, fifes, trumpets, lutes, and pipes. Once again, the defenders, with the help of some Venetian soldiers who had previously been stationed on the boats, drove off the attack. The stress of the siege now widened latent divisions among the defenders. Italian authors were particularly critical of the Greeks, with one echoing the traditional warrior's criticism of wallers: the Greeks, he said, were poor fighters who preferred plowing fields to manning their battle stations.

Underneath the no-man's-land between the lines, attacker and defender now played an ancient game of cat and mouse in the dark. Turkish and Greek sappers tunneled with fantastic speed, the one attempting to evade detection, the other to find and destroy. By May 16, the Turks had nearly reached the Kaligaria Gate, before vigilant defenders found their work and destroyed it. A second mine was destroyed on May 22 and a third on May 23. In all, seven mines were eventually found and destroyed, while the incessant cannonade rumbled on.

The sultan made use of every tool in the trade of siegecraft. In a single night, his men constructed a towering siege engine and rolled it against the walls. From this high perch, the Turks volleyed arrows over the battlements, terrifying the Constantinopolitans. The next night, intrepid defenders snuck out and blew up the causeway beneath the siege tower. The huge war engine collapsed in flames.

The Sea Walls received a scare. The city's seaside defenders watched with horror as Turkish sailors lashed together their boats to form a pontoon bridge spanning the Golden Horn. For the defenders of Constantinople, as for countless people before them, there was nothing more comforting than a wall, or more terrifying than a bridge. Greek and Italian chroniclers alike recalled the tale of the Persian king Xerxes bridging the Hellespont during his famous invasion of Greece. The thinly manned northern walls had now been made vulnerable to assault.

In the Turkish camp, expectations of victory—and plunder—soared. On Sunday, May 27, and Monday, May 28, the massive host prepared for a final attack with drums, shouts, and fire. For the Turkish soldiers, the racket and hubbub was a stimulant, exciting their mental state and producing surges of testosterone while they awaited their marching orders. To Nicolò Barbaro, behind the walls, it sounded as if their shouts came straight from hell.

The heroes of Constantinople spent their final days much as they had spent their final weeks: in hunger, unable to leave their positions. Those who had homes in the city worried that their families had run out of food.

Inside the walls, the Christians held a final religious procession in the dimming hope that divine intercession might yet rescue them from certain doom. The emperor addressed the throngs, with words to the effect that he was proud of the valiant deeds of the defenders and that they shouldn't lose heart just because part of their walls had been battered down. It was a short speech, but a brave one, cinematic in its own way, and inspiring—the kind of valedictory we expect from our heroes.

On Tuesday, May 29, in the dark hours of early morning, Mehmed launched his final assault. As if the roar of battle weren't enough, every church in the city rang its bells to wake up the sleeping. In the first wave, Mehmed sent in his most dispensable troops—fifty thousand Christian slaves and mercenaries. Like Xerxes at Thermopylae, he ordered them followed by men with whips, who lashed at anyone attempting retreat. Charging with their ladders, the attackers suffered heavy losses, and after two hours of fighting, Mehmed ordered their retreat. The cannons resumed their daily barrage, until Mehmed ordered a second assault, this time made by fifty thousand untrained Turks of the sort who had poured into his camp in hopes of booty.

The second wave struck all along the walls but was driven back. Even the monks were able to hold off the Turks from behind their intact fortifications. Then the Horrible Bombard struck a death blow, hitting the most vulnerable point on the line. A massive stone ball splintered the makeshift wooden palisade that the Genoese had erected to fill in for a stretch of demolished wall. Throngs of Turks streamed through the gap. For a while, the Genoese repelled them in desperate hand-to-hand combat.

By the time Mehmed launched his third wave, the Christian defenders—hungry, sleep deprived, and shell-shocked after fifty-three days of siege—had exerted themselves in unrelenting physical effort for several hours. Physically, and probably mentally as well, they were completely spent when the sultan's Janissary troops came screaming down on them. The defenders repelled an initial breakthrough with heavy losses, but the attackers kept coming. Concentrating their efforts on those areas where Orban's cannon had created breaches, the Janissaries fought as if they were expendable. Some thirty thousand reputedly fell around the Gate of Saint Romanus. The frenzied zealots were the first to penetrate the walls.

Giustiniani, having received a wound, now succumbed to the pressure of combat. In an act that appalled the siege's chroniclers and forever tarnished his legacy, the Genoese captain begged to be carried to safety. And so this "Justinian" would play his role, just as the spirit of Hadrian had in hosting Orban's foundry. The emperor begged the young commander to stand his ground, but Giustiniani had no stomach to die for a cause, noble or otherwise. In full view of his men, he was carried through a gate in the Inner Wall and spirited through the streets to the safety of a ship. Disheartened, the entire Genoese corps—the primary defenders of the shattered palisade—abandoned their posts.

The defection of the Genoese confirmed the fate of the city. As Turks poured over the palisade, the remaining defenders were pushed farther and farther back until they were massacred against the city's great Inner Wall.

Two groups of men—fleeing defenders and charging attackers—now fought to squeeze through the broken Gate of Saint Romanus. It was there that the emperor was last seen, in the company of his noble entourage, furiously fighting to drive the Turks back through the gate. Plunging into the throng of screaming zealots, Constantine Palaeologus exited the realm of history and entered that of myth.

After the breaching of the walls, there remained only the horror that Constantinopolitans had feared since the days of Theodosius II: the killings, the plundering, the dragging away of tens of thousands of civilians into slavery.

A few survivors scattered to spread the tale. Some wrote lugubrious poems, lamenting the loss of Constantinople, much in the same way the Sumerians had once lamented the fall of Ur. An embarrassed and somewhat self-absorbed Catholic Europe, which never sent the desperately needed aid for which the Byzantines had long pleaded, refused to concede the gravity of the event. Western writers tried to pass it off as the loss of just another city.

Historians see the fall of Constantinople somewhat differently. For most, May 29, 1453, marked a turning point in world history. The Roman-turned-Byzantine Empire had finally come to an end, never again to experience a Lazarus-like revival. The Turks had emerged as a world power. Islam had established a permanent presence in Europe. All these things were important. Perhaps none mattered quite so much as this: that the Turkish sultan and his Horrible Bombard had torn away mankind's ancient security blanket. For thousands of years, dating back to a time that predates empires and creeds, townspeople had found within their city walls the security to be civilized. They had voluntarily pitched in to build their city walls even while they dreaded the prospect of toiling away on the long walls of some imperial border. City walls were the one constant in the history of civilization. China, at the time of the fall of Constantinople, still had over two thousand walled cities. Worldwide, the total was beyond reckoning. They had all been rendered obsolete.

For some years, military engineers continued to labor over designs that they hoped would extend the usefulness of city walls, and these occasionally proved modestly effective, at least against smaller cannons. But after the fall of Constantinople, the defenders of walls were fighting a losing battle, locked in a contest they couldn't win. Their enemies were now civilized armies, just like their own, and equally well supplied with engineers, metallurgists, and ballistics experts. The city wall had originated as a defense against a different sort of foe, one equipped mostly with horses, arrows, and courage. That foe had largely disappeared from Europe and would soon be driven to extinction across Eurasia, defeated by an unlikely combination of modern weaponry and barriers so primitive they could hardly be distinguished as walls.

Beyond the Pale

IRELAND, SCOTLAND, AND THE RUSSIAN EMPIRE,
AD 1494–C. 1800

The end of the long wall came early to Western Europe. As one region after another succumbed to Christianity and the civilizing process, fewer and fewer warrior nations remained to wall out. The last Western barbarians were found on Europe's Celtic fringe, in Scotland and Ireland, where stubborn clans carried on in their ancient ways well into the eighteenth century. Samuel Johnson's nostalgic musings on the Highlanders, written shortly after the harsh repression of their culture when they had to surrender their swords and tartan plaid to the English crown, still recognized the ancient distinction between waller and warrior: "It affords a generous and manly pleasure," he wrote, "to conceive a little nation gathering its fruits and tending its herds with fearless confidence, though it lies open on every side to invasion, where, in contempt of walls and trenches, every man sleeps securely with his sword beside him." The barbarians had only just gone, and already the wall builders had started to miss them.

Ireland had never been Romanized, and the primitive manners of the Irish were a continual astonishment to foreigners even a thousand years after the fall of Rome. In an oft-quoted passage from his *Topography of Ireland*, Gerald of Wales (1146–1223) described the rough upbringing of Irish children, their meager diet, insufficient clothing, and infrequent, cold-water baths. This was a nurturing to do a Spartan mother proud, and to Gerald, the Irish are indeed the barbarians the Spartans once aspired to be: they live entirely off their cattle, hold farming in contempt, and have an aversion to town life. "They learn nothing, and practice nothing but the barbarism in which they are born and bred, and which sticks to them like second nature." What's worse, Gerard tells us, the Irish go about perpetually armed, battle-ax in hand, ever prepared to commit mayhem. Such appraisals weren't uncommon.

During the later Middle Ages, landowners across Ireland, despairing the lack of security, constructed stone towers for residences. When a roving war band came near, they retreated into their towers like turtles into their shells. In the late fifteenth century, the English Parliament adopted the same plan. Parliament listened to reports that English control of Ireland had effectively dwindled to little more than a small strip of land around Dublin and reacted as civilized states had for nearly four thousand years— by ordering the construction of a wall to keep the barbarians out. The resulting double-ditch barrier was topped with a palisade, giving rise to a new term for the small pocket of English control, the Pale (from Latin *palus*, "stake") and a new phrase, *beyond the pale*, for any uncivilized outsiders or their actions.

The Pale was an anachronism in the West, a final undistinguished testimony to the insecurity that had once motivated the construction of thousands of miles of walls across much of four continents. In truth, it was less of a border wall than a temporary admission that the English state was distracted with other things and couldn't then be bothered with the conquest of some stubborn hell-raisers. It had hardly been erected before another set of barriers, on the farthest fringe of the European world, eliminated the world beyond the pale forever.

In their homes north of the steppe, inhabiting a land that was in many ways the mirror opposite of the great southern civilizations, the Russians always resisted classification. They were in equal parts peasant and Cossack, builder and barbarian, Slav and Norseman. For every step they occasionally took toward the West, they took an equal and opposite step East. When modernity arrived in their harsh country, it had to share a seat with a resistant medievalism.

The wonder is that the Russian state survived. When Mother Russia first squatted and gave birth to her dark and hardy brood, she did so in a land that lacked any natural defenses. The early Rus might well have been swept away and very nearly were. The choices might have seemed binary: survival required either the creation of great walls or the development of a society so warlike it could drive off any threats. The Russians found instead a middle road. They formed a state that encompassed both wallers and warriors, the two halves working together to create a spectacle unique in world history: vast walls seemingly in motion, sweeping across the map, bulldozing peoples, and bringing an end to the long reign of the horsemen of the steppe.

In Ukraine (a term that originally meant "borderland" or "frontier"), the first Russian state conceived of the border walls that would eventually reverse the long cycle of warfare on the steppe. In the early Middle Ages, Russian settlers—cousins to the Slavic warrior peoples who had all but annihilated Byzantine Greece—raised the earliest of the so-called Dragon Walls in Ukraine. Dragon Walls are found in numerous locations around Ukraine, and their origins remain a mystery. However, the majority were built on the orders of the Kievan state, a late arrival to the fraternity of Eurasian wall builders.

Grandfather to the Russian Empire, the Kievan state rose to power in the late ninth and tenth centuries and immediately directed its energies toward establishing a physical barrier against the steppe. As usual, the name of a despot is attached to the great wall. Vladimir the Great (r. 980–1015) gets rather better press than most builders, but this is primarily due to his conversion to Christianity. He also mulled over conversion to Islam, but the religion's prohibition on alcohol gave him pause. We're Russians, he observed, alcohol is the only pleasure we have. This wasn't technically true, as Vladimir surely took at least some pleasure from his seven wives and eight hundred concubines. Either way, we can take those numbers as sure indication that Vladimir viewed everything in the state—and most especially every woman—as his to use, an attitude that would make possible the subsequent expansion of the Dragon Walls.

Under Vladimir and his successors, the Dragon Walls were extended over six hundred miles across the Ukrainian countryside. The earthworks alone stood over twenty feet high. At their base, they spanned some eighty-two feet in width, and a towering oak palisade brought the full height to a majestic thirty to forty feet. In the words of a visiting missionary, Vladimir's kingdom had been "enclosed on all sides with the longest and most solid of fences because of the roving enemy." The Grand Prince and his successors were well on their way to becoming czars. In the meanwhile, the Dragon Walls don't seem to have done much to improve the mood of the people. In folklore, Vladimir's greatest warrior is said to have been given a choice of three roads: one leading to riches, another to a wife, and a third to death. He chose death—a reasonable decision in the eyes of the average peasant, but hardly the strongest endorsement of life in the Kievan regime.

The Kievan state broke apart in the twelfth century, which put the Dragon Walls on that dubious roll of great walls rendered useless by the collapse of the empires that were supposed to be defending them. Consequently, the Mongols found little initial impediment when their campaigns turned west. In the 1240 sack of Kiev, virtually the entire population was slaughtered. A year later, in late December 1241, the frozen Danube—once the bane of Ovid's fearful existence—allowed the Mongols to cross in force, and Central Europe received a brief taste of Asia's agony. The heavy cavalry and infantry that dominated European warfare proved ineffective against the steppe men, and the Mongols hunted Hungary's king all the way to the coast of the Adriatic, while Hungary itself suffered terribly. According to contemporary descriptions, the invaders assembled the citizens of captured cities, stripped them nude, and massacred them. Only those possessing special skills were permitted to survive. In at least one town, where no skilled people were found, the Mongols slaughtered the townspeople until there was "nobody to piss against a wall." If, as is alleged, the Mongols turned the Danube red with blood, it merely added to growing roster of rivers so polluted by them. Roger of Varad visited the town of Gyula Fehérvár after its sacking and saw only bones and decapitated heads. Peasants were afraid to venture outside to work the land, and many villages and towns simply dried up due to the resulting famine. After the invaders had finally cleared out, a traumatized generation of Hungarians forever dated every event as having fallen either before or after the horrors of 1241 and 1242. Poland suffered equally savage attacks.

Beyond Poland and Hungary, where the forests were less hospitable to the Mongol herds, lay countless castles and town walls that may possibly have slowed the advance of the steppe men. However, there would be no final showdown at the walls. The fearsome Mongol armies began at last to dissolve on their own, defeated in no small part by the limitations of their own economy. The great hordes could only exist as ephemera. They had been willed into existence by charismatic khans and formed out of elements that could only briefly combine before the forces of repulsion—too many animals concentrated on too little pasture—forced them to fragment. Genghis had once commanded over one hundred thousand Mongol troops, and that figure excludes the Turks, Chinese, and others his horde had sucked into its great belly. Such numbers of men, sheep, and horses coexisted uneasily for a while, poking at the edges of forested regions, until they inevitably succumbed to centrifugal forces. By the end of the fourteenth century, the Mongol threat had dissipated. The great hordes spun out smaller fragments, such as the Crimean Tartars, who subsequently plagued Russia from the south.

For the Russians, whose northern land alternated between mud and ice, there would be no great walls of tamped earth or brick to arrest the raids of the Tartars. Russia was a world of wood, hacked out of the northern forests, sawed into lumber, and reassembled into towns where muck and marvel coexisted. Russian woodsmen—artists as much as laborers—carved their timber into exquisite onion domes but also laid their wood as planks across streets that turned so muddy after rain they might otherwise swallow a leg. As early as the twelfth century, the foresters of medieval Russia had begun felling trees across any open routes from the steppe. As the raids intensified, those local defenses coalesced into a single cooperative system, the Great Abatis Line, whose impassable barricades were often hundreds of yards deep.

By the late 1500s, the Great Abatis Line extended over six hundred miles from the Bryansk region, two hundred miles southwest of Moscow, to the edge of the deep forests that steppe horsemen found impenetrable. By then the ditches, earthworks, fortresses, log piles, and palisades were defended by rifle and artillery, but even gunpowder weapons hadn't yet sufficiently advanced to turn the tide against the armies of the steppe. Horsemen still terrorized peasants on either side of the Volga. The Tartars sacked Moscow in 1571 and attacked the city again in 1591. A year after Ivan the Terrible died in 1584, a Russian force employing cannons and firearms was defeated by traditional Tartar cavalry. Tartar raids became especially severe in the seventeenth century, when slave-raiding hordes could still penetrate Russian defenses and devastate settlements in the outskirts of Moscow.

In the face of these latter-day barbarians, spiritual descendants of those who'd brought down both Rome and Han China, Russia developed its own belated and northern version of an ancient empire. The country became a walled autocracy ruled by Caesars (corrupted in Slavic languages to *czars*).

The mid-1600s, an age of scientific revolution in the West, saw the Russians constructing hundreds of miles of seemingly anachronistic walls to safeguard their cities against raiders. While the Ming Chinese were building the Great Wall and Western Europeans were perfecting the artillery that was making walls militarily obsolete, Russians heaped up wood and earth for the thousand-kilometer Belgorod Line. That formidable barrier, composed of moats, mounds, wooden ramparts, forts, and fortified towns, subsequently begat the Simbirsk Line, the Trans-Kama Line, and the Izyum Line, to say nothing of its even more obscure offspring to the northeast.

The effort of corralling thousands of free Russian peasants into the labor forces required to construct so many border walls taxed even the czars. New laws were implemented that stripped peasants of their freedom. What good, after all, were workers who could say no? The emperors of China had never permitted peasants to opt out of the corvées, and neither would the czars. The beginning of many miseries was at hand. The seventeenth-century reforms that made it possible for nobles to organize peasants into gangs of wall builders transformed Russia. Peasants became serfs.

The serfdom that originated in Russia's belated era of wall building was among the most tenacious in the world. Not until the mid-nineteenth century, when freedom was in the air across the world, did the serfs finally receive their freedom. The czars liberated their peasant labor force in 1861—just two years before the emancipation of slaves in the United States. Prior to that, however, there had always been those peasants who wriggled and squirmed to freedom, even when it meant setting up camp in the deadly no-man's-land beyond the walls. For several centuries, peasants fleeing the enserfing efforts of Russia's czars and Poland's emperors (who were simultaneously establishing their own long walls in Silesia) found a home on the fringes of the Russian Empire. There they adopted a new identity and with it a new name: Cossack. The term derives, ironically, from a Turkish word, although the Turks were the sworn enemies of the Cossacks. Its original meaning was "free man," because freedom—from lords and czars—was the Cossacks' singular, defiant goal. Forever portrayed in art (and eventually photography) clutching their swords, muskets, or rifles, the Cossacks had broken the shackles of serfdom, given up farming, and taken up a life of hunting, fishing, and raiding. They tarnished their natural anarchy with only the most rudimentary of organizations, compelled by the threat of the Tartars to develop some large war bands that maintained permanent camps along the Dnieper River and later farther east along the Don. Few inhabited the Cossack camps except between campaigns, and in this fiercely masculine society, women were strictly forbidden.

For four hundred years, the Cossacks occupied the deadly no-man's-land between the Russian lines and the nations of the steppe. In that most ancient battleground, they became as barbaric and militarized as their barbarian oppressors. So thorough was the transformation of escaped serfs into Cossacks that by the early 1600s, they'd surpassed even the Tartars at raiding. In time, the Cossacks would inspire the literary imagination. Byron, the consummate Romantic, wrote a narrative poem about a Cossack despite never having visited Russia. Inside the Empire, where Cossacks were viewed as cowboys of sorts, the attraction was even stronger. Tolstoy once wrote that all Russians wished to be Cossacks, and this may well have been true, even if they were only trying to escape an assigned reading of *War and Peace*.

It took no less a figure than Peter the Great to finally bring the Cossacks to heel and put them to proper use clearing the steppe of the nomadic hordes that had forced so many cities and empires to construct walls. The hulking czar had an unusually intimate understanding of both workers and warriors. As a boy, he practiced woodworking and masonry with enthusiasm, and his fascination for the manual arts never faded, even as he reserved his greatest zeal for war games. Grown into a teenager, he organized his friends into regiments three hundred strong, which he supplied with balls, powder, and cannon. In these games, the future czar always played the common soldier, frequently taking up a shovel to help dig earthworks. In 1685, he and his playmates constructed an earth-and-timber fort only to watch it blasted by artillery.

In Peter, there was certainly no trace of xenophobia. Both privately and publicly, he disdained the customs of his native land, invariably preferring the companionship of those foreigners who largely composed his so-called Jolly Company, a hard-drinking, two-fisted entourage that added considerably to the general suspicion that the young czar might be the Antichrist. That the Company frequently mocked church ceremonies in its "All-Joking, All-Drunken Synod of Fools and Jesters" did nothing to assuage that belief. The Company's notoriety only grew after Peter dragged his band with him on a grand tour of Europe, where he pretended to be a ship worker (fooling no one) and saw sights that convinced him to remake Russia in a Western image. At home, Peter directed the efforts of his many laborers toward the construction of a new capital, St. Petersburg, a project he pursued with all the fervor of a despot building a great wall. Somewhere between twenty-five thousand and one hundred thousand workers died in the city's construction. By contrast, Peter put comparatively little effort into walls. His Tsaritsyn Line weighs in at a paltry forty-two miles—a hell of a wall, by ordinary standards, but not much by those of his vast country. However, the lines themselves were only one part of his evolving strategy. True to his bipolar identification with both workers and warriors, Peter revolutionized warfare, linking the walls, in their waning days, to gunpowder-equipped offensive forces.

The key to Peter's new strategy was the Cossacks, who, in combination with the extensive Russian lines, would sweep the raiders from the steppe. The unlikely pairing of wall, representing containment, and Cossack, the symbol of unfettered freedom, spelled the end for the steppe warriors. In the raids and counterraids of the seventeenth century, the Cossacks gave as good as they got. For the first time, the Tartars and other raiders found themselves in the unfamiliar position of being on the defensive. The czars repeatedly ordered the construction of massive walls that, bit by bit, with the help of the Cossacks who lived in front of them, blocked off the grasslands from raiders. The Belgorod Line repelled as many as two thousand attackers at a time, allowing large numbers of Russian peasants to settle behind it. In the meanwhile, the 150-mile-long Ukrainian Line curtailed the movement of the Crimean Tatars. Another series of fortified lines marked Russian progress in Siberia.

Russia had entered the game late, but soon its lines had far surpassed any efforts of the Romans and Persians and would rank second behind only the Chinese. The Trans-Kama Line, when elongated into the Orenburg Line, formed a defensive network totaling over sixteen hundred miles in length. Nowadays, only academic specialists remember the names of the various Russian barriers—the Irtysh Line, the Terek Line, the Mozdok Line, and so forth—but their geopolitical impact was tremendous. They were the last barriers that would ever need to be built against the steppe.

Horsemen and herds had rumbled across the steppe, stirring up drama and death for thousands of years. They were not accorded the honor of a climactic defeat. Threatened by the withering raids of the Cossacks, intimidated by the growing Russian lines, and lacking the leadership of a Genghis Khan, the raiders underwent changes of the sort that had previously spelled the end for the ancient

Gauls. In the late 1600s, the Crimean Tartars became increasingly civilized, with leaders who wrote poetry and patronized arts and education. By 1689, these former nomads had adopted that most characteristic tactic of settled peoples and, in a rare reversal of the old formula, dug a long ditch to fend off the Russians. The Khazars, once described as "sons of Magog . . . wild men, fearsome of face, savage in character," also began to settle. Before their downfall, they traded their roaming ways for massive fortress towns with stone towers and ditches. The barbarians were building walls, and with that, they ceased to be barbarians.

The steppe barbarian, who had inspired more walls than any other creature, died a largely unlamented death. Classical music lovers now hum the stirring Polovetsian Dances of the Russian composer Borodin without recognizing the Polovetsi as former steppe raiders or realizing that the lyrics translate, "Sing songs of praise to the Khan! . . . To his enemies the Khan is merciless. . . . Dance to entertain the Khan, slaves!" More distant Romantics, such as Lord Byron and Victor Hugo, tried their hand at memorializing the Mongols. But these few poems and songs paled beside the extravagant mourning of the Scottish Highlander, which itself paled compared to the lavish romanticizing of yet another set of unwalled warriors, long separated from Eurasia by ocean. Their discovery, largely concurrent with Russia's conquest of the steppe, set in motion a profound change in attitudes toward walls and the peoples outside them.

Fort Brokenheart

SOUTH, CENTRAL, AND NORTH AMERICA, PREHISTORY–AD 1800

A curious tale attends the French explorer La Salle's 1680 exploration of the Mississippi. It happens that La Salle, having run short on supplies, paused to establish a small fortified camp on frozen ground near Peoria, Illinois. He gave the tiny outpost a name—Fort Brokenheart (French: Fort Crèvecoeur)—which reflected the general mood of the expedition. Already, six of his original crew of thirty men had mutinied, fleeing into the woods rather than face the horrors of the Mississippi. It was a deadly river, or so the natives told them, teeming with serpents, surrounded by hostile peoples, and ending in an abyss. The Frenchmen wanted no part of it. La Salle placed Fort Brokenheart under the command of his Italian friend Henri de Tonti, a redoubtable veteran who'd lost his right hand in a grenade explosion and subsequently wore a glove to cover his iron hook. Leaving de Tonti with a skeleton crew, La Salle headed north to Canada for supplies.

The trip north was difficult. Often, after wading through icy waters, La Salle and his companions found their clothes had frozen to their bodies. When they arrived in Canada, they had little opportunity to relax. Messengers had followed the explorer north to apprise him of desertions from the fort. La Salle set off once more for the Mississippi, hoping to resupply his men before it was too late.

As La Salle made his way down the Mississippi, drawing closer to Fort Brokenheart, he came upon the remains of a terrible war. The feared Iroquois had swept through the region, wiping out any tribes that stood in their path. Nothing in La Salle's experience had prepared him for the sight of such carnage. The longer he searched, the more butchery came to light. In some villages, completely burned, nothing remained standing except for a few charred stakes, topped with trophy skulls. Half-burned cadavers had been left to the wolves, crows, and vultures that noisily squawked and howled amid the destruction. Some bodies lay partially cooked in kettles next to the carcasses of victims who'd been impaled and roasted. La Salle carried on with numb fortitude, meticulously examining skulls for signs that they may have been Frenchmen, until at last he found his tiny camp. A final chilling discovery awaited in the remains of Fort Brokenheart: a plank on which Tonti had left behind a message in French: NOUS SOMMES TOUS SAUVAGES. *We are all savages.*

The New World had a way of turning everything upside down. Here, where La Salle had landed, there were no walled sanctuaries where one might escape the brutality, the trophy killings, or the endless cycles of vengeance. Everywhere was war. The tiny company of Frenchmen had tried to wall off the horror, much as their prehistoric ancestors had back in Europe, but with insufficient labor at hand, their efforts failed miserably. Without the protection of their flimsy barriers how could they even hope to be civilized? To be there and to survive was to succumb to another way of life, to become a part of it, *un sauvage*.

If de Tonti could have seen more of the New World, he might have reconsidered his parting message. It wasn't all savagery, after all. There were, for example, the Maya, whose cities had certainly seen better days by then, but who could still look back, like the Europeans, on their own classical antiquity. Not too much earlier, they had written in hieroglyphs, built cities and pyramids, and developed fine systems of math and astronomy. Farther south lay the imperial world of the Incas, remarkable for engineering achievements. In Central America, the Aztecs commanded a massive empire, echoing the Eurasian models of Hammurabi, Theodoric the Great, and Kublai Khan, wherein former barbarians take over an urban civilization and build on it rather than destroy it. In all these lands, massive fortifications provided the sort of sanctuary La Salle and de Tonti couldn't find among the tribes of the Mississippi.

There were no shortcuts to civilization in the Americas, no skipping what had always been the rule in Europe and Asia. The march toward civilization in the Americas was everywhere preceded by the adoption of walls that secured the passage from warrior to worker. In Peru, the first steps were always higher, up the slopes of the Andes Mountains, where safety beckoned at ten thousand feet, even if not for long. The movement required an immense commitment of labor, carried out in thin mountain air that must have left the first unadapted arrivals gasping. Andeans moved stone and earth to create mountainside terraces where they could farm in safety. By the sixth century AD, the walled city of Kuélap looked down even on the clouds, a breathtaking example of labor converted into defense. Its cut-stone walls soared some sixty feet in height. Inside them, the inhabitants immediately became more advanced than their unwalled contemporaries and even performed the world's first bone surgery. Not far away, some forgotten Peruvian state established a line of border forts and then constructed the sixty-mile Great Wall of Peru. Eventually, the Andes bristled with fortified cities, such as Chan Chan, which had twenty-six-foot-high walls, and Hatunmarca, which was girded by three successive stone walls. When the Incas consolidated the region, they established yet another great wall, 150 miles long.

In Mesoamerica, workers contended against the jungle, and, in so doing, developed the patience to construct cities of stone. There, where nature swallows even pyramids and towns, history seeks to hide. Whole civilizations have dressed in camouflage and disappeared into the forest, becoming indistinguishable from the vegetation. Fortunately, archaeology has come a long way since 1839, when John Lloyd Stephens paid a skeptical local $50 for the ruins of Copán. Stephens hacked through vines with machetes to reveal a wondrous wall. Nowadays, laser mapping technologies hack away the jungle electronically, penetrating dense canopies to unveil what lies hidden beneath the tangle of earth, roots, vines, and branches. The new images disclose structures that were not supposed to exist: miles-long ramparts and ditches dating back to the Olmec and early Maya period. It seems that, contrary to what was once believed, the Mesoamericans required all the same protection as their counterparts across the Atlantic.

Fortifications of all types accompanied the rise of civilization in Central America. We now know that by the time Guatemala's El Mirador had grown to become the apparent capital of the first state in the western hemisphere, around the same time that Nebuchadnezzar was constructing the walls of Babylon, the city featured sixty-foot-high perimeter walls. El Mirador's inhabitants were still driven from their homes, but not before staging a ferocious last stand, fought atop a pyramid. In the meanwhile, settlers moved atop Monte Albán, fortified the flanks of the hill with a wall almost two miles long, and established the Zapotec civilization, which was instrumental in the spread of writing in Central America. A proliferation of walled cities accompanied the efflorescence of Mayan culture. When city walls were not sufficient, the Mayans established segmented border walls by fortifying the regions between hills and placing watchtowers on the hilltops.

The walls of Central and South America weren't found farther north, and neither were the mathematicians and astronomers. In North America, the tides of prehistory pushed in an entirely different direction. By the time of European discovery, the builders of heavily walled pueblos in the Southwest had largely been wiped out, remembered only as Anasazi, "enemy ancestors" or "ancient ones." Like the Andeans, they had once been committed to a life of labor. Those who built pueblos atop mesas had to tote supplies and even water up the steep slopes to their homes. Only a few survived to greet the Spanish.

At Cahokia, Illinois, another ancient nation, also long forgotten, constructed a one-and-a-half-mile palisade augmented by bastions. Like the Mesopotamians of ancient Iraq, these inhabitants of the lost "Mississippi Culture," whose city peaked around 1200 AD, covered their wall with plaster. Inside it, they left all the telltale fingerprints of an enormous civilian labor force, including the fourth-largest pyramid in the Americas, and some mysterious mounds, the largest of which once rose as high as a ten-story building. From time to time, other North American sites developed wooden palisades, but proper walls were rare. Of the nearly four hundred palisaded sites known, few consisted of anything more than screens of posts, carelessly spaced apart so that a determined invader could squeeze through.

On this vast continent, unwalled but for porous palisades, diversity prevailed, in the form of hundreds of distinct tribes, each with its own ways. The tribes spoke a variety of languages, wore a variety of clothes, and, having adapted to diverse habitats, practiced various ways of producing and acquiring food. They were as different from one another as the ancient German was from the Gaul, Hun, Mongol, or Turk—which is to say, they were hardly different at all. They were all warriors, just like their unwalled counterparts in Eurasia, and utterly unlike the wall builders of South and Central America.

Thomas Forsyth, who lived with the Sauks and Foxes, once made an observation on his hosts, that would have applied, without correction, to any of the unwalled warrior peoples of Eurasia. "Young Indians," he wrote, "are always fond of war, they hear the old warriors boasting of their war exploits and it may be said, that the principle of war is instilled into them from their cradles."

Forsyth's comment—by no means isolated—directs us to a history long buried, an image only now being rescued from that same ideological jungle that once resisted the hacking of anthropologists such as Keeley and Chagnon in their struggle against the entrenched belief in primitive pacifism. The thickets of a dubious orthodoxy—the myth of the peaceful "noble savage"—has long grown over the Native American past. The grip of the ideal has been so strong that even those Native Americans who seek to take pride in their warlike heritage have been largely ignored, an embarrassment to those who prefer the pacified image invented by white primitivists. But here we are, looking at a very different image recovered from the jungle: the unwalled Native Americans sharing the same warlike values as the Mongols and Huns.

Mulling over the American evidence, comparing it to that from another side of the globe, one wonders if we may have detected a glimpse of that skittish unicorn so fervently hunted by the social scientists: a hint of universality, evidence that perhaps human societies everywhere tend to fall into the same patterns of development. Independently, separated by miles of ocean, the New World had evolved along the same divergent paths as the Old. One path, beginning with walls, had led to writing, architecture, astronomy, and math. The other, open and unwalled, led only to militarism.

The centrality of war to the unwalled natives of North America was once noted even by their most ardent admirers, at least among those with firsthand knowledge. Henry Schoolcraft, the author of many an encomium on the Indians, and a man who spent years living among the tribes and was himself married to an Ojibwa wife, summed up with some force:

> Success in war is to the Indian the acme of glory, and to learn its arts the object of his highest attainment. . . . The whole force of public opinion in our Indian communities is concentrated on this point: the early lodge teachings (such as the recital of adventures of bravery), the dances, the religious rites, the harangues of prominent actors made at public assemblages (such as that called "striking the post"),—whatever, in fact, serves to awaken and fire ambition in the mind of the savage is clustered about the idea of future distinction in war. Civilization has many points of ambitious attainment. The Indian has but one prime honor to grasp: it is triumph in the war path; it is rushing upon his enemy, tearing the scalp reeking from his head, and then uttering his terrific *sa-sa-kuon* (death-whoop).

The observations of Schoolcraft and Forsyth find corroboration in countless other firsthand recollections by white and Indian alike. Warrior customs prevailed in nearly all native North American societies, extending across the full spectrum of habitats, economies, and language groups. It didn't matter if a tribe lived in forest, desert, or plain. It was enough simply that they occupied an open and insecure environment, in communities without walls. The importance of war to the unwalled societies of North America can be seen in the customs of the eighteenth-century Inuit, who drank the blood of their Cree enemies and gave breast-feeding babies a taste of blood "so as to instill in them the barbarism and ardour of war from the tenderest years," and those of the Mohave, who lashed and scratched their boys or pushed them into bees' nests to determine if they had the right stuff to mature into elite warriors. The Natchez Indians presented bows to their boys at the age of twelve and entered them into archery contests to determine who would receive the honor of being called "young warrior," or failing that, "apprentice warrior." Powhatan mothers refused to give their sons breakfast until they'd passed a morning archery test by hitting something that had been thrown in the air. When a Native American boy reached physical maturity, the passage to adulthood everywhere entailed a painful proof of endurance, the most famous of which, the Mandan *O-Kee-Pa*, culminated in being gouged with serrated knives, then suspended from sticks inserted in the wounds. There were dances to prepare for battles, colored feathers to commemorate kills, and sticks for "counting coup"—a way of demonstrating valor. Martial songs and folktales roused the warlike spirit. Bundles of charms provided sacred protection. Scalps provided proof of service. Tribal military societies, such as the Big Dogs, Crazy Dogs, and, for men who had become tired of life, Crazy Dogs Wishing to Die, created peer pressure to perform well in battle. If this weren't enough, young males who had not yet proven their courage were prevented from seeking a mate. Aging Cheyenne, interviewed in the 1960s, recalled how mothers would guard their daughters, querying would-be suitors about what deeds they had performed in battle. Girls would humiliate young men who had shown cowardice.

To the European, who came from a world where the way of the waller had prevailed over that of the warrior, it was all very strange. He couldn't make sense of those men who didn't define themselves by their work. The Indian male, it seemed, even to admirers such as Schoolcraft, was lazy. He was often observed standing around, smoking a pipe, and telling war stories, while the women did all the work. But, then, the Indians weren't especially impressed by these newcomers who couldn't fight their own battles and who busied themselves all day with women's work.

The confused reactions of Europeans and native North Americans to their initial interactions only hinted at the misunderstanding and conflict to follow. In many ways, that conflict wasn't new. It was a late and unwelcome encore to a long-running tragedy that had already shaped civilization on five continents. The wallers and the warriors had never understood one another, and there is little evidence that they ever had either the hope or the expectation of coexistence. Long before the arrival of European colonists, the conflict between native wallers and warriors had apparently already precipitated the decline of Mayan civilization, as well as that of the pueblo builders. That conflict—the origin of so many ancient border walls around the world—reached its bizarre, perverted apotheosis when, in a reversal of historical patterns, great masses of wallers, generally inept at warfare despite their access to gunpowder weapons, invaded an unwalled continent inhabited by warriors.

Being the only trained warriors in an age of conflict has immense disadvantages. There were plenty of wars to go around during the colonial period, and the Native Americans fought in all of them. They fought in their own intertribal struggles, which already crisscrossed the continent, and when the English and French imported Europe's intertribal wars to North America, the natives fought in those, too. Frequently, when the spread of European immigrants had become too great, the natives launched attacks on the newcomers. Invariably, they found the going pretty easy against the unwarlike settlers, until another faction of natives, eager for action, would join the whites and turn the tide. During King Philip's War (1675–76), the Wampanoags and their allies had all but driven the hymn-singing Puritans of New England into the sea until colonial governors hired Mohegan and Pequot to defend the settlers. A few decades later, when the Tuscarora nearly annihilated North Carolina in 1711, Colonel John "Tuscarora Jack" Barnwell rode to the rescue with a force of 30 whites and 925 Indians—typical numbers for these early conflicts and a critical reason for the rapid demographic decline of the tribes who were supplying soldiers for both sides of every conflict.

George Washington, who learned a great deal while fighting against and alongside Native Americans in the French and Indian War, once made a comment that, while rarely quoted, marks, as well as any stone monument, a turning point in history. Observing the rapid disappearance of the Native Americans, the first president suggested to his secretary of state that the United States might need to build a "Chinese wall" to protect the Indians from further encroachment.

Washington's remark was not intended as a policy proposal. He preferred that Indian men should learn farming, reckoning this would transform warriors into workers and reduce conflict with farming settlers. In a broad sense, the comment belongs in the same category as Johnson's nostalgic ruminations on the Highlanders, who had "in contempt of walls and trenches" lived in "fearless confidence." The two eighteenth-century men both knew that an ancient way of life was becoming extinct, even if one romanticized it somewhat more than the other. They had seen the last of the unwalled, or very nearly so.

The remorse expressed by Washington and Johnson would only grow as the world's great walls, battered by wind and rain and robbed of their stone by farmers, receded into the landscape. As the walls gradually disappeared, so, too, did their histories. Ancient conflicts were forgotten, and perhaps that was for the best.

Ironically, the Native Americans, who had played little part in the history of walls, became, in the popular imagination, symbols for all the outsiders who had once inhabited the world beyond the pale. Romanticized by Elizabethan poets, Restoration playwrights, eighteenth-century novelists, essayists, and travel writers,

Enlightenment *philosophes*, early-American political philosophers, and the authors of early Broadway plays, the Native Americans were endowed in literature with an aura so great that its excess light spilled over even onto the unwalled outsiders of ages past.

A fascination for the lost world beyond the walls consumed Western thinkers during the Romantic era, with its love for all things natural and exotic. Enthralled and often titillated by glamorized images of the brooding nomad, a series of Western travelers, most of them women, set out for dusty, faraway lands in hopes of observing the very peoples whose ancestors had once terrorized the ancient cities, forcing the construction of the great walls. Despite the experience of being robbed or made witness to robberies, murders, and raids, Isabella Bishop, Mrs. E. R. Durand, and Vita Sackville-West penned romantic, adulatory encomiums on the nomads of Persia. Several other women, meanwhile, sought out nomads in Arabia, where Lady Hester Stanhope, Jane Digby, and Lady Anne Blunt arrived as enchanted admirers of the Bedouins. Digby married a sheikh. Far to the east, Beatrix Bulstrode sought out the Mongols, her fervent wish being for "primitive life among an unmistakably primitive people." If she could have found Gog and Magog, she would have paid them a visit as well.

By the 1920s, the parade of intrepid ladies had paved the way for the arrival of those redoubtable silent-era documentarians Ernest Schoedsack and Merian C. Cooper, whose *Grass* introduced the tent-dwelling Bakhtiari to film audiences. The movie was accompanied by a book, which includes, among other things, a wistful soliloquy by the Bakhtiari khan, in which he explains how he would gladly trade his chiefly rank for the opportunity to live in New York. He had briefly attended school in Manhattan, and he remembered it as a place of theaters and pretty girls. "You come be boss of Baktyari," he said. "I go dance on Broadway." *Grass* was a groundbreaking film, but it wasn't Schoedsack and Cooper's masterpiece. Eight years later, the adventurous duo produced another movie, this one fictional, about an island where the inhabitants had constructed a giant wall to restrain a great primitive beast that lived on the other side. The movie was remade in 1976, then again in 2005, then again in 2017.

A particularly fond childhood memory of mine was formed on a day that several friends and I were crammed into a Volkswagen Bug, then dropped off at the old Tennessee Theatre in downtown Knoxville, where we watched a special matinee of the original *King Kong*. Happy as only nine-year-olds can be in that ornate old movie palace, we cheered heartily when Schoedsack and Cooper's great ape, which had just killed dozens of innocent New Yorkers, swatted down a biplane that had taken to the air to defend the city. Nine years old and we already knew we were supposed to root for the primitive over the civilized. We didn't give a damn about New York. We just wanted to see the other side of the wall, where dinosaurs fought giant gorillas.

When had it become so ingrained to dream of the other side of the wall? Was it when the artist Gauguin sailed off to Tahiti "to see no one but savages"? Or when Freud wrote *Civilization and Its Discontents* to inform us that we were all, despite what we might think, miserable, as long as we lived the civilized life? Or had it begun much earlier, perhaps around the time Johnson rued the subjugation of the unwalled Highlanders?

For the first time in our story, we have arrived at that point where the protagonists begin to remind us of ourselves. They have emerged victorious over the forces they once walled out, and it has filled them with remorse. They worry that they may have lost more than they ever won. Having forgotten the reason for the old walls, they regret ever having built them. Rebelling against the models of the past, they might have stopped building walls altogether. But it wasn't yet time for that.

PART FOUR

A CLASH OF SYMBOLS

The Last Battles

In their verse, the Chinese speak of ghosts and skeletons inhabiting the Wall. These phantoms are the remains of workers, according to the poets, but some must also be soldiers, and if their spirits have eyes and ears, they surely would have roused from their sleep to the familiar sound of battle at Xifengkou on a late winter day. The Xifengkou pass was critical to the defense of the Wall. It had been targeted by a superior force, which could threaten the entire region if it breached the defenses. Wave after wave of assaults tested the Chinese; only furious close-quarters combat and the advantage of fortifications prevented the pass from being immediately overrun. Nightfall brought only temporary relief. As their enemy retired to sleep, Chinese officers selected their most skilled fighters for a counterattack. The elite troops carried *dadao*s, the machete-like swords favored by the military because their use could be mastered easily and quickly by conscripts. Sneaking down trails created by local woodcutters, the Chinese soldiers, temporarily abandoning the protection of the Wall, arrived at the enemy camp without warning and went to work quietly, slashing their foes in the dark. In the melee that erupted, they destroyed the enemy's machines for battering the Wall, then slipped back behind the fortifications for safety. It was March 11, 1933—arguably the beginning of the Second World War—and China was defending the Great Wall, perhaps for the final time, against a Japanese army armed with machine guns, artillery, tanks, and bombers.

In a different era—a dozen different eras, in fact—the Wall had been built to defend against just such attacks from the north. But time and war and weapons—especially weapons—had passed the venerable monument by. The Wall had become a relic.

The Wall's last war had begun only two months earlier, when a rogue Japanese army launched an unprovoked attack on the monument's easternmost pass. Japan's Kwantung Army was experienced, highly disciplined, and fully modern. By 1933, it was also infamous for its independence. Its name came from the Chinese term for "east of Shanhaiguan," referring to the Great Wall pass that so irritated the army's aggressive and imperialist generals because it blocked their territorial ambitions. Politically, the Kwantung Army's leaders had long been at odds with their own civilian government. In 1931, they ignored Tokyo when, on their own initiative, they invaded Manchuria and established a menacing Japanese presence on the Chinese border. In the views of the army's imperialist generals, China—then deeply weakened by political divisions—made a rich and tempting target. The Wall was no longer viewed as a significant obstacle.

The Kwantung Army chose as its initial target the hated pass at Shanhaiguan, long the physical limit to its expansionist plans. After orchestrating an apparent "false flag" bombing incident, the Japanese commander denounced the Chinese defenders of the pass as terrorists and launched a massive combined-forces attack. Tanks, bombers, and offshore warships battered the "First Pass under Heaven," while Japanese troops charged with bamboo ladders. The sheer organization of the attack on Shanhaiguan put to lie any protests that the incident had been anything but carefully planned. An assault by land, sea, and air spontaneously brought together in less than a day? The rest of the world wasn't buying it. Ambassadors lined up to object to the seizure of the pass. Western journalists also expressed outrage, or at least as much as they could muster for events that still seemed to them distant and detached from anything of real importance. A writer for the *Saturday Evening Post* dutifully reported signs of impending war while logging his travels to the Wall—"the most stupendous construction work of man, ancient or modern." The Chinese army, he observed, was frantically at work repairing roads to the Wall, but this hardly attracted more notice than the bleakness of the Chinese countryside or that the author had been gypped in a heroin deal.

To the Chinese, the preparations were far more serious. In Beijing, just south of the Wall, the army commandeered cars and trucks, along with ten thousand rickshaws and their drivers. The makeshift convoy made its way north to the famous monument, singing, "Go! Go! We must go together to the front to resist! . . . The bloodstained Great Wall is glorious!" Chinese citizens living north of the Wall were also streaming toward the ancient monument, but when they arrived, they found it closed to them, already buttoned-up and prepared for battle.

After taking Shanhaiguan, the Japanese general Sosaku Suzuki had given his assurance that Japan wouldn't advance beyond the Great Wall—a statement carefully worded to exclude Jehol, the Chinese province that lay north of the Wall. Less carefully worded was his unreassuring response to world condemnation: "We have nothing to be ashamed of. The Chinese must come to us on bended knee." The Kwantung Army wasted little time in moving against Jehol.

When the Japanese arrived to clear out the province, the poorly prepared Chinese troops could do little more than take pot shots at them while the Japanese disembarked their trains. The defense of Jehol had devolved upon the province's opium-growing warlord, Tang Wulin. A brash and somewhat colorful figure, Tang had established two heroin factories on the grounds of an old imperial palace. As the Japanese drew closer, he entertained foreign correspondents by performing acts of ambidextrous marksmanship while riding a Mongolian pony. He couldn't do much about the Japanese, but at least his displays did less to provoke the enemy than the words of the Chinese foreign minister, who boasted that China had more people than the Japanese had bullets, saying, "Lives are our ammunition!" In reality, the defense of Jehol crumbled quickly as Chinese generals deserted their troops or displayed welcome flags for the invaders. Tang Wulin escaped, as drug lords so often do, disappearing forever from the world stage, where he'd enjoyed his brief flirtation with fame. He was last seen "staring vacantly out the window at some deer."

The fall of Jehol brought the war to the Wall, General Suzuki's assurances notwithstanding. On March 10, the Japanese attacked Xifengkou, where the Chinese swordsmen would make their daring night raid. Incredibly, the defenders held their position, despite their severe disadvantage in weaponry. The Japanese, unable to make any headway, abandoned the attack. Similarly, at Luowenyu the defenders also succeeded in stopping the invaders. The Great Wall, called out of a long retirement and hustled out onto the battlefield for one last mighty effort, had held.

More than a week passed before the mechanized and industrialized Japanese, with their state-of-the-art weaponry, finally made a critical breakthrough. The April 11 breach of the pass at Engkoo, after fierce fighting in which the pass changed hands several times, effectively marked the end of the Wall's military career. Once Japanese troops had penetrated the line in force, the Wall's remaining defenders could easily be surrounded and attacked from the rear. The entire line became indefensible. Chinese troops withdrew from the Wall on the very roads they'd so recently repaired. To their south lay some two thousand walled cities, defenseless against bombers, and inhabited by tens of millions of civilians who could still remember the waning days of an ancient empire.

The Great Wall in 1933 may have been "bloodstained" and "glorious," but it could barely slow down a technologically superior attacking force. By then, the venerable structure had already completed its transition from viable military fortification to worldwide celebrity and symbol. These were only the latest entries on the long résumé of a monument that had already served in many capacities. To the ancient inhabitants of the steppe, the Great Wall—and all its pre-Ming predecessors—had been a formidable barrier. To the Chinese laborer, forever liable to imperial conscriptions, it symbolized oppression. To the distant Romans, it was a model that their own emperors might emulate. To millions of Eurasians who'd never actually seen the Wall, couldn't be certain where it was, and knew nothing of its history, it was a source of myth, usually associated with the apocalyptic trio of Alexander, Gog, and Magog.

The emergence of the Wall as an international symbol had resulted from many of those same forces that had elsewhere led to the colonization of the Americas. In the sixteenth and seventeenth centuries, the Wall drew the attention of Jesuit missionaries to China. The Jesuits were never especially successful at converting the Chinese to Christianity. However, they dazzled the imperial court with novelties of Western manufacture—pumps, clocks, sextants, telescopes, cannons, even steam-powered automobiles—and in turn the Jesuits were dazzled by the Great Wall of the Ming. To Father Verbiest, whose accounts of China were widely read in Europe, the Wall surpassed all the Seven Wonders of the World put together. Western mapmakers enthusiastically, but inaccurately, depicted it enclosing the entire Chinese Empire. References to a great Chinese wall became common in Western literature. In the nineteenth century, when Western powers forcibly pried open the once-guarded nation, China became a tourist destination, and the Wall its greatest attraction.

For all its celebrity, the Great Wall would not, in modern times, continue to serve as a model to foreign powers, as the Han Walls had for the emperors of Rome and Persia. The early-modern period had not been kind to fortifications. The tales of Orban's Horrible Bombard battering down the walls of Constantinople had changed attitudes toward walls. Western visitors to the Wall continued to marvel, but homebound critics adopted a more skeptical view. Daniel Defoe, in his hasty sequel to *The Adventures of Robinson Crusoe*, had his titular hero visit the Wall only to rudely inform his guide that the monument was nothing, that it was outdated, had never worked, and that a train of British artillery could make short work of it, obliterating the whole thing inside of ten days. Voltaire agreed. Despite his enthusiasm for China as a convenient vehicle for the Western self-loathing he did so much to popularize, the Frenchman eventually declared the Wall futile. The same Wall that he had, just a few years earlier, praised in the most hyperbolic terms, he described in later works as "a monument to fear."

Even as the Wall was acquiring its questionable associations with futility, obsolescence, and cowardice, it was becoming connected to yet another negative trait in Western eyes: that of wrongheaded isolationism. The Western rediscovery of China coincided precisely with the growth of capitalism, which would give rise to an ideology of open borders and free trade. The reluctance of China—still an ancient empire, playing by ancient rules—to open its markets appalled and annoyed Western traders, who made the Wall a symbol for backwardness and isolation. Before long, they'd dismissed the entire nation as introverted oddballs, freakishly addicted to walls.

The latter point needs addressing. In writings on China, it is customary, even among leading sinologists, to observe that the Chinese possess an innate predilection for isolationism and wall building. Western writers detect the alleged trait in the construction of China's earliest walled cities, in the use of walled courtyards by architects, and especially in the Empire's repeated attempts to secure its borders with walls. Thus, when Cambridge sinologist Julia Lovell speaks of China's "impulse to wall-building" or a "Chinese love of enclosing walls," she stands in good company alongside Owen Lattimore, the much-admired dean of Eurasian frontier studies, who believed that "there must have been something inherent in the historical process of the state in China that favored the evolution of walled frontiers, irrespective of hostile relations between the Chinese and peoples whose ways of life were incompatible with them." Such statements can be multiplied indefinitely: "Wall is what makes China," observes one scholar. "Even today the cultural power of the 'wall' runs deep in the national psyche," writes another. The Chinese are thus singled out for having behaved no differently from any other civilized nation in world history. Nothing about China's efforts to wall off its northern borders from the steppe was unique. Cimmerians, Greeks, Romans, Byzantines, Persians, Khwarezmians, Slavs, Russians, Koreans, and others constructed similar walls for the same purpose, generally to defend against the same peoples—and this is to say nothing of analogous long walls built in other regions, by Sumerians, Egyptians, Babylonians,

Peruvians, Nigerians, Indians, and Vietnamese. Walled cities were even more universal. The Chinese differentiated themselves solely by the impressiveness of their efforts, but this was enough that they became attached to the idea of "wall" when that idea was, during the ages of cannons and capitalism, brought into disrepute.

Still more walls were being built during the twilight of their usefulness, and these, too, sometimes acquired greater significance as symbols than as concrete barriers. The smoke had hardly cleared from the last battles of the Great Wall before another type of wall—a newer breed, utterly unlike any of its ancient ancestors—fought its first. The new wall would never have the opportunity to develop a military record to compare with that of its older Chinese kin, much less a comparably hoary folk history. The Maginot Line was not even ten years old when German tanks scooted around it, hastening it on its own transformation from fortification to symbol.

Like so many other European institutions, the Maginot Line had its origins in the confused aftermath of the First World War. A late Allied offensive, made possible by the arrival in 1918 of 2 million American troops, had driven the Germans from the contested regions of Alsace and Lorraine and convinced the German government to accept what would turn into an infamously punitive peace. The French gained territory but not an accompanying sense of security. Not even the harsh terms of the Versailles Treaty—which stripped Germany of its best industrial regions, crushed the German economy with punitive reparations, drastically limited the size of the German army and air force, and encircled Germany with newly created hostile states—could bring peace of mind in those days. Victory had hardly been celebrated before hand-wringing generals and politicians had begun debating how to prevent future invasions.

Nearly a century later, it is difficult to imagine the spirit of those times, when memories of the last war still jostled with fear of the next. French generals turned into bestselling authors with titles such as *L'invasion, est-elle encore possible?* (*Is Invasion Possible Again?*). Ministers and military men achieved fame for their positions on issues of national security. Who was Maginot, after all, except an obscure governmental minister, before his name became attached to his eponymous line?

Prior to Maginot, the French had been tiptoeing around the possibility of a great wall for fully three hundred years—ever since 1636, the infamous Year of Corbie, when the Austrian capture of a French fortress at Corbie had left Paris directly imperiled. That kind of scare wasn't easily forgotten. In 1678, France's original general-turned-author, the self-promoting military theorist Sébastien Le Prestre de Vauban, had proposed, as an alternative to a wall, a frontier guarded by technically advanced border fortresses. Vauban's designs were only the latest in a long series of efforts to extend the viability of the ancient technology of city walls, some two hundred years after the fall of Constantinople had proven them obsolete. The history of technology is replete with such rearguard actions, and Vauban's fortresses fared no better than the typewriter or 8-track tape when their time had come and gone. Still, the French persisted in their pursuit of fortified borders. During the 1702–15 War of the Spanish Succession, when English and Dutch forces threatened from the east, the French established the palisades and earthworks of the seventy-five-mile-long Lines of Brabant. They subsequently constructed the longer and more intimidatingly named Ne Plus Ultra Lines, which stretched some two hundred miles. French desire for an impermeable border peaked after the nation's rapid and humiliating defeat in the 1870–71 Franco-Prussian War. This led to yet another attempt to tweak an apparently obsolete technology, the final result being the cast-iron and reinforced-concrete fortifications of the Barrière de Fer (Wall of Iron).

It was the Barrière de Fer that most intrigued French policy-makers in the 1920s. The Wall of Iron, unlike the Lines of Brabant or the Ne Plus Ultra Lines, never entirely failed. At Verdun, its modernized forts had withstood a fantastic battering during World War I, even at the hands of Germany's massive Big Bertha guns. The Battle of Verdun, where André Maginot received the wound that left him with a limp and Marshal Philippe Pétain earned his reputation as a hero of France, was intensely studied during the interwar years. It planted the notion of a new type of fortified boundary, something that would *not* resemble the Great Wall of China. In the fierce debates over whether or how to fortify France's borders, even proponents jockeyed to distance themselves from the Chinese symbol. Marshal Joffre argued that France would be "doomed to defeat for seeking to establish a new Wall of China." Maginot himself stated, "We could hardly dream of building a Great Wall of France," deeming it too costly. What they designed was a new prototype, a Great Wall for the twentieth century, or so it was hoped.

The Maginot Line, as it emerged from the French drawing boards, placed little emphasis on continuous physical barriers. It included exactly two: a long zone of dense barbed wire to stall infantry movements, and, in front of that, thousands of metal rails, projecting from the ground to stop tanks. The real essence of the Line was its network of fortified bunkers and gun placements. *"Le feu tue!"* Pétain had argued—"Firepower kills!" This revolutionary principle was embodied in the design. The Maginot Line would not resemble any wall of brick, tamped earth, or even iron. It was a wall of fire. By Pétain's reasoning, if he could just protect the guns, the guns would protect France.

Never before had a defensive barrier taken such form. The Maginot Line dispensed with even the traditional fort. In its place, the French designed *ouvrages* ("works") that lay almost entirely underground. Each *ouvrage* contained miles of tunnels, barracks, munition dumps, hospitals, and mess halls, all connected to a series of guns encased in either concrete bunkers or steel turrets that only peeped out of the ground during battle. The gun crews, living fifty feet underground in impenetrable mazes, were never exposed to enemy fire, and there was a welcome committee for anyone who managed to breach the seven-ton steel doors of the *ouvrages*: machine-gun bunkers were positioned to mow down intruders. If all else failed, the tunnels were rigged with explosives for self-destruction.

Work on the new design proceeded quickly. In 1926, the French government undertook the construction of the first experimental units for the proposed Line. A few years later, in 1930, with international relations deteriorating and a grim pessimism taking root in the early days of the Depression, the Chamber of Deputies allocated funds to realize the entire plan. André Maginot, whose lobbying had been crucial in generating support for the project, died a year later, in 1932, three years before the first newspaper attached his name to the Line.

For almost the last time, masses of workers contributed to the construction of a barrier intended to defend their nation from military attack. Their numbers were oddly small—fifteen thousand, hardly a fraction of the workforces once employed by the ancient empires—but the Depression-era French had the advantage of backhoes, excavators, dump trucks, bulldozers, and cement mixers. Over the next several years, they poured more than a million cubic yards of concrete and placed 150,000 tons of steel. By 1939, they had completed the Line.

In its final form, the Maginot Line shared one conspicuous attribute with its more ancient Chinese cousin: it covered only a small portion of the border it was intended to defend. Like the Romans, the French believed they could rely on the Rhine River to prevent intrusions across much of their eastern border. Along the Rhine, they placed only a rudimentary array of defenses—a few machine-gun bunkers and fortlets, augmented by mines and barbed wire. Only in the region above the Rhine, principally in Alsace and Lorraine, the two territories that Germany and France had contested for decades, did the French deem the full panoply of the Line necessary. They left unfortified the "impassable" Ardennes Forest, as well as the border with the Low Countries, working on the assumption that the Germans would avoid either route.

On the eve of world war, the defenders of the Maginot Line settled into their subterranean world like groundhogs. Wearing khaki uniforms emblazoned with the optimistic motto *On ne passe pas* ("None shall pass"), they moved through their tunnels on trolleys, taking advantage of wine cellars, barbershops, and chapels as they awaited the inevitable coming of the Germans.

In May 1940, the Germans at last launched their assault on France. They addressed the Maginot Line in exactly the same way the Manchu had addressed the Great Wall: by avoiding it. Confounding French expectations, German tanks swarmed through both the Low Countries and the Ardennes, where they took ordinary roads, finding the forest not at all impassable. The rapidity of the German advance enabled the invaders to surround the French armies, while the khaki-clad troops of the Maginot Line had no targets for their intact firepower.

The fall of France came swiftly, and it was with equal rapidity that the Maginot Line joined the Great Wall in that growing list of symbols that compose our mental shorthand when thinking about walls. For the next fifty years, at least, writers could speak of a "Maginot Line psychology" when dismissing some misplaced faith in the power of sanctuary. Historians applied the term retroactively. The great Persianist Richard Frye spoke of Sasanid Persia's "Maginot Line mentality" when describing its system of walls. Arthur Waldron compared the Great Wall of China to the Maginot Line. Writers and politicians invoked the Maginot Line to condemn all manner of policies. Even poets piled on. As recently as 2004, the unfortunate Line became the subject of a poem by Harold Rosen. The poem is set in 1939 and introduces us to a Frenchman in a straw hat and sunglasses who is going off to service. Along the way, he picks up a hitchhiker, for whom he puts on a brave face:

> The Maginot Line. He utters it like a charm,
> Warding off catastrophe.
> "Couldn't be in a safer place"
> Than in his concrete labyrinth.

Lost in the general disdain of historians, poets, and politicians is the underreported and now somewhat ironic reality of the Maginot Line: there was, when the Germans invaded in 1940, in fact no safer place in France than in the concrete labyrinth. If the Line had only been extended farther, the German invasion of France, Hitler's Europe, and perhaps, by extension, the Holocaust, all could have been stopped.

The combat record of the Line is brief but exemplary. In mid-June 1940, after the Germans had secured control of France, Hitler ordered his Wehrmacht to turn back and destroy the Maginot Line. In this action, dubbed Operation Tiger, the Germans had every advantage, being able to attack the Line simultaneously from the front and the rear. The Germans pounded the Line with aerial bombing and artillery. In reply, the French popped up in their steel domes, pivoted, and fired. Not a single *grand ouvrage* was destroyed or captured. The defenders, unharmed in their underground world, but slowly working through their three-month supply of food, surrendered only reluctantly, when ordered to do so by the French commander in chief.

The Germans, who had been taught the value of the Line, studied it and perhaps borrowed from it an idea or two in the design of their own late-war bunkers. The French, stunned by the collapse of their army in the field, immediately began assigning blame. Pétain, the hero of Verdun, had supported the Maginot Line, but then made peace quickly with the Germans. Postwar, he was branded a traitor. The Line's leading prewar opponent, Charles de Gaulle, was elected president of France. As for the Line, it remained exactly where it was, as ineradicable as it was indestructible. It was not fated to command the awe reserved for the Great Wall. A few *ouvrages* have been opened to tourists, but they rarely figure in postcards from France. The Line's real legacy was symbolic, a universal byword for folly, and a hardy example of the misuse of history.

Perhaps somewhere there is a club where old walls gather to commiserate, grumbling about their obscurity or their ill-deserved infamy. If such a place exists, the Maginot Line is surely there, sharing a stiff drink with the Great Wall, and they have reserved a curse or two for another wall, which, for a while, eclipsed them both, dragging down their reputations even further, until the very name *wall* had become anathema. That wall was in Berlin.

"A Hell of a Lot Better Than a War"

As I approach the finish of this book—with new border walls being constructed or proposed all around the world even as I type—a fear nags at me: I can't help but wonder if the fate of Peter Wyden might soon be mine. A former *Newsweek* correspondent, Wyden spent more than four years interviewing eyewitnesses and scouring written sources for his narrative history of the Berlin Wall. When he was done, the finished product ran a magnificent 762 pages. He finished just in time for Simon & Schuster to release *Wall* in late 1989. It was obsolete almost before it hit the shelves.

Wyden had assembled a meticulous history, but how could he have known what was about to happen—that the Wall's spectacular climax would occur in the penultimate month of 1989, televised live around the world on MTV? He'd wrapped up his opus on a curiously subdued note. Life, he observed, had grown up around the Berlin Wall like weeds on an ancient ruin. West German families held picnics in the shade of the Wall, enjoying the lack of traffic; joggers raved about how pleasant it was to run alongside the concrete barrier; cabdrivers were bored of taking questions about it from tourists. "What have we learned from the Wall?" Wyden asked. "Not a great deal."

In his conclusion, Wyden quoted a retired American official, a veteran of the Kennedy administration, ruefully recalling the lethargic Western response to the news that the first coils of barbed wire had been rolled out across the streets of the city in August 1961. "Nobody thought for a minute it would be permanent," the official recalled. At the time of his statement in the late 1980s, the official could hardly envision a world without the Berlin Wall.

Of course, the Wall wasn't permanent, and neither is anything else. The Mesopotamians, watching their mud-brick walls repeatedly wash away, had figured out that much four thousand years earlier. They concluded that even humans were made of clay and that when we die, we simply return to clay, sinking back into the ground, as if repaying a loan from the earth. Berlin's infamous concrete barriers, like the great walls of Mesopotamia, gave only the illusion of permanence. If the American official had waited just a bit longer before giving his interview, he might have felt less disappointed by the Kennedy administration's obtuseness back in August 1961. The Wall had proven temporary after all. It had just required a little more patience than anticipated.

But patience was every bit as elusive as permanence in those atom-obsessed days, and the Cold War was a time of bomb shelters and duck-and-cover drills, when news magazines still regularly enumerated the strengths of the two superpowers, laid out in colorful graphics, detailing the numbers of soldiers, airplanes, missiles, and warheads. In such an atmosphere, it was inconceivable that all we had to do was wait, that the Wall, and indeed the Cold War itself, would prove to be brief and historically insignificant. We still wrestle with that reality today. A hundred years from now, the Berlin Wall will be forgotten, as obscure as Shulgi's Wall of the Land or the fortified lines of czarist Russia. The number of those who remember watching the Wall fall on MTV grows smaller every year. The number of those who once lived behind the Wall is smaller still. Future generations may wonder what all the hubbub was about.

For the time being, however, the Wall refuses to subside into the clay. It has firmly attached itself to our historical memory. In modern debates on walls, the Berlin Wall figures in almost every utterance. It is the universal example, perpetually at hand, perpetually tossed into discussions of barriers with which it had absolutely nothing in common. In its afterlife, it has assumed an importance out of proportion to its reality.

The story of the Berlin Wall turns out not at all what we expected it to be. It retains its gripping elements of international diplomacy, nuclear brinkmanship, fatal miscalculations, and brave escapes. However, the great players rarely seem in control. Seizing the narrative from them are the journalists, filmmakers, and news correspondents. The storytellers themselves have become bigger than the story, converting concrete and barbed wire into a symbol of such power that it has affected us ever since. They have played God with the Wall and with it our imaginations.

The preconditions for the Berlin Wall developed in the last months of World War II, when natural enemies who'd been made allies by the necessity of defeating Hitler met awkwardly at conferences to coordinate their final offensives. The Race to Berlin was no real race at all. The Soviets gobbled up great swaths of territory in their drive to dominate postwar Europe. Eisenhower, heedless of Churchill's plea to advance quickly to "shake hands with the Russians as far East as possible," took a more measured approach. In Eisenhower's thinking, there was little to be gained by seizing territory that Roosevelt had already promised to the Russians. Germany was to be divided, and the Supreme Allied Commander wasn't about to start a third world war by overrunning the Soviet sector.

A million and a half Berliners died during the war. No sooner had it ended than the survivors endured the systematic looting of their industrial base, as the Soviets—for a while the sole occupiers of the German capital—shipped nearly all the city's heavy equipment to Russia. By the time US and British troops arrived to assume their role in administering the former capital, the bombed-out city could no longer feed itself.

In the tug-of-war over Berlin, the Cold War commenced almost immediately. Wartime treaties had already determined the city's future: Berlin was to be divided into four sectors, with the British, French, Americans, and Russians each administering one. In accordance with the agreements, all of Berlin—even the Western sectors—lay deep in Soviet-controlled East Germany. It was an impossible design, all but guaranteeing friction.

In writing about Cold War Berlin, I'm probably not the first author to recall the story in which the biblical King Solomon is said to have resolved a maternity dispute by ordering a baby split in half. He averted the actual tragedy by swiftly awarding the child to the woman who objected most strenuously to his plan. In the case of Berlin, the baby died. In 1946, the Russians vetoed Berlin's first free elections since the days before Hitler. Two years later, they adopted a more extreme strategy, attempting to starve the allies out of Berlin. The Berlin blockade could well have sparked a war, if the Western powers hadn't been so sick of fighting. For nearly a year, the American-, French-, and British-controlled areas subsisted as an island, supplied only by air. A new city—West Berlin—was born.

The bifurcated city occupied a unique position in Cold War Europe. It was the most vulnerable point in both the Eastern and Western systems. To Nikita Khrushchev, the bombastic Soviet premier who succeeded Stalin, Berlin was "the testicles of the West." He needed only to squeeze them from time to time to make the West howl. But Berlin was equally problematic for Khrushchev and, before him, Stalin. The realization that the Russians intended to lay permanent claim to Eastern Europe horrified those who recalled the scourge of Communist political violence in the twenties and thirties. Hundreds of thousands of East Germans fled west. Within a year, more than a million had made their escape. Stalin, having looted East Germany of its industrial capital, now saw it looted of its human capital. Forced to deal with an exodus that threatened to hollow out the Soviet zones altogether, he finally turned to an ancient strategy, twisting it toward a new and perverted end.

It is a measure of the hold that the Berlin Wall still has on our imaginations that few people today—and indeed even few specialists outside the affected countries—are aware that much longer Cold War walls preceded the enclosure of West Berlin. The curtain that separated East and West Germany was not, for the most part, iron, but close enough. It consisted of 870 miles of concrete, barbed wire, trip alarms, guard towers, and electric fencing. Similar barriers separated Hungary and Austria. The Iron Curtain evolved rapidly during the Cold War, but it was always a tangible, physical barrier. By the end, it had attained a form that now serves as the prototype for many of the controversial border walls of the twenty-first century.

The walls of the Iron Curtain preceded the Berlin Wall by more than a decade. On December 1, 1946, East German border police established roadblocks and barbed-wire fences between East and West Germany. Stalin took additional steps toward concretizing Cold War borders in May 1952. By 1959, the border was manned by tens of thousands of border police stationed in concrete guard towers. Local patrols augmented those of the feared East German secret police, the Stasi. Neighbors were encouraged to report on neighbors.

The early Iron Curtain had one gaping hole. In Berlin, where East and West still freely comingled, it was still quite easy for an Easterner to apply for freedom. The more formidable the border walls became, the more people took advantage of this last remaining opening. By 1961, the number of escapees had surpassed 4 million, and the figure would have been even higher had the West Germans not regularly tested the refugees and returned those deemed less desirable. Fewer and fewer skilled workers remained in the East, where the exodus exacerbated economic hardship. The Russians sold more than fifty tons of gold to prop up their tottering East German satellite, but no amount of cash could slow the tide of émigrés.

In late 1958, a frustrated Khrushchev squeezed "the testicles of the West" with fury. He demanded the Western powers withdraw from Berlin altogether, threatening to sign a separate treaty with East Germany that would essentially allow Russia to control all access to West Berlin. In the tense atmosphere of the atomic age, this was widely viewed as a threat of nuclear war. The crisis, however, passed without escalation.

Three years later, confronted by an unproven, young US president and dealing with a worsening emigration crisis, Khrushchev renewed his threats. The first year of the Kennedy administration had raised Cold War tensions to a new peak. Kennedy's attempt to overthrow Fidel Castro with the ill-fated Bay of Pigs invasion had left the impression that the inexperienced president was not up to his task. While the hot-tempered Khrushchev contemplated the humiliation of his American counterpart, Walter Ulbricht, the squeaky-voiced and notoriously friendless leader of East Germany, pressed for a resolution to the emigration crisis. A lifelong Communist ideologue who wore his beard in the style of Lenin, Ulbricht frequently played the devil on Khrushchev's shoulder, whispering into the Soviet premier's ear plans that could potentially provoke nuclear war. Ulbricht dreamed of starving West Berlin into submission by severing all access to the city. He proposed clogging the air above West Berlin's airport with giant balloons and jamming the channels used by the flight controllers. He also made plans to imprison West Berlin with walls.

In March 1961, Ulbricht ordered his trusted deputy Erich Honecker to stockpile barbed wire and concrete slabs in preparation for the construction of a massive barrier around West Berlin. Like Ulbricht a committed ideologue, Honecker had joined his first Communist youth organization at the age of ten, and his entire education had been acquired at Communist institutions such as the International Lenin School in Moscow. He'd envisioned walls around West Berlin since at least 1953, when reports of Communist youths fleeing the country in the aftermath of a worker's revolt had shaken him.

The summer of 1961 brought a gradual escalation of tensions. A June meeting between Kennedy and Khrushchev left the American leader shaken. "He beat the hell out of me," Kennedy confessed. In the aftermath of the summit, Khrushchev spoke openly of "freeing" West Berlin, and Ulbricht expressed his desire to strangle the Western enclave. Nuclear war seemed closer than it had ever been.

Kennedy addressed the crisis in a televised address on July 25. "We cannot and will not permit the Communists to drive us out of Berlin, either gradually or by force," he declared. Khrushchev—having to consult a written transcript of Kennedy's address in this last year before Telstar made satellite broadcasts possible—flew into a rage. With characteristic intemperance, he threatened a US diplomat with a "thermonuclear" response. A week later, he convened a meeting of Warsaw Pact leaders at the Kremlin.

While Western intelligence fished for news from that August 3–5 Warsaw Pact meeting, the future of Berlin was being decided in Moscow. Unbeknown to the CIA, Khrushchev rejected Ulbricht's more inflammatory proposals. The East German leader succeeded in attaining only one concession: Khrushchev would allow him to seal West Berlin with barbed wire. The wire barrier would subsequently be transformed into a proper wall while the West, in Khrushchev's words, would "stand there like dumb sheep."

Ulbricht and Honecker had planned for this moment in strict secrecy. Berlin in 1961 was one of the most compromised cities of the Cold War, crawling with CIA agents who could still freely cross the border. East German leaders had taken to communicating only orally or in handwritten notes, all of which came from the hand of the same police colonel.

On the evening of August 12, Willy Brandt, the mayor of West Germany, gave a campaign speech in which he addressed the refugee issue. "They fear being shut into an enormous prison," he said. That prophecy was just hours from being realized.

At midnight, August 13, 1961, a Sunday, Honecker phoned the army with a terse command: "You know the assignment! March!" Trucks roared alive and rumbled around the streets and countryside surrounding West Berlin. East German soldiers and police hammered fence posts into the ground and began stringing up fencing. They rolled out miles of barbed wire. At the famous Brandenburg Gate, where Napoleon had once marched into the city, workers jackhammered the street that had only hours earlier permitted routine border crossing by commuters and shoppers.

The shock was most keenly felt by those who had been living in denial. In the final days before Barbed Wire Sunday, many East Germans had sensed something was afoot. Observing the hasty deployment of police units, they had calculated daily, even hourly, whether the time had come to make their dash. Thirty thousand had escaped in July and another twenty-two thousand in early August. On the last day before the unrolling of the barbed wire, more than twenty-five hundred escaped. Now the procrastinators had run out of time. The clanging and roar of construction machinery roused a sleepy Berlin. In the middle of the night, panicked East Berliners hastily dressed themselves and embarked on belated and mostly doomed bids for freedom. Hundreds thronged the Friedrichstrasse Station, desperately trying to board trains that would never leave. At Bernauer Strasse, where the facades of apartment buildings still marked the border, East Berliners leaped from their windows to the Western streets below.

Desperation turned quickly to hysteria. "The West Is Doing Nothing!" blared the headline of the West German tabloid *Bild*. Within days, Berlin had been blanketed by posters comparing Western inactivity to the betrayal of Czechoslovakia at the Munich Conference of 1938. Thirty thousand West Berliners took to the streets in demonstrations.

The event that so many Berliners viewed as the brink of apocalypse engendered little initial response from the West. The next morning, the *New York Times* reported the events of Barbed Wire Sunday with a sleepy notice about commuting being shut down in Berlin. US secretary of state Dean Rusk gave the matter little attention in his midmorning briefing. That afternoon, he attended a baseball game. Harold Macmillan, the prime minister of England, carried on with a hunting trip.

Incredibly, the birth of the Berlin Wall had passed nearly unnoticed in Washington. Years later, Wyden would observe that few of the president's top advisers even remembered the event:

> They hardly remembered what they did on Sunday, August 13, 1961. Nor did they make records of that historic day, and I refer to such busy note-takers as McGeorge Bundy, Ted Sorensen, Arthur Schlesinger, Pierre Salinger, and Maxwell Taylor. Walt Rostow, in charge of the National Security Council that day, showed me his appointment book; to his consternation, it was blank.

For his part, the president actually welcomed the barbed wire, viewing it as the end of the Berlin crisis. In his opinion, the other

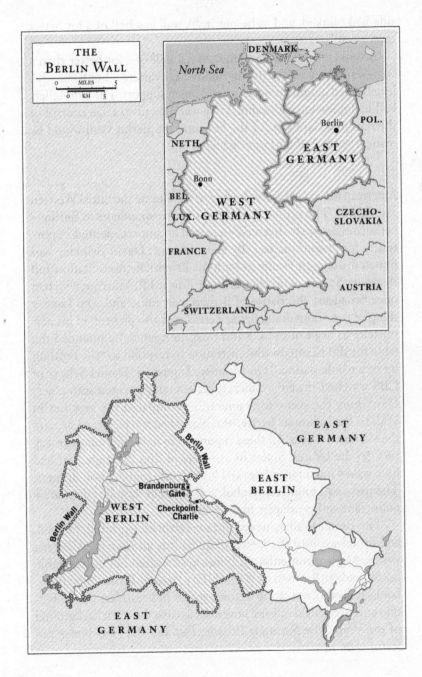

THE
BERLIN WALL

0 MILES 5

0 KM 5

DENMARK

North Sea

NETH.

BEL.

LUX.

FRANCE

SWITZERLAND

Bonn

WEST
GERMANY

Berlin

EAST
GERMANY

POL.

CZECHO-
SLOVAKIA

AUSTRIA

EAST
GERMANY

EAST
BERLIN

Berlin Wall

WEST
BERLIN

Brandenburg
Gate

Checkpoint
Charlie

Berlin Wall

EAST
GERMANY

side had blinked, and as he put it, "A wall is a hell of a lot better than a war."

A wall is, by almost any measure, a hell of a lot better than a war—especially war of the thermonuclear variety—but Kennedy's levelheaded judgment never gained much support. The storytellers had had quite enough calm. They were about to seize control of the narrative, and not for the last time the Berlin Wall would be made a symbol of far larger issues.

American journalists were the first to recalibrate the initial Western assessment. The presence of Western correspondents in Berlin—eyewitnesses to the hysteria—created an unprecedented opportunity for sensationalism. By sheer chance, David Brinkley had filmed the chaotic scenes at both the Friedrichstrasse Station and Bernauer Strasse. The old warhorse Edward R. Murrow, who had once broadcast the Battle of Britain over radio and who knew a thing or two about dramatizing a crisis, was also present. In his new capacity as head of the US Information Agency, he pounded the table for the Kennedy administration to respond to "the bottling up of a whole nation." On Monday, August 14, Daniel Schorr of CBS watched the first concrete slabs being lowered into place. Describing the scene for cameras, he compared the new Berlin Wall to the infamous barrier the Nazis had once erected around the Warsaw Ghetto. All these reports were now winging their way back to the United States in canisters of film and tape that had been tossed into orange bags and loaded onto transatlantic airliners. The press had found its symbol, and it would soon be adopted by politicians and producers in every media.

The Berlin Wall achieved instant celebrity—printed, radioed, and broadcast into the hearts of audiences all over the Western world. Almost immediately, publishers rushed out coffee-table books with titles such as *Barbed Wire Around Berlin*. Adventure books followed, narrating heroic escapes in breathless detail. Fiction authors rushed out spy novels set against the stark background of the Wall. The *Saturday Evening Post* and the *New Yorker* ran features on it.

Television found the Wall especially irresistible. Against the objections of an embarrassed Kennedy administration, both CBS and NBC financed the digging of tunnels in exchange for exclusive film rights to the escapes. CBS eventually caved to pressure and dropped their project, although they did produce a fictional version, "Tunnel to Freedom," which aired as an episode of the popular *Armstrong Circle Theater*. NBC's enterprise carried on as planned. Twenty-nine East Germans escaped through the 150-yard tunnel before it was discovered and shut down. The resulting documentary dominated nightly ratings.

In California, a middle-aged actor watched such reports with interest. His Hollywood career all but over, he'd already commenced that inevitable transition when, midlife, a man's view of the world turns inevitably more critical and dyspeptic, his ambitions focus less on comfort than position, and his interests narrow increasingly to the political. To Ronald Reagan, the Berlin Wall was a burning symbol of the Communist ideology he viewed as the immediate threat to the American way of life. Two decades later he would play a small but highly visible role—the most famous of his career—in bringing down the Wall. Meanwhile, the Hollywood establishment that had generally lost interest in Reagan was also taking a keen interest in the Wall.

The first director to deal with the Berlin Wall had a decidedly personal beef. Billy Wilder, already famous for *Double Indemnity*, *Sunset Boulevard*, and *Some Like It Hot*, was in Berlin filming the forgettable Cold War comedy *One, Two, Three* on Barbed Wire Sunday. The sudden change of conditions forced him to relocate production to Munich. Four months later, the movie debuted with a preface, written by the famously apolitical director and narrated by the film's star, James Cagney:

> On Sunday, August 13, 1961, the eyes of America were on the nation's capital, where Roger Maris was hitting home runs #44 and 45 against the Senators. On that same day, without any warning, the East German Communists sealed off the border between East and West Berlin. I only mention this to show the kind of people we're dealing with—*real shifty*.

This was only Hollywood's first salvo. Dozens followed. Within a year of Barbed Wire Sunday, MGM had rushed out *Escape from East Berlin* (aka *Tunnel 28*), based on a breakout that had occurred in January of that year. The film premiered at a festive opening in West Berlin. British studios, having already warmed up with such pre-Wall Iron Curtain films as *Beyond the Curtain*, embraced the genre as well. In 1965, Britain's Salem Films turned the John le Carré thriller *The Spy Who Came in from the Cold* into a film featuring Richard Burton. By then, images of Berlin were already so familiar that the movie's opening images required no narration; the audience was expected to recognize the Wall immediately. From that point on, Berlin Wall movies became something of a staple. The next year alone brought *Funeral in Berlin*, starring Michael Caine in an adaptation of Len Deighton's spy novel, as well as Alfred Hitchcock's *Torn Curtain*, which starred Paul Newman. By 1972, even the Philippines had produced its first Berlin Wall movie—*Escape from East Berlin*—featuring dialog in Tagalog.

As movies and television lavished attention on Cold War Berlin, the Wall became a must-see for foreign travelers. Western tourists who might otherwise have skipped Berlin altogether now made pilgrimages to the Wall. As early as 1962, exasperated Berliners were already complaining about the parade of tour buses. Meanwhile, the Wall continued to evolve. By the 1970s, the famous concrete slabs, covered in graffiti, represented only the outermost portion of a barrier system that was mostly hidden from Western eyes. Given a bird's-eye view, tourists could have seen that behind the Wall lay a death zone that included beds of raised nails, booby traps, land mines, and barbed wire. The Western side—and let us not forget that the Wall technically enclosed West Berlin, not East—was considerably more approachable. Kids played by it, and neighborhood families held parties in its shade. Tourists were mostly routed to the Potsdamer Platz, where street vendors hawked sausages and souvenirs, and guides recited stories of harrowing escapes. In 1978, a particularly famous pair of Americans arrived: Ronald and Nancy Reagan, accompanied by a television crew, just months before the launch of Reagan's successful presidential campaign.

By the time Reagan made his famous demand that the barrier be torn down, the Berlin Wall had been trotted across Western pages and screens for over two decades. Shock had gradually turned to familiarity and then something else again. As late as 1981, the Wall, by then somewhat typecast, was still starring in the tense made-for-TV thriller *Berlin Tunnel 21*, which featured a dramatic reenactment of Barbed Wire Sunday. But audiences were growing tired. In the mid-eighties, the once-chilling symbol of Communism had been reduced to a bit part in the spy comedy *Gotcha!* Somewhere between the quiet command of Richard Burton and the stammering of Anthony Edwards in *Gotcha!* the Wall had reached the end of its practical life span as a symbol of terror.

Long before Reagan's demand that he "tear down this wall," Mikhail Gorbachev had been laying the groundwork for just that. In the final chapter of the Wall's history, Gorbachev was the one indispensable figure. Made leader of the Soviet Union in 1985, he quickly introduced reforms. In Russia, he liberated political prisoners, allowed open elections, and introduced market-based economic reforms. He also repudiated the so-called Brezhnev Doctrine, which had reserved for the Soviet Union the right to intervene in the affairs of any Soviet Bloc state. In Poland, Czechoslovakia, Bulgaria, Hungary, and Romania, Soviet-supported dictators realized that they could no longer count on Russian support. In East Germany, Erich Honecker—who'd once been whisked to safety and saved by Soviet tanks during the workers' revolt of 1953—unhappily confronted the same realization.

East Germany had fared poorly behind the Iron Curtain. Lost in so many daring escapes were many of the nation's best—the risk takers, the problem solvers, the freethinkers, and the creators. They were the sort who persevered at difficult tasks until they'd completed long tunnels or fashioned homemade hot-air balloons. In the annals of the escapes, one searches in vain for escapees motivated by materialism, economic need, or a lust for Western goods. They came West seeking only freedom, fleeing a regime where propagandists controlled both the media and the schools. German reviewers excoriated *Tunnel 28* because it depicted refugees fleeing simply to experience the material culture of the West. Now Gorbachev's reforms threatened to undermine the East German leaders who'd clung to power partly by driving such creative people out.

The first changes occurred quietly, far from Honecker's Berlin, on the border of Hungary and Austria. There, a state-of-the-art border-security system had gradually fallen into disrepair, a victim of the struggling Communist economy's inability to cover the costs of maintenance. Electrified wires rusted and malfunctioned. Rabbits and birds set off thousands of costly false alarms. In 1988, the Hungarian government deemed its stretch of Iron Curtain too expensive. On May 2, 1989, with Gorbachev's approval, the Hungarians announced their intention to dismantle their border wall.

Western leaders, conditioned for more than a quarter century to believe that only one wall mattered, responded predictably. "Let Berlin be next," said President George H. W. Bush. The books, the documentaries, and the movies had always focused solely on the divided city. Who wanted to be known as the president who brought down the Austria-Hungary border fence?

In Eastern Europe, however, where the walls were something more than mere narrative, the Hungarian announcement was electrifying. East German tourists already in Hungary refused to vacate their campgrounds. Thousands crowded the West German embassy at Budapest, seeking asylum and escape. When the number of refugees overwhelmed the embassy, the Holy Family Roman Catholic Church began taking them in. The dreaded East German secret police were in Budapest all along, observing the asylum seekers from the roofs of nearby buildings, but they could only watch impotently as the encampments swelled by the thousands.

That August, a conservative Hungarian party received permission from the government to open the gates of the still-standing, still-guarded border so that a small crowd of Austrians and Hungarians could mingle for a few hours and celebrate the historic ties between their countries. The crowd that arrived for the picnic in Sopron stunned both the event organizers and the local border guards. In command of the Hungarian guards that day was Lieutenant Colonel Arpad Bella, pulling a Saturday shift on his wedding anniversary. Bella had been briefed to expect only a small ceremonial event. He was completely unaware that the decisions that would be forced on him would someday make him a minor celebrity, still sought out for interviews decades later.

A quarter century after the event there is no shortage of politicians eager to claim responsibility for what became known as the Pan-European Picnic. Bella's account has at least remained consistent. As throngs of East German asylum seekers approached the gate, the Hungarian officer elected to ignore standing orders to fire a warning shot. His friend and counterpart on the Austrian side of the border, Johann Götl, was apoplectic. "Are you out of your mind?" he shouted. "We already discussed this, and then you send me six hundred people out of a cornfield!"

Hungary's leaders were now racing to catch up to the forces they had inadvertently unleashed. For the next several weeks, they continued to police their still unopened borders, fearful that they had undermined the position of Gorbachev. Hungary's prime minister, Miklós Németh, met with West Germany's chancellor, Helmut Kohl, and agreed to bus the remaining refugees to West Germany. Within six weeks, nearly thirty thousand East Germans had escaped through Hungary, and the exodus only accelerated when Czechoslovakia opened its borders as well. By early October, some twelve thousand East Germans were camped out on the grounds of the German embassy at the baroque Lobkowicz Palace in Prague. Honecker, losing his grip, responded by closing East Germany's borders even against other Soviet states, but the move came too late. Freedom was in the air—literally, in the form of former *Knight Rider* (and later *Baywatch*) star David Hasselhoff's reissue of a seventies-era German pop song, which had been given new lyrics and retitled "Looking for Freedom." Hasselhoff's singing was, to be sure, an acquired taste, but the song held the top place on the charts for eight weeks and prompted a summer concert tour in which the singer drove a car through a mock Berlin Wall. Bootleg copies of the hit circulated around the East, providing the peppy earworm of the revolution.

By mid-autumn, the demonstrations had spread to East Germany. The crowds in Leipzig swelled ominously that October—

first to 70,000, then 120,000, then 300,000. Erich Honecker, the architect of the Wall, who had just that January declared defiantly that the Wall would last another "fifty or one hundred years," resigned under pressure from his party. On November 4, some half million protesters flooded the streets of Berlin. Five days later, it was all over.

Fittingly, the Wall, which had starred in so many books and movies over the years, saved its most memorable performance for last. On November 9, the media spokesman for East Berlin's Communist Party read an obtuse policy announcement on new border regulations established by the politburo. A roomful of journalists pressed for clarification, none of them certain of the announcement's meaning. Hours later, an Associated Press summary attempted to put the announcement in more straightforward terms: "The GDR is opening its borders." This was probably not at all what the government intended, but it did have the effect of rendering the government's intention's moot, and the reality of a new era struck East Germans when they tuned in to the evening news. The response was electric. East Berliners poured out of their homes, crowding the still-closed gates. Crowds formed at every checkpoint, demanding to cross. Initially, the guards allowed only the more boisterous individuals through, and only after checking their documents. This created bottlenecks, frustrating the crowds even more. By 10:00 p.m., Egon Krenz, Honecker's successor, knew that there was little he could do to reverse the damage from the AP story except to call out the tanks.

The nightly news broadcasts only worsened the government's position, announcing that "the gates of the Wall stand wide-open." This declaration was no more accurate than the AP report, but the words nevertheless galvanized the people. Was anyone still asleep in Berlin? It would hardly seem possible, judging from the crowds that streamed into the streets. The only Berliners left inside were the tank crews.

At 11:30 p.m., one of the Wall's guard units, at a loss for orders and fearing it was about to lose control, opened the first checkpoint.

By midnight, every checkpoint along the Wall had been thrown open. Exuberant youths scaled the Wall and chiseled off chunks of concrete. Across the seas, stunned Americans watched the fall of the monument whose rise, twenty-eight years earlier, had found them sleepy and oblivious. MTV broadcast the scene free and unencrypted to the newly popular satellite systems located around the world, especially in those areas not yet reached by cable.

In retrospect, the life of the Berlin Wall seems oddly short, a time span unbefitting a monument so thoroughly ingrained in our consciousness. The rest of the Iron Curtain was dismantled without fanfare. Local museums commemorate the old barriers. In Germany, an elongated green space has taken the place of the old Inner German border. Outside of those living in the immediate neighborhoods, few now recall that those barriers even existed. Our selective amnesia is embarrassing. The Western specialists in modern Eastern European history with whom I consulted were all entirely unaware of the physical barriers that once made up the Iron Curtain. But Berlin? They knew all about Berlin.

The Berlin Wall had always hogged the stage. When the Cold War died an unexpected death, the city held a spectacular wake, then the mourners all separated and went off to the only real business of the nineties: making money. A single relic—the star of books, tabloids, and movies—lingered behind, clinging to the spotlight like a fading diva, loath to relinquish her celebrity.

Lucky tourists carried off chunks of the Wall to display to their friends. Bill Roedy, the head of MTV Networks International, recalls carting off "suitcases and suitcases" of Wall fragments, later stamped with MTV's logo and given away. Larger sections of the Wall were sold at auction to be displayed in the homes of wealthy buyers. Rock stars descended on Berlin to host me-too concerts. The English rock band Pink Floyd even emulated the Hasselhoff wall-busting stunt. Hasselhoff himself made a triumphant return.

Once the initial buzz had subsided, it might have seemed that the Berlin Wall would go the way of Ozymandias. Television specials on the Wall were ratings poison. And one can only imagine how quickly the rich must have tired of displaying dirty concrete slabs in their living rooms. Meanwhile, the movies and the novels of the Cold War faded into oblivion. *The Spy Who Came in from the Cold*, *Funeral in Berlin*, and *Torn Curtain* only rarely resurface on cable nowadays, invariably seeming quaint and dated. The last VHS copies of *Gotcha!* went unsold at yard sales. Two thousand years from now, archaeologists sifting through our trash will perhaps find copies of it. With any luck, they'll lack the technology to play it. Meanwhile, newsmagazines have stopped running infographics on Soviet and American troop numbers. For a while, they were replaced by articles about "the End of History."

Of course, the key to celebrity survival is always reinvention, and this would hold true in the case of Berlin. The first books written about the Wall after its fall still highlighted the usual features: its tense beginnings, the daring escapes across it, and so forth. However, Hollywood had moved on in search of fresher stories. Communism had collapsed. The two Germanies were united. Russia had opened a stock exchange. A world obsessed with its new electronic toys forgot about the Cold War. History wasn't dead, just forgotten. The Wall shed its former role as a symbol of Communist oppression and acquired an entirely new image in a foggy-minded popular imagination that remembered the Wall but couldn't quite recall who'd built it or why.

The Berlin Wall had always had impeccable timing—making its grand appearance at the height of the Cold War and bowing out in spectacular fashion to bring the Cold War to its conclusion. It would now embark on its second career with similar timeliness, returning to the stage as a symbol of *all* border walls, just as they were about to make a reappearance around the world.

Epilogue: "Love Your Neighbor, but Don't Pull Down Your Hedge"

May Rindge was a tough old bird. She'd owned almost the entire Malibu coastline since 1892, when her husband acquired it for $10 an acre, and she wasn't about to let anyone take it from her. Not an inch. Malibu was her sanctuary—an "earth paradise" in her late husband's words—a pristine realm of mountain and shore, and with sentimental attachments besides. She intended to preserve forever this reminder of the kindly, Christian man who'd rescued her, a plain, prospectless schoolteacher, from a Michigan farm, whisking her away to a sunny Eden.

May's enemies were legion, and they had declared war on the Rindge family even while her frail husband was still alive. To begin with, there were the homesteaders, crusty, uncouth squatters, living in tin-roofed shacks on state land in the Santa Monica Mountains. They didn't pay much attention to property lines when they tramped across the Rindge ranch, stealing cattle and produce, hunting, and using the ranch trail as a shortcut to Santa Monica, where they traded for bullets at the general store. When the homesteaders encountered a fence, they weren't inclined to become good neighbors. These were rough men, men who would, and sometimes did, shoot a man over a fence they didn't like. Rindge had other enemies, too. They came from Los Angeles, in the form of grasping county and state government officials who saw in Malibu something they didn't have and wanted it. They weren't as hotheaded as the homesteaders, but they wielded more power.

231

The real troubles began in 1895, when May's husband, Frederick, dismayed by the crowds of Los Angeleno day-trippers invading his land to sightsee, ordered locked gates installed at both ends of his vast ranch—Las Flores Canyon in the east and Point Dume in the west. Frederick obligingly supplied the homesteaders with keys to the gates, allowing them free passage, but to these ruffians, accustomed to coming and going as they pleased, the new arrangement was an insult. The arguments, fights, and lawsuits that commenced in 1895 would last another thirty years.

Life in paradise was never quite the same after the gates went up. After a November 1903 fire—which May blamed on arson—consumed the ranch, May was consumed with a fire of her own. When her frail husband succumbed to his illnesses in 1905, she all but declared war on his enemies. She would allow no one to ruin his beloved Malibu. May instructed her ranch hands to construct five gates on the ranch's coastal trail, and when trespassers kept destroying them, she responded by beefing up her security patrols, adding dozens more men, armed with shotguns. May herself stalked the grounds with a gun holster slung across her hip, a terrifying sight to the homesteader children who occasionally encountered her. But she couldn't scare off the state, which won a lawsuit demanding she open her trail to the public. Hundreds of automobiles soon clogged her Malibu beaches, while homesteaders mutilated ranch cattle and uttered death threats. May bought a gun for her teenage daughter to wear while she was playing and another gun for her daughter's friend.

In 1917, May celebrated an appeals court victory by shutting down the coastal trail yet again and enclosing the entire ranch with fifty miles of fencing. A group of homesteaders unsuccessfully tried to kill her by blocking the ranch road with three cars, connected by chains, behind which they waited in ambush with their guns. A few months later, they poisoned two hundred of May's sheep. She ordered several homesteaders' trails dynamited the very next day. By 1918, the battle between her ranch hands and the homesteaders had escalated to shooting.

It was a battle that May Rindge could never win. In 1923, the US Supreme Court, in a landmark decision that proved pivotal in establishing the reach of eminent domain, ruled that the state could seize land from the Rindge ranch to build a coastal road—the Pacific Coast Highway. May stayed in denial for a while: when the construction crews arrived, she held them off for three days with a force of forty guards, mounted on horseback. But paradise was lost, and May knew it. In 1926, strapped for cash after decades in court and defeated in her dream of preserving the estate of her beloved husband, she agreed to lease some property on the Malibu beaches.

It is here that Anna Q. Nilsson enters the story. The Jazz Age movie star was coming off a rough year. In 1925, she had divorced her second husband, an alcoholic, then suffered a serious accident while riding a horse. She'd been making a dozen films a year and was badly in need of a break when she elected to check out the new lots for lease in Malibu. In 1926, Anna passed through the guarded gate at Las Flores, where May's trail turned off the Pacific Coast Highway, drove down the one-lane dirt road to the shore, and fell in love. May's private Eden enchanted Anna just as it had once enchanted Frederick. She saw in it the ideal place to relax and perhaps even duck the fans who deluged her with thousands of letters each month. Anna signed a lease for $75 a month and built a summer home. Soon after came her peers—first Marie Prevost and Raoul Walsh, then Clara Bow, Gloria Swanson, Ronald Colman, Bing Crosby, and others. Past the gates and down the private road, movie-studio carpenters, accustomed only to building temporary backdrops for film productions, constructed flimsy cottages for Hollywood royalty, creating what would soon become known as the Malibu Motion Picture Colony. Movie stars had discovered that they liked living in a private world, walled off from the hoi polloi.

Who were the wall builders?

It's a good question. More than four thousand years of history have passed before us since we first posed it while puzzling over the mystery of Syria's Très Long Mur. In some ways, the problem remains as baffling as ever. Who were the wall builders? Whoever they were, they're still at it. In the seventy-odd years since the surrender of the Maginot Line, border walls have proliferated around the world, and their resurgence has only accelerated since 1989. Berlin Walls have grown into Great Walls. Razor wire, motion sensors, electrified fencing, and concrete slabs consume horizons, rolling across countrysides for hundreds of miles. By some recent estimates, there are as many as seventy extant border walls, although the number changes annually, if not weekly. The new walls, no longer expected to withstand military assaults, most commonly take the form of specialized fences. Otherwise, they have much in common with their mud-brick ancestors.

When we search contemporary maps for walls, familiar names and places poke at our memories, as if to underscore just how little has changed. The Iraqis, whose Mesopotamian ancestors struggled incessantly against the impermanence of their mud-built world, still fight against impermanence. They have constructed a wall against the water that is so vulnerable to erosion that teams of workers have to shore it up daily lest their world finally be washed away in an epic deluge. The Chinese, who constructed long walls to protect their trade routes and even longer walls to isolate and protect themselves from their enemies, carry on much the same today, with protectionist economic policies guarding their trade, border fences guarding against North Korea, and a great internet firewall maintaining their cultural isolation. The Persians, whose erstwhile emperors once built elaborate systems of walls against their enemies, still place barriers on their borders. So, too, do the people of Uzbekistan, whose Silk Road ancestors once constructed hundreds of miles of walls enclosing oases or defending borders. Migrating Syrians, terror of whom once inspired the world's first border walls, continue to inspire fear and walls around the world. Even distant European nations have fortified their borders against them.

The players are the same, but the story line has been revised. Walls can no longer stop armies or even slow them down. Cities are no longer contained by walls, either. They sprawl unchecked over the surrounding countryside, gobbling up farmland and becoming more and more reliant on a fantastically wasteful long-distance trade in food. The unity of the walled city has become a thing of the distant past, too, replaced by ghettoization and neighborhoods walled against neighborhoods.

In the early years of the new millennium, the world entered its Second Age of Walls. Few of us even noticed. It all happened quickly, like a worldwide Barbed Wire Sunday, but drawing far less interest from Western observers than the earlier walling of Berlin. Two factors—mass immigration and the rise of Islamic terrorism—were the immediate precipitators of the new walls, and both tended to affect other countries before reaching Europe or America. If the West had snoozed for a full day after Berlin was enclosed in 1961, it hibernated during the first decade of the new age, when non-Western nations from Saudi Arabia to Malaysia embarked on wall-building projects that quickly surpassed the combined efforts of the Romans, Persians, and Chinese.

The coming of the walls was so sudden and simultaneous that it is difficult to pinpoint its inception. The Middle East, home of the world's earliest border walls, has, in the past fifteen years, become a honeycomb of fences and walls. Saudi Arabia, in particular, has come as close as any nation since Nebuchadnezzar's Babylon to realizing the dream of a fully enclosed state. In 2003, the kingdom commenced work on a barrier along its eleven-hundred-mile border with Yemen. Hearkening back to so many ancient walls situated on the fringes of wastelands, the Saudi structure cuts across Arabia's desolate Empty Quarter, the uninhabitable home of the world's largest oil deposits. Designed to stop illegal immigration, as well as terrorism and sectarian violence, the Saudi barrier uses the sort of materials that were unavailable to the shahs of ages past, who built walls facing the other direction, against the Arabs. Ten-foot-high steel pipes, filled with concrete, provide the structure, the sides of which bristle with razor wire. Tunnels run deep underneath to prevent terrorists from circumventing the barrier from below. A sister wall—this one stretching six hundred miles along the border with Iraq—supplements a preexisting twenty-foot-high sand berm. The Saudi-Iraq barrier includes five layers of fencing, spaced some hundred meters apart and rendered uncrossable by razor-sharp concertina wire. Underground sensors detect any movement, and sentinels in guard towers maintain watch with the aid of night-vision technology.

Tracing their course on a map, the walls lead only to more walls. The Saudi-Iraq barrier ends at Kuwait, whose 120-mile-long border with Iraq was fortified by the United Nations. The Kuwaiti structure, initially an electrified barbed-wire fence, has recently been upgraded to a steel wall. Not far away, the United Arab Emirates has fortified its border with Oman.

More prominently, Israel has enclosed itself with walls. The tiny nation, long sequestered from its neighbors by fenced towns and kibbutzim, constructed its second-most-famous wall in response to the Second Intifada, a Palestinian uprising that lasted from 2000 to 2005. In the first years of the Intifada, frequent reports of bombings and other attacks traumatized Israeli citizens. By 2002, the government had commenced work on a barrier that would eventually stretch 450 miles and spawn several more walls totaling hundreds more miles. The West Bank Wall—to its critics, the Wall of Occupation or even the Apartheid Wall—features various technological advances, many cribbed from the old Iron Curtain barriers. Infrared night sensors, radar, seismic sensors, balloon-borne cameras, and unmanned, remote-controlled Ford F-350 trucks, equipped with video cameras and machine guns, augment the wall's concrete slabs and concertina wire. The technologies have acquired admiring notice from American politicians and drawn close attention from other nations seeking to secure their borders, leading one skeptic to label Israel "the biggest exporter of cages in the world." For Israeli companies, such as Elbit Systems, border security has become a $100 million international business. The technology so impressed outsiders that some politicians have argued that it obviates the need for a physical structure, a suggestion strenuously resisted by the wall's architect, Dany Tirza: "Virtual fence? I don't believe it. It's not realistic. It cannot catch a man. And even if you do, what to do with him? He can just say he didn't know he had crossed the border."

The Israel–West Bank barrier was soon replicated on other borders: In 2011, work began on a 45-mile wall along Israel's

Syrian border. Two years later, Israel had completed a 150-mile barrier facing Egypt to its west. More recently, construction has started along the borders of Lebanon and the Gaza Strip, and 2017 saw the creation of a partial and—by Israeli standards—somewhat halfhearted fence on the Jordanian border. Proponents of the walls point out that the barriers have effectively eliminated illegal immigration and brought about a drastic decline in terrorism. Critics, however, charge that the borders themselves are invalid.

In the meanwhile, Israel's neighbors have been building walls of their own. On its border with Gaza, Egypt constructed a steel wall that extends more than sixty feet below the ground. Jordan, too, has erected barriers, with a little help from friends. From 2008 to 2016, the Obama administration provided over $500 million, in addition to more than $2 billion in loan guarantees, to support construction of a high-tech 287-mile barrier along Jordan's border with Syria. The Obama administration also supplied technical support, and the work was largely contracted through the US company Raytheon.

New walls haven't been limited to the Middle East. In Southeast Asia, the borders of India are no older than those of Israel, although they haven't inspired the same level of scrutiny from Westerners (whose interest waned shortly after a harried British mapmaker drew up the boundaries of India, Pakistan, and Bangladesh in 1947). Only after the rise of Islamic terrorist organizations in Pakistan and Bangladesh galvanized the world's largest democracy were the long-fuzzy lines turned to concrete and steel.

For the past fifteen years, India has rivaled Saudi Arabia and Israel as a consumer of razor wire. India's fences now gobble up thousands of miles of often spectacular terrain, occasionally bisecting regions whose traditional identities predate their modern "nationalities." In a feat of engineering surpassing even the works of the ancient Chinese, Indian workers climbed into thin air in 2004 and snaked twelve-foot-high, partly electrified barriers across some of the world's highest mountains, securing part of India's absurdly placed border with Pakistan. Around the same time, the Indians constructed over two hundred miles of fencing and walls along the border with Bangladesh—a first step toward what quickly grew into two thousand miles of barbed wire and concrete. In 2013, the Indians picked up their climbing gear anew and trudged into the Himalayas to wall off another region of the Pakistan border. Rather than relaxing after these fantastic efforts, they've taken up wall building with a growing perfectionism. In 2016, the Indian home minister visited Israel to observe state-of-the-art border technology; the lessons were to be applied on borders in the northwestern states of Punjab and Jammu. Later that year, India added Maginot-like underground bunkers to some of its borders. By then, India's relative success at stemming terrorism was being emulated by Thailand and Malaysia, whose governments agreed to cooperate on the creation of a mutual border wall after Thailand had suffered over sixty-five hundred deaths at the hands of Malaysia-based Islamic militants.

On the other side of the world, Africa reacted to the spread of terrorism and mass immigration with walls. After an April 2015 attack by the Islamic terror organization al-Shabab left 148 dead at Garissa University, the Kenyan government initiated work on a 440-mile barrier along its border with Somalia. Morocco and Algeria built walls primarily to slow illegal immigration and drug smuggling. And, in 2016, the United States quietly provided funding for a 125-mile barrier along the Tunisian border with Libya to prevent the movement of jihadists. This was the second such wall funded by the United States under President Barack Obama, who in April 2016 publicly dismissed border walls as "wacky."

The rapid expansion of walls across Asia and Africa was historically unprecedented. In its first fifteen years, the Second Age of Walls eclipsed the First in nearly every metric. More countries had built longer border walls than at any other time in history. The movement affected countries whose populations totaled over 4 billion people, and even this estimate excludes those distant nations whose emigrants could cross several borders before reaching a physical barrier. However, the massive expansion of border walls was, in its first decade, a movement that largely bypassed the West, whose borders remained, until recently, conspicuously open. Consequently, the re-walling of the world attracted little notice except from a handful of academic specialists.

Only one Western nation matched the early efforts of the Asian and African countries. Well before plans had even been drawn up for the long walls of Israel, Saudi Arabia, and Egypt, a series of Clinton administration initiatives, aimed at tightening security on the porously fenced Mexican border, led to the extension or enhancement of physical barriers in California, Arizona, New Mexico, and Texas. The earliest of the Clinton walls was rolled out just four years after the fall of the Berlin Wall. Operations Blockade and Hold the Line in 1993, Gatekeeper and Safeguard in 1994, and Rio Grande in 1997 were succeeded in 2006 by the passage of the Secure Fence Act, which saw the Clinton-era walls extended by hundreds of miles under the Bush and Obama administrations.

The American barriers made for some potentially awkward criticisms. Even seventeen years after the events of 1989, the Berlin Wall remained a potent symbol, and politicians were careful to avoid any use of the term *wall* in reference to the southern border. The eighty senators who voted for the Secure Fence Act—a bipartisan majority, which included two junior senators with presidential aspirations, Barack Obama and Hillary Clinton—thus sought to escape the taint of unseemly historical comparisons.

The insistence on a largely meaningless semantic distinction between two functionally identical structures provided an early foretaste of debates that would soon be waged primarily with symbols, slogans, and inaccurate historical generalizations. In public comments on the 2006 act, proponents commonly resorted to the folk-saying "Good fences make good neighbors." The phrase had strong positive connotations in American society, being widely attributed to the nation's bland former poet laureate Robert Frost. It was bandied about frequently in congressional debates, and even Israeli prime minister Ehud Barak, picking up on the pithy aphorism's evident popularity, quoted it while lobbying for his West Bank wall. Ironically, Frost had been given credit for an axiom that was already a trite cliché when he wrote "Mending Wall" in 1914. By then, local versions of the venerable proverb were already common throughout the world, in languages ranging from Hindi to Japanese.

An 1840 edition of *Blum's Farmer's and Planter's Almanac* is believed to have carried the first known American appearance, although Americans initially preferred the cheekier "Love your neighbor, but don't pull down your hedge." The sentiment was quite ancient. In fact, neighboring Roman farmers were so convinced of the value of well-marked property lines that they venerated the stones that bound their fields, seeing them as manifestations of the god Terminus.

By 2009, the United States had walled off—or at least Securely Fenced—some seven hundred miles along its southern border. Mikhail Gorbachev, whose English apparently didn't include the use of euphemisms, had his doubts, remarking, "Well, I am not going to repeat what President Reagan once said, but I think the Great Wall of China or the Berlin Wall have not been very effective, nor particular efficient." Gorbachev's comment wasn't unique. It had been more than twenty years since Reagan's famous speech, and its original anticommunist context was already long forgotten, allowing Reagan's words to experience a second life as an anti-wall manifesto. Wherever walls went up, they were spray-painted with Reagan's exhortation or Kennedy's "*Ich bin ein Berliner*."

Two events finally drew attention to the worldwide rise of border walls. The first was the expansion of mass migration into Europe. The second was an American presidential campaign that sensationalized the issue worldwide.

The walling of much of North Africa, the Middle East, and Southeast Asia during the early 2000s had an unintended yet profound impact on Europe. The Somalis, Sudanese, and Ethiopians who annually arrived in Saudi Arabia through Yemen, the Afghan and Pakistani migrants who sought entrance into India, and the would-be Syrian migrants to Jordan all found they could no longer cross borders that had once been porous. Subsequent waves of migrants sought detours around the razor wire. The alternative routes took them across the Mediterranean or through Turkey into the Balkans and eventually into northern Europe. Meanwhile, their numbers swelled with the addition of refugees displaced by the outbreak of civil war in Syria.

The timing of the new wave of immigration was inauspicious, coming on the heels of the stock market collapses of 2008. Before reaching the promised lands of Germany, France, Sweden, and the United Kingdom, migrants passed through a series of nations that were still reeling from economic crises and were ill equipped to handle the flow of so much human traffic. In 2011, Greece, the chief entry point into Europe from the Middle East, started construction on a fence along its border with Turkey. The fence was completed in 2012, cutting migration through the area by 90 percent. However, the closing of Greece's borders only forced new detours, rather than reducing the numbers of migrants. Many new arrivals traveled by sea to Italy or the Greek islands, which couldn't be walled off. Others found new land routes through Turkey. All across southeastern Europe, cash-strapped nations, unable to afford the policing and social services necessitated by the sudden arrival of hundreds of thousands of migrants, played a furious game of whack-a-mole, erecting walls wherever migrants entered in great numbers. The dominoes fell quickly: starting in 2013, Bulgaria built a fence along its hundred-mile border with Turkey. The new fence lay just north of Edirne, the old Adrianopolis. The newly fenced-off "city of Hadrian," named for the Western world's greatest wall-builder, had also produced the cannon that ended the age of city walls. Irony was now biting its own tail. A year later, Turkey began construction on its own five-hundred-mile barrier, a ten-foot-high concrete wall topped with razor wire, which shut off its border with Syria. The walling crept north in 2015, when Hungary constructed a 109-mile electrified fence along its border with Serbia, Austria constructed a barrier on its border with Slovenia, Slovenia commenced work along its four-hundred-mile border with Croatia, and Macedonia added a second line to its preexisting barrier facing Greece.

Locally, the new walls succeeded at their goals. The success of Turkey's Syrian wall prompted the country to announce plans for future walls along its Iran and Iraq borders. In areas walled by Hungary, the number of migrants plummeted from as many as ten thousand a day to as few as forty. From a more global perspective, the walls had merely shifted the burden. Migratory routes evolved yet again, putting even more strain on Italy as a primary point of entry for immigrants arriving from Africa by sea. In 2016, Austria began work on a barrier along its Italian border. Italy, unable to wall its coastline, is, as I write in 2017, contemplating closing its ports to migrants, while a cash-strapped Spain grimly anticipates the bulk of the mass migration shifting to Gibraltar.

As the first walls finally reached northern Europe—most famously the Great Wall of Calais, a thirty-foot-high concrete barrier designed to protect automobile traffic from attacks by migrants encamped in the so-called Calais Jungle, on the coast of northern France—the US presidential election, keenly watched throughout the world, brought walls to the forefront of public consciousness.

The presidential race saw walls enmeshed for the first time in broader debates on borders and immigration. Perhaps never before had a single issue created more confusion or witnessed more frantic reconfiguring of positions. As the campaign unfolded, both major Democratic candidates initially expressed skepticism over open borders. Hillary Clinton boasted that she had, as a senator, voted "numerous times" for barriers against illegal immigration, arguing that it was important to "control your borders." Vermont senator Bernie Sanders dismissed open-border policies as "a Koch brothers' proposal," linking the idea to the billionaire businessmen famous for funding right-wing causes. Sanders was correct in highlighting the influence of lobbying, which had not been widely noticed by the electorate. Prior to 2016, support for open borders came chiefly from corporate interests. The *Wall Street Journal*—often considered a mouthpiece for its right-wing owner, Rupert Murdoch—was particularly relentless in editorializing for unfettered immigration. The *Journal* was originally opposed by liberal economists, such as Paul Krugman, as well as unions and environmentalists. The former calculated that immigration reduced wages, while environmentalists stressed the impact of immigration on natural resources. However, some left-wing immigration activists opposed border controls, and the power of the checkbook had muddied the voice of environmentalists after billionaire David Gelbaum pressured the Sierra Club, an American environmentalist organization, to support open borders in return for a $100 million donation.

Against this confused backdrop, the entry of Donald Trump into the US presidential race brought sudden, artificial clarity to the issues of borders and walls, forcing politicians and voters alike to rethink their traditional positions. Trump's announcement that he would build a "big, beautiful wall" on the US border with Mexico became one of the most controversial events in modern political history, galvanizing supporters and opponents equally. Ironically, Trump himself had originally been indifferent to the idea, picking it up only after observing the wildly enthusiastic response it drew from an Iowa crowd in January 2015. Later, Trump eliminated references to the wall from his prepared remarks, but his supporters—crowded by the thousands into auditoriums, convention centers, state fairgrounds, and airport hangars—refused to let the issue die. Joyfully chanting, "Build that wall!," they interrupted Trump's speeches until he would respond, "Oh, we're going to build that wall. Believe me, we're going to build that wall." To the objective observer—and there were few of these to be found—it was clear that, whatever second thoughts Trump might have harbored after interacting with pro-immigration Republican donors and party bosses, his constituents would have none of it. The wall had outgrown the candidate.

Previous administrations had built miles of concrete walls, corrugated steel walls, and flat steel walls along the Mexican border, always careful to refer to all barriers as "fences." Trump, with no patience for semantic distinctions—"Nobody builds walls better than me, believe me"—left his proposals open to all the criticisms that the Clinton, Bush, and Obama administrations had labored to avoid. In 2016, the Berlin Wall was no longer a fading celebrity, clinging to the limelight. It was in full comeback, making splashy cameos in endless articles and commentaries. The former symbol of Communist oppression had seamlessly morphed into a bogeyman for a new age. To a new generation, largely sympathetic to the ideology that had brought about such abject misery to those living behind the Wall, Communism was no longer the great evil. The Wall itself was.

In the endless opinion pieces written about Trump's proposals, the Berlin Wall shared the stage primarily with its new partner, the

Great Wall, which, by virtue of its monumental size, had been recast as a symbol for all that was preposterous or impossible in human endeavors. That Saudi Arabia had, in short order, constructed barriers longer than those proposed by Trump, or that Israel—a country with less than 3 percent of the population of the United States and just a fraction of the landmass—had constructed barriers half the length proposed by Trump was not widely known. Senators scoffed authoritatively at the notion that the United States could ever accomplish what Saudi Arabia had done in less than a decade.

"Good fences make good neighbors" experienced early retirement. In its place came the untested phrase "Build bridges not walls." If nothing else, the new slogan seemed designed to give military historians fits. Throughout history, bridge building had been recognized as an act of aggression. Since at least the time of Xerxes bridging the Hellespont, Caesar the Rhine, or Trajan the Danube, bridge building had preceded invasions, enabling troop movements across natural barriers, and as late as the twentieth century, military uses had figured prominently in the thinking behind the bridges of Germany's autobahn and the American interstate highway system. None of this was enough to slow the rise of a hot catchphrase. The slogan showed up on T-shirts, wristbands, and banners. It became a popular hashtag on Twitter. Protesters chanted it. Politicians invoked it. Even Pope Francis paraphrased the sentiment.

In the eighteenth century, Voltaire had dismissed the Great Wall as a "monument to fear." Nearly three hundred years later, the French *philosophe* was hardly more than an afterthought in a Western Civilization lecture, but his comment lived on, unattributed to him, echoed in a thousand different combinations and permutations.

And yet the walls kept coming—even if we didn't always recognize them.

Let us return to California. Whatever became of the glamorous Anna Q. Nilsson? The Swedish-born actress had started quite a trend. Her Malibu home, sequestered behind the Colony's locked and guarded gates, was later bought by Robert Redford, then Bob

Newhart. Nowadays, even a cursory search for similar gated communities yields an avalanche: endless gushing lists of the hippest, the most expensive, the most celebrity filled, or the most exclusive private neighborhoods. There's Beverly Park, reputedly the richest, competing with Hidden Hills, legally incorporated behind its massive fence. There's Mulholland Estates, Bel Air Crest, Beverly Ridge Estates, and dozens of others, all reputedly fabulous.

Walled neighborhoods are no longer the exclusive prerogative of movie stars. When the Seal Beach, California, retirement community Leisure World opened—or, more accurately, *locked*—its gates in 1962, it established a new trend: walled enclaves for the masses. In short order, there were hundreds of gated communities in the United States, followed by thousands, then tens of thousands. By 1997, authors Edward Blakely and Mary Snyder had concluded that Americans were "forting up"—a rather overwrought hyperbole for a retiree who enjoys living in a country club by the putting green, but we get the drift.

The trend hasn't been limited to the wealthy—many of whom have no need for community gates as they write their pious homilies on immigration and border policy from behind the confines of their personal walled compounds—or to the United States. Gated communities are found among every class and ethnic group. Abroad, gated communities are common in countries with border walls, such as India, Saudi Arabia, and Malaysia, but they're equally common in nations that face walls built by others. Mexico is filled with walled neighborhoods, as is Pakistan.

The total number of people worldwide living in walled communities is not known. However, if a 2009 estimate of 6 to 9 million in the United States is at all accurate, that still leaves over 90 percent of us to judge and criticize them. With a little flair for the dramatic, we can describe them, as some academics have, as *dreading the world outside their gates*, even if they don't seem so fearful when we see them shopping for socks at Walmart.

A funny thing happens when you tell an acquaintance you're writing a book on walls. He or she almost immediately forgets that walls are tangible, physical structures and starts asking you if you've ever thought about all sorts of metaphorical barriers. Firewalls, for example, or antiviruses. Some suggestions have a physical dimension, such as the ubiquitous home-security system, a business expected to grow to $35 billion by the end of 2017. Others are entirely immaterial, such as the mental walls we erect, or at least we imagine other people erect when we wish to feel superior to them. But there has always been more brick, stone, tamped earth, wrought iron, corrugated steel, and barbed wire than most of us realize.

Are we forever building "monuments to fear"? It strikes me as an ironic testimony to the lingering influence of our primeval warrior past that cowardice remains the harshest and most stigmatizing opprobrium that can be cast on another human being. Those are fighting words, or would be if we weren't afraid to fight. Perhaps we should at the least take a breath and consider what they might mean. Can we build things out of fear?

The idea doesn't seem too unreasonable. In many ways, fear is the most powerful of all human emotions. When fully roused, it lords over happiness, anger, sadness, and even love. Its power derives from its direct link to the survival instinct, a connection that makes fear the most practical and necessary weapon in the emotional arsenal of living creatures. In its extreme form, fear becomes panic, but in its chronic state—insecurity—it allows for a degree of deliberation and planning and still exerts a powerful influence on decision making.

Biologists tell us that animals have but two choices when they feel threatened: fight or flight. History suggests that human societies have developed other options. Of these, the oldest was surely this: that men were trained not to fear. They were forced to undergo lifelong exposure to desensitization exercises—beatings, vision quests, periods of forced deprivation, pubertal circumcisions and other tests of pain tolerance, as well as times forcibly spent alone and in the dark—so they could function as soldiers without succumbing to the urge to flee. Desensitization worked, as long as it was measured only by its capacity to win wars.

As an alternative to desensitization, some societies built walls.

In the preceding chapters, we've seen that, over the last four thousand years, the struggles between those who built walls and those who assaulted them have frequently decided which states have endured and which have disappeared. Those same struggles have influenced the spread of languages and religions. They've brought about the economic dominance of some areas and the desolation of others. They've affected our thinking about matters that have little to do with politics, war, or walls.

Of equal importance, however, is how the walls themselves transformed us. As we've seen, walling provided certain advantages—we might call them evolutionary, although certainly not in the biological sense. The psychologist Abraham Maslow proposed, in his famous "hierarchy of needs" (usually presented to us as a pyramid), that once humans achieved security they could then concentrate on more elevated needs, eventually achieving "self-actualization." That may be a tad far-fetched, but history has demonstrated that the sense of security created by walls freed more and more males from the requirement of serving as warriors. Walls allowed them to engage fully in civilian pursuits—making things, building things, thinking, creating—whether or not they ever got around to actualizing themselves. By releasing men to the agricultural labor force, walls also freed women from bearing the sole responsibility for food production.

However, the wall builders sacrificed something of themselves in gaining these freedoms. They would never again possess the same immunity to fear. The wall builders would endure countless defeats by the people outside their walls. The resulting feelings of insecurity were paired with equal feelings of inferiority. The builders suffered a chronic failure of confidence that had them forever hiring soldiers from the ranks of their unwalled enemies. The apparently superior courage of the outsiders shamed the wall builders, repeatedly causing them to dream of returning to a more primitive lifestyle that might restore their manly virtue. As early as ancient Sparta, or the time of those Old Testament prophets who exhorted the Israelites to return to their tents, the wall builders dreamed they might be stronger in a world without walls. In time, this admiration for the unwalled and the longing for a life of courage lived outside the walls evolved into one of the most powerful and pervasive belief systems in the Western world. It crystallized into what philosophers have deemed primitivism.

Primitivism is one of the quiet cornerstones of Western thought, so deeply embedded in our thinking that we are rarely even aware of its influence. We might define it as that philosophy by which wild, natural things—even wild, natural people—are regarded as inherently more virtuous than civilized, artificial ones. It is the reason we instinctively opt for a product that is marketed as "natural" rather than "artificial," the reason we prefer our crafts handmade rather than machine produced, the reason we camp and hike when perfectly good hotels are available, the reason that so many books have rehashed the argument that hunter-gatherers are wiser, healthier, happier, and in every way superior to their miserably wrongheaded brethren from the tribe of civilization. Recently, there has been some excitement over the "Paleolithic diet"—and this, too, merely exposes our primitivist inclinations acting on us. On a confessional note, I once nearly crippled myself, injuring both of my Achilles tendons after becoming swept up in a primitivist fad for barefoot running. The seductions of primitivism can snare us at any time.

In the end, we restrain most of our primitivist impulses because although toughness sounds fun, achieving it hurts, and none of us want to slide backward down Maslow's pyramid. We *could* learn to fight for survival, but it's a lot easier to close the door, lie on the couch, and watch some television in a space we know is physically secure.

And so we build walls—metaphorical ones, as acquaintances constantly remind me, but mostly real ones—while we wait on everyone else to become just as civilized as we are.

Who are the wall builders?

We are the wall builders.

It was us all along.

Acknowledgments

There are no prizes for finishing a book. Nevertheless, it has become customary that an author, at the end of a work, step up to the podium and thank various agents, editors, colleagues, family, and friends, like an Academy Award winner nervously reading his acceptance speech while the orchestra attempts to drown him out. And so, with the haunting "Love Theme to *Walls*" welling up from the orchestra pit, I offer the following thanks, but with the crucial caveat that any flaws in this book are everyone's fault but mine. I accept responsibility only for the good parts.

Well before I even knew where this project was heading, I received CSU Research Grants that funded my participation on three archaeological excavations. I learned a great deal from the archaeologists with whom I worked at Vindolanda—Andrew Birley, Robin Birley, and Justin Blake—and, at Sibot-3, Andre Gonciar, Paul Damian, Adela Baltec, Corina Bors, and Alexandru Ratiu.

Roland Clark of the University of Liverpool kindly performed a close read on an early draft, as did my team of gentle readers: Ian Cheney, my wife, Noelle, and my parents, Otha and Virginia Frye. Wayne Lee of the University of North Carolina also read an early draft and provided valuable encouragement. Four undergraduate research assistants—Shawn Batchelder, Michael Zarcone, Samantha Dobbyn, and Jessica Kokoszka—have aided me in various capacities.

I have benefited a great deal from my association with my agent, Peter Steinberg, and the entire team at Foundry Literary + Media, as well as my editor, Rick Horgan, along with Emily Greenwald and the rest of the team at Scribner. I would also like to thank

Laura Hassan and the team at Faber & Faber for their work in preparing the UK/Commonwealth edition.

Finally, I have profited from many discussions on the theme of walls and other topics with various university colleagues, students, and friends. As the orchestra approaches its deafening crescendo, I provide a list in alphabetical order: Kate Alexander, Benjamin Andreotta, Tom Balcerski, Alan Bennett, Dan Brewer, Caitlin Carenen, Kristine McQuarrie Charles, Mike Christina, Joe Corso, John Cox, Brad Davis, Pete DeOrio, Maggie Downie, Margaret Eliason, Craig Emmerthal, Scott Erick, Tim Ferraro, Packy Frye, Kelly Gillette, Al(an) Gore, Mike Greer, Tyler Hewes, Anne Higginbotham, Stefan Kamola, Anya Kirchmann, Allen Lungren, Kevin MacVane, the Mafia Princess, Zach Marotte, Scott McCulley, Joan Meznar, Scott Moore, Asa O'Brien, Jamel Ostwald, Joe Petre, Bill Priest, John Regan, Norm Riley, Jeff Rose, Steve Ross, Sara Schneider, Kristen Sixby, Joe St. Amand, Ashley Stevens, Jason Taraskiewicz, Barbara Tucker, Nick Ugolik, Chris Vasillopulos, the Warrior Princess, John Watt, Bowen Weyel, and Mark White.

Notes

Notes are keyed to phrases in the text, listed by page numbers below. For a full bibliography, consult the author's website, www.davidfrye.org, which also contains resources for educators wishing to assign the text in their classes.

Introduction: A Wall against the Wasteland

9 "What is the theme of my song?": *Ars Amatoria* 1.34, in *Ovid: The Art of Love*, trans. Rolfe Humphries (Bloomington: Indiana University Press, 1957), 106.

10 "played to the moon": Julia Lovell, *The Great Wall: China Against the World, 1000 BC–AD 2000* (London: Grove Press, 2006), 152.

Midwife to Civilization: Wall Builders at the Dawn of History

18 "Wall of the Land Was Built": The Cuneiform Digital Library Initiative has made available a full list of Shulgi's year names at cdli.ox.ac. uk/wiki/doku.php?id=year_names_Shulgi.

19 three successive sets of walls: Builders of walls for Ur include Ur-Nammu, Ibbi-Sin, Warad-Sin, and Samsu-iluna. Kings who provided walls for Babylon include Sumuabum, Sumulael, Apil-Sin, Yawium, and, much later, Nebuchadnezzar. Three consecutive kings— Izbi-Irra, Szu-liliszu, and Bur-Sin—constructed walls at Isin, shortly to be followed by Damiq-liszu and Samsu-iluna.

19 lifted it out of the mold: D. O. Edzard, "Deep-Rooted Skyscrapers and Bricks: Ancient Mesopotamian Architecture and Its Imaging," in *Figurative Language in the Ancient Near East*, ed. M. Minndlin, M. J. Geller, and J. Wansbrough (London: University of London School of Oriental and African Studies, 1987), 16–17. The source is from the reign of Gudea.

19 inhabited Mesopotamia in great numbers: Judging from the numbers of animals, the territory around cities must have swarmed with sheep. At Ebla the king alone possessed flocks numbering more than eighty thousand. A city the size of Ur—which processed 421 tons of wool in a single year—probably maintained over half a million sheep. Weaving was done on an industrial scale in factories. Lagash employed some six thousand women and children in a single mill and an estimated fifteen thousand workers in all its mills combined. Alfonso Archi, "The Royal Archives at Ebla," in *Ebla to Damascus: Art and Archaeology of Ancient Syria: An Exhibition from the Directorate-General of Antiquities and Museums, Syrian Arab Republic*, ed. H. Weiss (Washington, DC: Smithsonian Institution Traveling Exhibition Service, 1985), 146; D. T. Potts, *Mesopotamian Civilization: The Material Foundations* (Ithaca, NY: Cornell University Press, 1997), 43–44; Robert McC. Adams, "Shepherds at Umma in the Third Dynasty of Ur: Interlocutors with a World Beyond the Scribal Field of Ordered Vision," *Journal of the Economic and Social History of the Orient* 49/2 (2006): 163.

20 hardly kept track of them: Adams, "Shepherds at Umma," 151, 157.

20 "vitality ebbs away": Glenn Schwartz, "Pastoral Nomadism in Ancient Western Asia," in *Civilizations of the Ancient Near East*, ed. Jack Sasson (New York: Charles Scribner's Sons, 1995), 251.

20 sheep-stealing carnivores: The Puzrish-Dagan (Drehem) archives record sheep lost to lions—Adams, "Shepherds at Umma," 156. Babylonian lions still stalked Mesopotamian sheep in the late nineteenth century AD. Lions only became extinct in the Zagros in the twentieth century. See John Ure, *In Search of Nomads: An Anglo-American Obsession from Hester Stanhope to Bruce Chatwin* (New York: Carroll and Graf, 2003), 44, 100.

20 temptation to drift away: Adams, "Shepherds at Umma," 149, 152, and 155, where he notes that only eight of seventeen shepherds recorded in one set of accounts were still on the rolls after five years.

21 she prefers a bad boy: The courtship of Inanna and Dumuzi has been synthesized into a single poem in Diane Wolkstein and Samuel Noah Kramer, *Inanna, Queen of Heaven and Earth: Her Stories and Hymns from Sumer* (New York: Harper and Row, 1983), 29–49.

21 "I am a shepherd!": For the praise poem of Shulgi, see J. A. Black et al., *The Electronic Text Corpus of Sumerian Literature* (hereafter abbreviated *ETCSL*) (Oxford, 1998–2006), c.2.4.2.03, http://etcsl.orinst. ox.ac.uk/. The equation of kings with shepherds was formulaic in the ancient Near East. Artists perennially depicted shepherd-kings hunting, killing, or wrestling with dangerous animals. Deviations from the formula are exceedingly rare—and probably deserving of more attention. Lipit-Eštar briefly added farmers to the formula with royal inscriptions beginning, "I, Lipit-Eštar, humble shepherd of Nippur,

true farmer of Ur, unceasing [provider for Eridu], *en* priest suitable for Uruk, king of Isin, king of the lands of Sumer and Akkad." His successors dropped the reference to farming and returned to identifying themselves as shepherds of Nippur and herdsmen of Ur. Rīm-Sīn is one of the few later kings to adopt the formula identifying with farmers. The inscriptions are in Douglas Frayne, *The Royal Inscriptions of Mesopotamia Early Periods*, vol. 3/2: *Ur III Period (2112–2004 BC)* (Toronto: University of Toronto Press, 1997), 64–105, 289.

22 digging of wells: In the Sumerian myth "Gilgamesh and Aga," the elders of Uruk advise Gilgamesh against going to war because wells need to be dug. "Gilgamesh and Aga," *ETCSL*, 1.08.01.01.

22 "What I need are soldiers": Paraphrased from *ETCSL*, t.3.1.15.31–33.

23 "birds in a cage": The king of Gubla, Rib-Hadda, frequently complained of being trapped behind his city walls "like a bird in a cage." See, for example, EA 74, 13–19; EA 78, 7–16; EA 79, 34–37, in William Moran, ed. and trans., *The Armana Letters* (Baltimore: Johns Hopkins University Press, 1992).

24 "like a throw stick!": Jeremy Black, "The Sumerians in Their Landscape," in *Riches Hidden in Secret Places: Ancient Near Eastern Studies in Memory of Thorkild Jacobsen*, ed. Tzvi Abusch (Winona Lake, IN: Eisenbrauns, 2002), 54–55.

24 An Egyptian writer: The unknown author of the *Papyrus Anastasi I*. An English translation is available in Alan Gardiner, *Egyptian Hieratic Texts, Series I: Literary Texts of the New Kingdom. Part I: The Papyrus Anastasi I and the Papyrus Koller Together with the Parallel Texts* (Hildesheim, Germany: Georg Olms Verlag, 1964).

24 "acted with violence against the gods": Victory of Utu-hegal, *ETCSL*, t.2.1.6.

25 the so-called *Cuthean Legend*: O. R. Gurney, "The Sultantepe Tablets (Continued). IV. The Cuthean Legend of Naram-Sin," *Anatolian Studies* 5 (1955): 93–113; Michael Astour, "Ezekiel's Prophecy of Gog and the Cuthean Legend of Naram-Sin," *Journal of Biblical Literature* 95/4 (1976): 576–79.

25 Umman Manda: As late as the mid-first millennium, it was still being applied to Cimmerians, Medes, or any "ferocious enemies ignorant of moral rules." Florence Malbran-Labat, "Le nomadisme à l'époque néo-assyrienne," in *Nomads and Sedentary Peoples, XXX International Congress of Human Sciences in Asia and North Africa*, ed. Jorge Silva Castillo (Mexico City: Colegio de México, 1981), 60.

25 "come down on my people": A. Kirk Grayson and Donald Redford, *Papyrus and Tablet* (Englewood Cliffs, NJ: Prentice-Hall, 1973), 89.

26 "killer out of the highlands": Thorkild Jacobsen, *The Harps That Once . . . : Sumerian Poetry in Translation* (New Haven, CT: Yale

University Press, 1987), 233–72; William Hamblin, *Warfare in the Ancient Near East to 1600 BC: Holy Warriors at the Dawn of History* (New York: Routledge, 2006), 122–25.

26 "like a net": Jacobsen, *Harps That Once*, 252.

26 ancient wall of King Lugalbanda: Lugalbanda and the Anzud Bird, *ETCSL*, t.1.8.22.

26 peaceful dwelling places: Letter from Shulgi to Puzur-Sulgi about the Fortress Igi-huraga (version B), *ETCSL*, t.3.1.08.

27 Shulgi's surviving correspondence: Letter from Aagdu to Shulgi about the Fortress Igi-huraga, *ETCSL*, t.3.10.6; letter from Puzur-Sulgi to Shulgi about the advance of the enemy, *ETCSL*, t.3.1.07; letter from Shulgi to Puzur-Sulgi about the Fortress Igi-huraga (version B), *ETCSL*, t.3.1.08.

27 Word soon arrives: Letter from Sarrum-bani to Su-Suen about keeping the Martu at bay, *ETCSL*, t.3.1.15.

28 heads like clay pots: The Lament for Sumer and Urim, *ETCSL*, 2.2.3.

28 Egyptian cities were not open: Nadine Moeller, "Evidence for Urban Walling in the Third Millennium BC," in Barry Kemp et al., "Egypt's Invisible Walls," *Cambridge Archaeological Journal* 14/2 (2004): 259–88. The earliest Egyptian cities possessed mud-brick walls even during the allegedly safe Old Kingdom period—a time (roughly 2686–2181 BC) when Egypt was politically unified and any military threat could only have come from outside. There is evidence for the walled cities at Elephantine, Edfu, Dendara, Kom Ombo, and Elkab. See Barry Kemp, "Unification and Urbanization of Ancient Egypt," in Sasson, *Civilizations*, 687.

28 maintained a careful watch: As early as the Old Kingdom, pharaohs appointed officers styled as "overseer[s] of the barriers, the deserts, and the royal fortresses of Heliopolis." James Hoffmeier, "'The Walls of the Ruler' in Egyptian Literature and the Archaeological Record: Investigating Egypt's Eastern Frontier in the Bronze Age," *Bulletin of the American Schools of Oriental Research* 343 (2006): 1–20, 2.

28 "teams as they ploughed" . . . "I must stay awake!": James Pritchard, trans. and ed., *The Ancient Near East: An Anthology of Texts and Pictures* (hereafter abbreviated *ANE*), 2 vols. (Princeton: Princeton University Press, 1958), 1:252; William Hallo and K. Younger, eds., *The Context of Scripture* (hereafter abbreviated *COS*), 3 vols. (New York: Brill, 1997–2002), 1:93–98, 1:106–10.

28 Pyramid texts speak of defenses: Hamblin, *Warfare*, 361.

28 Wall of the Ruler: James Breasted, *Ancient Records of Egypt: Historical Documents from the Earliest Times to the Persian Conquest, Collected, Edited, and Translated with Commentary*, 5 vols. (Chicago: University of Chicago Press, 1906–7; repr. 1988), 1:493; *ANE*, 1:5.

29 circuit around an entire country: On these walls, see Rocío Da Riva, "BM 67405 and the Cross Country Walls of Nebuchadnezzar II,"

in *The Perfumes of Seven Tamarisks: Studies in Honour of Wilfred G. E. Watson*, ed. N. Wyatt, G. del Olmo, and J. Vidal (Münster, Germany: Ugarit Verlag, 2012); Rocío Da Riva, "Just Another Brick in the Median Wall," *Aramzid: Armenian Journal of Near Eastern Studies* 5/1 (2010): 55–65; and R. G. Killick, "Northern Akkad Project: Excavations at Habl As-Sahr," *Iraq* 46/2 (1984): 125–29.

29 long walls to the north and south: Killick, "Northern Akkad Project," 125, calculates the distance as 47 km. Da Riva, "Just Another Brick," prefers 54 km.

30 "made Babylon a mountain of life": IM 516231, quoted in Da Riva, "Just Another Brick," 61.

30 "fuel for flames": Jeremiah 51:58.

30 so-called Umm Rus wall: The Umm Rus wall cannot be definitively dated, and scholars have placed it anywhere from 401 BC to AD 363. Julian Reade, "El-Mutabbaq and Umm Rus," *Sumer* 20 (1964): 83–89, at 87.

30 defended the Tigris plain against bedouins: Reade, "El-Mutabbaq and Umm Rus," 83–87. For the suggestion of a later date and attribution to the Caliph Ma'mun, see R. D. Barnett, "Xenophon and the Wall of Media," *Journal of Hellenic Studies* 83 (1963): 1–26, at 6.

30 one-sixteenth their former size: Robert McC. Adams, "Contexts of Civilizational Collapse: A Mesopotamian View," in *The Collapse of Ancient States and Civilizations*, ed. N. Yoffee and G. Cowgill (Tucson, AZ, 1988), 37–38.

To Wall or Not to Wall?

35 In the late thirteenth century BC: Oscar Broneer, "The Cyclopean Wall on the Isthmus of Corinth, Addendum," *Hesperia: The Journal of the American School of Classical Studies at Athens* 37/1 (1968): 25–35.

35 securing their water supplies: Nancy Demand, *The Mediterranean Context of Early Greek History* (Malden, MA: Wiley-Blackwell, 2012), 198, 204.

38 do away with it all: This material transformation has been described by many scholars, including E. N. Tigerstedt, *The Legend of Sparta in Classical Antiquity*, 3 vols. (Stockholm: Almquist and Wiksell, 1965–78), 1:40, 1:44; Paul MacKendrick, *The Greek Stones Speak: The Story of Archaeology in Greek Lands*, 2nd ed. (New York: W. W. Norton, 1982), 166; Oswyn Murray, *Early Greece*, 2nd ed. (London: Fontana Press, 1993), 171–73; Paul Cartledge, *Spartan Reflections* (Berkeley: University of California Press, 2003), 182.

38 been a city at all: Thucydides 1.10.

41 golden hair clasps: Ibid., 1.6–7.

42 Athenian men underwent: The evidence has been collected in W. Kendrick Pritchett, *The Greek State at War*, pt. 2 (Berkeley: University of California Press, 1975), 209ff. See also Everett L. Wheeler, "*Hoplomachia* and Greek Dances in Arms," *Greek, Roman, and Byzantine Studies* 23/3 (1982): 229; and Jason Crowley, *The Psychology of the Athenian Hoplite: The Culture of Combat in Classical Athens* (Cambridge: Cambridge University Press, 2012), 81: "The Athenian hoplite did not receive any military training, basic or otherwise, and so he arrived on the battlefield, for better or worse, exactly as his society had made him."

42 brief period of mandatory exercise: When Plato, *Republic* 5.466e–467e, suggested that children should start being trained for war, he only proposed that they should attend battle as observers, carefully shielded from danger and mounted on horseback so that they could flee from peril. As regards the date of the *ephebeia*, which briefly provided military training for males who had turned eighteen, one of the few scholars to argue that the full institution existed earlier than the fourth century is Chrysis Pélékidis, *Histoire de l'éphébie attique des origines à 31 avant Jésus-Christ* (Paris: Éditions E. de Boccard, 1962), 50–79. Oscar Reinmuth, "The Genesis of the Athenian Ephebeia," *Transactions and Proceedings of the American Philological Association* 82 (1952): 34–50, believes that particular elements of the institution existed in earlier times. Pierre Vidal-Naquet, "The Black Hunter and the Origin of the Athenian Ephebeia," in *Structuralism in Myth: Levi-Strauss, Barthes, Dumezil, and Propp*, ed. Robert Segal (London: Routledge, 1996), 277–98, compares the *ephebeia* to primitive initiation rituals, but does concede it is a fourth-century novelty. Peter Siewert, "The Ephebic Oath in Fifth-Century Athens," *Journal of Hellenic Studies* 97 (1977): 102–11, argues that the *ephebic* oath taken by Athenian citizens predated the system of training by at least a century.

42 fulfill all combat roles: For example, Plato, *Timaeus* 17c–18b; also *Critias* 110c–d, where Plato attributes such a system to a mythical, prehistoric Athens. At the time of Plato's writing, a trend toward military professionalism was generally under way. See Pierre Vidal-Naquet, "La tradition de l'hoplite athénien," in *Problèmes de la guerre en Grèce ancienne*, ed. Jean-Pierre Vernant (Paris: Mouton, 1968), 173ff.

42 physical education: Christian Laes and Johann Strubbe, *Youth in the Roman Empire: The Young and the Restless Years?* (Cambridge: Cambridge University Press, 2014), 104ff; Nigel Kennell, "The Ephebeia in the Hellenistic Period," in *A Companion to Ancient Education*, ed. Martin Bloomer (Malden, MA: Wiley-Blackwell, 2015), 172–83.

43 supply their needs entirely by sea: Thucydides 1.143, 2.13.

44 "does not make us soft": Ibid., 2.40; Thucydides, *History of the Peloponnesian War*, trans. Rex Warner (New York: Penguin Books, 1982), 147.

46 "Not a man in the city was idle": Lykourgos, *Against Leokrates* 44, cited in John Camp, *The Archaeology of Athens* (New Haven, CT: Yale University Press, 2001), 143.

"Cries of Pain and Sadness"

47 "good at weeping": Wilt Idema, *Meng Jiangnu Brings Down the Great Wall: Ten Versions of a Chinese Legend* (Seattle: University of Washington Press, 2008), 5.

47 "men and of mud": Ibid., 10.

48 "cries of pain and sadness": Lovell, *Great Wall*, 175.

48 "work without complaining": Ibid., 109–11.

49 "simply exhaust them": Ibid., 167.

49 width of eighty feet: Ralph Sawyer, *Ancient Chinese Warfare* (New York: Basic Books, 2011), 19–30; William Watson, "The City in Ancient China," in *The Origins of Civilization: Wolfson College Lectures, 1978*, ed. P. R. S. Moorey (Oxford: Clarendon Press, 1979), 54–56; Robin Yates, "Early China," in *War and Society in the Ancient and Medieval Worlds: Asia, the Mediterranean, Europe, and Mesoamerica* (Washington, DC: Center for Hellenic Studies, 1999), 9.

50 towers of ice and snow: Ruth Meserve, "The Inhospitable Land of the Barbarian," *Journal of Asian History* 16/1 (1982): 52–53.

54 "feared that royal decree": *The Shi King: The Old "Poetry Classic" of the Chinese, a Close Metrical Translation with Annotations*, trans. W. Jennings (London: Routledge, 1891), 182–83. Nan-Chung is dated to around 800 BC in *The Book of Songs*, trans. Arthur Waley (1937; repr., London: Routledge, 2005), 122.

58 "the four ends of the earth": René Groussett, *The Rise and Splendour of the Chinese Empire* (Berkeley: University of California Press, 1964), 44.

59 "never reach them in time": Sima Qian, *Records of the Grand Historian*, rev. ed., trans. Burton Watson (New York: Columbia University Press, 1993), 2:194.

59 "Chinese soldiers are not so good": Cited in Nicola Di Cosmo, *Ancient China and Its Enemies: The Rise of Nomadic Power in East Asian History* (Cambridge: Cambridge University Press, 2002), 203.

59 "grabbing at a shadow": Sima, *Records of the Grand Historian*, 2:195.

60 forked over the tribute: A Hun king paid homage to the emperor in 51 BC and was given 5 kg of gold, 77 suits of clothes, 8,000 bales of silken fabric, 1,500 kg of silk floss, 15 horses, 680,000 liters of grain, and some cash. A half century later, "tributary" kings received up to 30,000 bales of fabric. Meanwhile, the Chinese court debated whether

payments to tributary barbarians were bankrupting the state or were their only hope of preventing raids.

60 "rouge has melted from her cheek": Po chu-I, cited in Stuart Legg, *The Barbarians of Asia* (New York: Dorset Press Reprints, 1990), 128–29.

Wallers and Warriors: Life outside the Walls

63 "live with birds and beasts": Lovell, *Great Wall*, 112.

69 "die in a battle": Ure, *In Search of Nomads*, 70.

69 "Raids are our agriculture": Louise Sweet, "Camel Raiding of North Arabian Bedouin: A Mechanism of Ecological Adaptation," *American Anthropologist* 67/5 (1965): 1142.

69 "torn in anguish by their nails": Quoted in Hugh Kennedy, *The Great Arab Conquests: How the Spread of Islam Changed the World We Live In* (Philadelphia: De Capo Press, 2007), 41.

69 Some German youth: Tacitus, *Germania*, 31.

70 "loss of a little blood": Ibid., 14.

70 Huns: Priscus fr. 10; Scythians: Herodotus 4.64; Lusitanians: Diodorus 5.34.6ff.

70 word for "man" sufficed: Denis Sinor, "The Inner Asian Warriors," *Journal of the American Oriental Society* 101/2 (1981): 135.

70 Banquet: Herodotus 4.66. Skinning of enemies: Ibid., 4.64ff, and Ammianus Marcellinus 31.2.14. Chinese accounts: "When they fight in battle," wrote one Chinese historian, "those who have cut [enemy] heads or captured prisoners are presented with a cup of wine, and all the booty that they have taken is also given to them; the people they capture are made into slaves" (Di Cosmo, *Ancient China and Its Enemies*, 278, citing Shi chi 110, 2892). The author of this passage, Ssuma Ch'ien (Sima Qian), had never encountered the earlier writings of Herodotus, written thousands of miles away.

72 "to make soldiers": A widely cited remark. See, for example, Nicola Di Cosmo, introduction to *Military Culture in Imperial China*, ed. Nicola Di Cosmo (Cambridge, MA: Harvard University Press, 2009), 18.

Prologue to the Great Age of Walls: Alexander's Gates

77 "land of unwalled villages": Ezekiel 38:11–12.

78 gates that Alexander had built: Josephus, *Jewish War* 7.7.4.

Walls Connect Eurasia

83 He described his team: Mark Aurel Stein, *On Ancient Central Asian Tracks* (repr., Delhi: Book Faith India, 1998), 30.

84 Stein once recalled: Ibid., xvii, 30.

87 "skeletons prop each other up": Cited in Thomas Barfield, *The Perilous Frontier: Nomadic Empires and China* (Oxford: Oxford University Press, 1989), 96.

87 still being sung: Ibid.

89 Balkh: Arezou Azad, *Sacred Landscape in Medieval Afghanistan: Revisiting the Fada il-i Balkh* (New York: Oxford University Press, 2013), 92–95.

90 Iron Gates: The wall reached at least 5.5 meters (eighteen feet) in height and had platforms for archers, inner corridors for troop movements, and loopholes for shooting. S. A. Rakhmanov, "The Wall between Bactria and Sogd: The Study on the Iron Gates, Uzbekistan," in *New Archaeological Discoveries in Asiatic Russia and Central Asia* (Saint Petersburg: Russian Academy of Sciences, 1994), 75–78.

90 reports of nations: Full tale of Zhang's reports in Sima, *Records of the Grand Historian*, 2:231–46.

Hadrian's Walls

94 Stanegate Frontier: For an overview, see N. Hodgson, "The Stanegate: A Frontier Rehabilitated," *Britannia* 31 (2000): 11–22.

96 "separate the Romans and barbarians": Historia Augusta, *Hadrian* 11.2.

99 "the open plain": Tacitus, *Agricola* 3.7.

100 old-growth oaks: David Breeze, *The Frontiers of Imperial Rome* (Barnsley, UK: Penn and Sword Military, 2011), 4, 12, 78.

101 Trajan's Walls: The series of three barriers carry the name Trajan's Rampart, the Valu lui Traian, or sometimes Trajan's Wall, although no connection to Trajan has yet been demonstrated. Several other fortifications in southeastern Europe are unfortunately known by the same name. The interpretation of the walls as Roman is argued in W. S. Hanson and Iona Oltean, "The 'Valu lui Traian': A Roman Frontier Rehabilitated," *Journal of Roman Archaeology* 25 (2012): 297–318. For the less convincing case that the walls were constructed by medieval Bulgarians, see Paolo Squatriti, "Moving Earth and Making Difference: Dikes and Frontiers in Early Medieval Bulgaria," in *Borders, Barriers, and Ethnogenesis: Frontiers in Late Antiquity and the Middle Ages*, ed. Florin Curta (Turnhout, Belgium: Brepols, 2005); and Uwe Fiedler, "Bulgars in the Lower Danube Region: A Survey of the Archaeological Evidence and of the State of Current Research," in *The Other Europe in the Middle Ages: Avars, Bulgars, Khazans and Cumans*, ed. Florin Curta (Leiden, Netherlands: E. J. Brill, 2008), 162–66. As for the Roman date, it seems entirely implausible that Hadrian, while erecting vast defenses in relatively placid areas, would have left untouched and unimproved

a region where the barbarian threat was constant, menacing, and so threatening to Constantinople that subsequent emperors spent the next several hundred years redoubling their efforts to fortify it.

101 lines of fortresses and watchtowers: S. T. Parker et al., *The Roman Frontier in Central Jordan: Final Report on the Limes Arabicus Project, 1980–1989*, 2 vols. (Washington, DC: Dumbarton Oaks Research Library and Collection, 2006); Philip Mayerson, "The Saracens and the Limes," *Bulletin of the American Schools of Oriental Research* 262 (1986): 35–47; Procopius, *Buildings* 5.8.5.

Paradise Lost

103 an end to war: P. Aelius Aristides, *The Complete Works*, vol. 2: *Orations XVII–LII*, trans. Charles Behr (Leiden, Netherlands: E. J. Brill, 1981), 26, 67ff.

103 schools filled the cities: Ibid., 26.104.

103 "universal and clear to all": Ibid., 26.81, slightly altered to fit the sentence.

107 towns entirely abandoned: Similar abandonments occurred in Angers, Aix-en-Provence, and countless other cities. Ambert saw complete abandonment; Javols and Angers saw particularly brutal destruction. Joseph Gagnaire, "Ambert," *Villes et agglomérations urbaines antiques du sud-ouest de la Gaule: Histoire et archéologie, Deuxième Colloque Aquitania: Bordeaux, 13–15 septembre 1991* (Bordeaux: Éditions de la Fédération Aquitania, 1992), 19; Françoise Prévot, "Javols-Mende," *Topographie chrétienne des cités de la Gaule des origines au milieu du VIIIe siècle*, vol. 5, ed. Nancy Gauthier and Jean-Charles Picard (Paris: De Boccard, 1986), 82; Michel Provost, *La carte archéologique de la Gaule 49: Maine et Loire* (Paris: Académie des Inscriptions et Belles-Lettres, 1988), 87–88; A. Desbat, "Note sur l'abandon de la ville haute de Lyon," *Récentes recherches en archéologie gallo-romaine et paléochrétiennes sur Lyon et sa région*, ed. S. Walker (Oxford: BAR, 1989); M. E. Bellet et al., "Orange: Cours Pourtoules," *Gallia Informations* (1987–88/2): 321–25; D. Busson, "Paris: Place André Honnorat et rue Michelet," *Gallia Informations* (1993/1–2): 29–30. Tours: Michel Provost, *La carte archéologique de la Gaule 37: Indre-et-Loire* (Paris: Académie des Inscriptions et Belles-Lettres, 1988), 78, 85, 90, 92. Aix: J.-P. Nibodeau, "Aix-en-Provence: Boulevard de la République," *Gallia Informations* (1987–88/2): 225.

108 wall at the narrow isthmus: Zonaras 12.23. This was but one in a long series of attempts to wall off the Peloponnesus, the best known of which is the so-called Hexamilion. See Timothy Gregory, *The Hexamilion and the Fortress (Isthmia)* (Princeton, NJ: American School of Classical Studies at Athens, 1993). For a suggestion of a slightly

later date, pertaining to the threat of Attila, see Robert Hohlfelder, "Trans-Isthmian Walls in the Age of Justinian," *Greek, Roman, and Byzantine Studies* 18 (1977): 173–79.

108 *birds in a cage: The Anonymous Continuator of Cassius Dio* fr. 9.2, cited in *The History of Zonaras: From Alexander Severus to the Death of Theodosius the Great*, trans. Thomas Banchich and Eugene Lane (New York: Routledge, 2009).

108 sacked five hundred cities: Zonaras 12.21, and Banchich and Lane, *History of Zonaras*, 101n5, for related sources and the claim of five hundred cities sacked.

108 regions were abandoned altogether: The Agri Decumates were once guarded by twenty thousand troops, Raetia by ten thousand, and Dacia by fifty thousand. See Lawrence Okamura, "Roman Withdrawals from Three Transfluvial Frontiers," in *Shifting Frontiers in Late Antiquity*, ed. R. Mathisen and H. Sivan (Brookfield, VT: Variorum, 1996), 11. All three provinces were abandoned in the reign of Gallienus.

108 Gaul survived the turbulence: Luce Pietri, "Angers," in Gauthier and Picard, *Topographie chrétienne*, 5:1; C. Sintès, "L'évolution topographique de l'Arles du Haut-Empire à la lumière des fouilles récentes," *Journal of Roman Archeology* 5 (1992): 141; G. M. Woloch, "A Descriptive Catalogue of Roman Cities," in Pierre Grimal, *Roman Cities*, ed. and trans. G. M. Woloch (Madison: University of Wisconsin Press, 1983), 129; Charles Bonnet and C. Santschi, "Genève," in Gauthier and Picard, *Topographie chrétienne*, vol. 3 (Paris: De Boccard, 1986), 41; F. Prévot, "Limoges," in Gauthier and Picard, *Topographie chrétienne*, vol. 6 (Paris: De Boccard, 1989), 72; L. Pietri, "Rennes," in Gauthier and Picard, *Topographie chrétienne*, 5:62; F. Prévot, "Rodez," in Gauthier and Picard, *Topographie chrétienne*, 6:44; N. Gauthier, "Trèves," in Gauthier and Picard, *Topographie chrétienne*, vol. 1 (Paris: De Boccard, 1986), 20; L. Pietri, "Troyes," in Gauthier and Picard, *Topographie chrétienne*, 5:71.

109 For nearly three hundred years: A few cities had been granted the protection of walls during the early Empire. For a list of walled cities in early imperial Gaul, see C. Goudineau, "Les villes de la paix romaine," in *Histoire de la France urbaine*, ed. George Duby, vol. 1: *La ville antique* (Paris: Seuil, 1980), 244.

109 Buildings in the paths: For example, J.-M. Fémolant, "Senlis: Ancien palais épiscopal, Musée d'Art et d'Archéologie," *Gallia Informations* (1989/1): 240; Bonnet and Santschi, "Genève," 41; H. Sivan, *Ausonius of Bordeaux: Genesis of a Gallic Aristocracy* (New York: Routledge, 1993), 41.

109 torn down simply to provide stone: In general, see Grimal, *Roman Cities*, 79; Ramsay MacMullen, *Soldier and Civilian in the Later Roman*

Empire (Cambridge, MA: Harvard University Press, 1963), 129; Louis Maurin, "Remparts et cités: Les provinces du Sud-Ouest de la Gaule au Bas-Empire (dernier quart du IIIe siècle—debut du Ve siècle)," in *Villes et agglomérations*, 368; T. F. C. Blagg, "The Reuse of Monumental Masonry in Late Roman Defensive Walls," in *Roman Urban Defences*, ed. J. Maloney and B. Hobley, Council for British Archaeology Research Report 51 (London: CBA, 1983).

109 broke apart tombs, temples: In Paris, the city walls contained materials drawn from the old amphitheater, theater, and baths. The walls of Rennes included blocks from a Hadrianic temple to Mars. At Sens, the walls incorporated columns and panels from the public baths, and the walls of Senlis contained sections from a temple of Jupiter. Portions of a victory monument, a temple of Mars, and a monumental arch all found their way into the walls of Mainz. The walls of Bordeaux incorporated stones from a number of public buildings. Metz incorporated stones from its old baths. Temple fragments were in the foundations of the walls at Tours. Even the tiny town of Alzey used stones from a column to Jupiter and a temple of Apollo. The walls of Avignon seem to have included large blocks of inscriptions, sculpted fragments, and the debris of a triumphal arch. For Paris, Sens, Senlis, Mainz, Bordeaux, and Alzey, see Blagg, "Reuse of Monumental Masonry," 131–34. For Rennes: Pietri, "Rennes," 61. Bordeaux: Hagith Sivan, "Town and Country in Late Antique Gaul: The Example of Bordeaux," in *Fifth-Century Gaul: A Crisis of Identity*, ed. J. Drinkwater and H. Elton (Cambridge: Cambridge University Press, 1992), 133; and Sivan, *Ausonius of Bordeaux*, 39. Metz: N. Gauthier, "Metz," in Gauthier and Picard, *Topographie chrétienne*, 1:40. Tours: Provost, *Carte archéologique de la Gaule* 37, 81. Avignon: J. Biarne, "Avignon," in Gauthier and Picard, *Topographie chrétienne*, 3:17.

110 fragments of ancient architecture: M. Gauthier and P. Debord, *Bordeaux, Saint-Christoly: Sauvetage archéologique et histoire urbaine* (Bordeaux: Direction des Antiquités Historiques d'Aquitaine, 1983), 19–24.

110 the extraction of gravel: Roblin, "Paris: 14, rue Pierre-et-Marie-Curie," *Gallia Informations* (1993/1–2): 23. In Arles, townspeople pulled marble veneers off the walls of abandoned buildings and used the marble to cover holes in the ground. See Sintès, "L'évolution topographique de l'Arles," 144.

110 In Fréjus: I. Béraud and C. Gébara, "Fréjus: Porte d'Orée," *Gallia Informations* (1987–88/ 2): 271–72.

110 surrounded as it now was by lean-tos: Sintès, "L'évolution topographique de l'Arles," 141–44; William Klingshirn, *Caesarius of Arles: The Making of a Christian Community in Late Antique Gaul* (Cambridge: Cambridge University Press, 1994), 51, 175–76; C. Sintès, "Arles:

Institut de Recherche en la Provence Antique-Musée," *Gallia Informations* (1990–91/1–2): 146.

110 reduced pitifully in size: Walls surrounded by sturdy temples and town houses, even abandoned ones, offered little defense; attackers could simply find shelter in the extramural buildings. Consequently, workers throughout the western provinces tore down any peripheral building that might provide a besieging army with cover, creating a no-man's-land around the walls. J. Hubert, "Évolution de la topographie et de l'aspect des villes de Gaule du Ve au Xe siècle," in *La città nell'alto medioevo, Settimane di studio* 6 (Spoleto, Italy: Centro italiano di studi sull'alto medioevo, 1959), 535.

111 workers who destroyed it: The excavations are described in J.-M. Sauget and J.-C. Claval, "Clermont-Ferrand: Ancienne confiturerie Humbert," *Gallia Informations* (1989/1): 39.

111 evacuated five grand houses: Excavations and dates of abandonment in Bérard, "Aix-en-Provence: Les Chartreux," *Gallia Informations* (1990–91/1–2): 131–35.

111 Iron Age predecessors: For example, Bazas and Geneva: L. Maurin, "Bazas," in *Villes et agglomérations*, 42; Bonnet and Santschi, "Genève," 41.

111 days before Caesar: The final numbers attest to the near collapse of urban life. Walled Autun covered only one-twentieth its former area, yet its walls surpassed those of Auxerre, Troyes, Tours, Rennes, Anges, Loudon, Bayonne, and Périgueux. Few cities encompassed more than 30 acres. Bayeux, Dax, Limoges, Soissons, Mâcon, Agen, Albi, Beauvais, Evreux, Le Mans, Rennes, Auxerre, Grenoble, Embrun, Meaux, and Geneva each occupied between 17 and 30—pitifully small, but nowhere near the nadir. Senlis, Anger, Vannes, Vermand, Périgueux, Auch, St. Bertrand, St. Lizier, and Noyon were between 7 and 15 acres. Clermont-Ferrand, which had once sprawled over 494 acres, occupied only 7 by the later third century. Adrien Blanchet, *Les enceintes romaines de la Gaule: Étude sur l'origine d'un grand nombre de villes françaises* (Paris: E. Leroux, 1907), 14–19 (for Autun), 58–60 (Auxerre), 71 (Troyes), 39–44 (Tours), 50–53 (Rennes), 53–56 (Angers). For Bayonne, Dax, Loudon, Périgueux, see Maurin, "Remparts et cités," 367. For acreages (converted from hectares), see Ferdinand Lot, *La Gaule: Les fondements ethniques, sociaux et politiques de la nation française* (Paris: Fayard, 1947), 397; O. Barraud et al., "Origin et développement topographique des agglomérations: Agen, Angoulême, Bourdeaux, Périgueux, Poitiers, Saintes," in *Villes et agglomérations*, 208; S. T. Loseby, "Bishops and Cathedrals: Order and Diversity in the Fifth-Century Urban Landscape of Southern Gaul," in Drinkwater and Elton, *Fifth-Century Gaul*, 150.

111 as if they were tombs: Ammianus 16.2.12.

111 occupy prehistoric hill forts: Edward James, *Europe's Barbarians, AD 200–600* (New York: Pearson Longman, 2009), 40.

112 a new twenty-seven-mile wall: This is near the site of modern Obzor, starting at the Eleshnitsa River valley and ending at the Black Sea. Andrew Poulter, "An Indefensible Frontier: The *claustra Alpium Iuliarum*," *Jahreshefte des Österreichischen Archäologischen Institutes in Wien* 81 (2012): 120.

113 forty Rhineland towns: Zosimus 3.1.

Defenseless behind Walls

117 just admitted its own ruin: Ammianus 31.4.6.

118 Synesius: Synesius, *On Imperial Rule*, opposition to luxury: 11.2–5; 12; 13. Opposition to walls: 11.6. Draft civilians rather than hire mercenaries: 14.6–8.

120 rubble of cities: Procopius, *Wars* 3.2.24.

120 "died with one city": Brian Ward-Perkins, *The Fall of Rome and the End of Civilization* (New York: Oxford University Press, 2005), 28.

121 all four of her children: Olympiodorus fr. 29.2.

121 bodies washed ashore: Eugippius, *Life of Saint Severinus* 20.1–2.

121 countless snakes: Procopius, *Wars* 8.20.42–46.

122 complaining when it didn't come: Synesius, ep. 125.2; 132.2.

122 The barbarians seized: Ibid., 61.2; 73.4; 107.1; 125.1–2; 130.4–6.

122 the manufacture of weapons: Ibid., 107.1; 133.6.

122 purchased from traders: Ibid., 133.7.

122 patchwork arsenal: Ibid., 108.1–2.

122 evening patrols: Ibid., 125; 132.

122 They were curious: Ibid., 108.3.

123 no help from Rome: Priscus, fr. 40, depicts the Roman governor Boniface as a resolute barbarian-fighter who not only fended off their hordes but occasionally engaged them in single combat. He was, however, often at odds with the central government.

123 stench of putrefaction: The chief chronicler of these depravities is Victor of Vita, *History of the Vandal Persecution*, trans. John Moorhead (Liverpool: Liverpool University Press, 1992). See especially at 1.3–4, 1.6, 1.8, 1.10, and 1.12. See also Possidius, *Life of Augustine*, 28, and Quodvultdeus, *In Barbarian Times*, cited in P. J. Heather, *The Fall of the Roman Empire: A New History* (London: Oxford University Press, 2005), 289.

123 Bishops debated: Possidius, *Life of Augustine*, 30.

123 Talk of Gog and Magog: James Palmer, *The Apocalypse in the Early Middle Ages* (Cambridge: Cambridge University Press, 2014), 37.

123 Carthaginians went to the circus: Daniel Van Slyke, "The Devil and His Pomps in Fifth-Century Carthage: Renouncing Spectacula with

Spectacular Imagery," *Dumbarton Oaks Papers* 59 (2005): 58. Richard Lim, "The *Tribunus Voluptatum* in the Later Roman Empire," *Memoirs of the American Academy in Rome* 41 (1996): 168.

123 heroics were rare: The final generation of Romans rallied somewhat. It was their emperors who let them down. In the western provinces, one city after another held off the invaders, assuming an imperial army would eventually race to their rescue, but that relief generally never came. The Franks, who gave their name to France, took over Gaul in a series of sieges, the longest of which, the siege of Paris, reputedly lasted ten years. Around that same time, the Goths were seizing Roman cities farther south, and they sometimes held out also. At the city of Clermont-Ferrand, besieged townspeople were reduced to eating the grass that grew in the cracks of the city walls. The city's leading citizen assembled a small force that succeeded in temporarily driving off the Goths, but the city was soon enough lost, surrendered without a fight by the imperial government.

123 abandoned in favor of more secure hill forts: David Frye, "Aristocratic Responses to Late Roman Urban Change," *Classical World* 96/2 (2003): 185–96.

124 long walls of the Dark Ages: The most powerful Dark Age state was that of the Franks, and it responded to the invasion of Magyar horsemen by restoring the original Devil's Dykes, the old Roman walls of Hungary, also known as the *limes Sarmatiae* or *Csörz árok*. Eszter Istvánovits and Valéria Kulcsár, "The History and Perspectives of the Research of the Csörsz Ditch ('*Limes Sarmatiae*')," in *Limes XVIII. Proceedings of the XVIIIth International Congress of Roman Frontier Studies Held in Amman, Jordan (September 2000)*, vol. 2, ed. P. Freeman et al. (Oxford: British Archaeological Reports, 2002), 626; Charles Bowlus, *Franks, Moravians, and Magyars: The Struggle for the Middle Danube, 788-907* (Philadelphia: University of Pennsylvania Press, 1995), 13.

125 average of once every decade: In 422, 442, 447, 481, 486, 493, 499, and 502. Brian Croke, "The Date of the Anastasian Long Wall," *Greek, Roman, and Byzantine Studies* 20 (1982): 68–69.

126 Anastasian Long Wall: I have split the difference between the estimate of 56 km given by J. Crow and A. Ricci, "Investigating the Hinterland of Constantinople: Interim Report on the Anastasian Long Wall," *Journal of Roman Archaeology* 10 (1997): 239, and the 65 km estimate of Croke, "Date of the Anastasian Long Wall," 60. The wall was built of uniform blocks, standing five meters (sixteen feet) high. Up-to-date field reports of excavations are available at the Anastasian Wall Project website, www.shca.ed.ac.uk/projects/longwalls/anastasianwall.htm.

126 six times in one ten-year period: In 577, 583, and 587, and the Slavs in 581, 584, and 585. See Croke, "Date of the Anastasian Long Wall," 69–70.

127 stone-and-clay houses: Florin Curta, *Southeastern Europe in the Middle Ages, 500-1250* (Cambridge: Cambridge University Press, 2006).

127 "Scythian desert": Procopius, *Secret History* 18.20–21.

128 He rebuilt cities: Justinian's southeastern-European fortifications are the theme of Procopius, *Buildings* 4. Procopius emphasizes, especially at 4.1.4 and 4.1.6–7, that the new walls were necessitated by the unprovoked attacks of barbarians. Their archaeology is discussed in Curta, *Southeastern Europe*, 40–48.

129 sorrow and dejection: Procopius, *Secret History* 26.5ff.

129 "demolishing their own property": Agathias 5.13.5–6, quoted in Crow and Ricci, "Investigating the Hinterland," 239–40.

129 shifted toward other strategies: On the development of Byzantine strategy, see Edward Luttwack, *The Grand Strategy of the Byzantine Empire* (Cambridge, MA: Harvard University Press, 2009), passim; John Haldon, *Warfare, State, and Society in the Byzantine World, 565–1204* (London: Routledge, 1999), 36.

129 "not allowed to use my freedom": J. B. Bury, *History of the Later Roman Empire from the Death of Theodosius I to the Death of Justinian*, 2 vols. (New York: Dover Publications, 1958), 2:73.

Cycles of Walls and Despots

132 "trust in virtue, not in walls": Helmut Langerbein, "Great Blunders?: The Great Wall of China, the Berlin Wall, and the Proposed United States/Mexico Border Fence," *History Teacher* 43/1 (2009): 14.

134 "anxiety about border defense": Arthur Waldron, *The Great Wall of China: From History to Myth* (Cambridge: Cambridge University Press, 1990), 45.

135 "smile to kill people": Ming Dong Gu, *Translating China for Western Readers: Reflective, Critical, and Practical Essays* (Albany: State University of New York Press, 2016), 160.

136 historians logged numerous complaints: Arthur Wright, "Sui Yang-Ti: Personality and Stereotype," in *The Confucian Persuasion*, ed. A. Wright (Stanford, CA: Stanford University Press, 1960), 66.

136 "a hundred million people": Lovell, *Great Wall*, 133.

136 aphrodisiac-driven sexual desires: Wright, "Sui Yang-Ti," 66–71.

136 "Emperor Yang exhausted the country": Lovell, *Great Wall*, 143.

137 "process of military training": David Morgan, *The Mongols* (Cambridge: Basil Blackwell, 1986), 84.

137   raping his women: René Grousset, *The Empire of the Steppes: A History of Central Asia*, trans. Naomi Walford (New Brunswick: Rutgers University Press, 1970), 249.

137   adopting a sedentary life: Anatoly Khazanov, *Nomads and the Outside World*, trans. Julia Crookenden, 2nd ed. (Madison: University of Wisconsin Press, 1994), 241.

137   no value to the Mongol soldier: Mongol religion, such as it was, consisted of a sort of halfhearted shamanism. See Morgan, *Mongols*, 40–41.

138   "earthen-walled cities": *The Secret History of the Mongols: The Origin of Chingis Khan*, adapt. and trans. Paul Kahn (Boston: Cheng and Tsui, 1988), 114, 116.

138   "the walls of their cities": Ibid., 161.

139   cowed tribute-payers: Morgan, *Mongols*, 74.

139   The population of China: Herbert Franke and Denis Twitchett, eds., *The Cambridge History of China, Vol 6: Alien Regimes and Border States, 907–1368* (Cambridge: Cambridge University Press, 1994), introduction.

139   Heaven is weary: Grousset, *Empire of the Steppes*, 249.

140   maintain a strong defense: Edward Farmer, *Zhu Yuanzhang and Early Ming Legislation: The Reordering of Chinese Society Following the Era of Mongol Rule* (Leiden, Netherlands: E. J. Brill, 1995), 83.

140   rebuilt the city walls: Yinong Xu, *The Chinese City in Space and Time: The Development of Urban Form in Suzhou* (Honolulu: University of Hawaii Press, 2000), 123.

140   sea link between Europe and Asia: On Chinese maritime history, see Edward Dreyer, *Zheng He: China and the Ocean in the Early Ming Dynasty, 1405–1433* (New York: Pearson, 2006); Gang Deng, *Chinese Maritime Activities and Socioeconomic Development, c. 2100 BC–1900 AD* (Westport, CT: Greenwood, 1997); John Wills Jr., ed., *China and Maritime Europe, 1500–1800: Trade, Settlement, Diplomacy, and Missions* (New York: Cambridge University Press, 2011).

142   nearly two hundred wars: Alastair Johnston, *Cultural Realism: Strategic Culture and Grand Strategy in Chinese History* (Princeton, NJ: Princeton University Press, 1995), 184.

142   "groaning in bed": David Spindler, "A Twice-Scorned Mongol Woman, the Raid of 1576, and the Building of the Brick Great Wall," *Ming Studies* 60 (2009): 66–94.

143   as late as 1805: On this wall, see Yonglin Jiang, "The 'Southern Great Wall of China' in Fenghuang County: Discovery and Restoration," *Ming Studies* 68 (2013): 57–82; and Magnus Fiskesjö, "On the 'Raw' and 'Cooked' Barbarians of Imperial China," *Inner Asia* 1/2 (1999): 139–68, at 148–49.

144   "Endlessly they built walls": Lovell, *Great Wall*, 260.

Walls and the Apocalypse

146　Babylon in 1811: Claudius Rich, *Memoir on the Ruins of Babylon* (London: Longman, Hurst, Rees, Orme, and Brown, 1818).

147　riding, archery, and truth telling: Herodotus 1.136.

148　"swallow the Greek poison": Roman Ghirshman, *Persian Art: The Parthian and Sassanian Dynasties, 219 B.C.–A.D. 651*, trans. Stuart Gilbert and James Emmons (New York: Golden Press, 1962), 261.

148　protecting the entire Empire with walls: R. N. Frye, "The Sasanian System of Walls for Defense," in *Studies in Memory of Gaston Wiet*, ed. Myriam Rosen-Ayalon (Jerusalem: Hebrew University of Jerusalem, 1977), 7; Hamid Mahamedi, "Wall as a System of Frontier Defense during the Sasanid Period," in *The Spirit of Wisdom [Mēnōg ī Xrad]: Essays in Memory of Ahmad Tafazzoli*, ed. Touraj Daryaee and Mahmoud Omidsalar (Costa Mesa, CA: Mazda Publishers, 2004). There is one allegedly Achaemenid-era wall, located in northern Afghanistan and named, like several others, *kam pirak*. Unfortunately, little is known of this wall, which ran 60 km (37 miles) from Dilbarjin toward Balkh, and given that linear barriers seem to have been utterly foreign to the Achaemenids, I am skeptical that the date will withstand scrutiny. See Warwick Ball, *Archaeological Gazetteer of Afghanistan*, 2 vols. (Paris: ADPF, 1982), 145; Warwick Ball, *Rome in the East: The Transformation of an Empire* (London: Routledge, 2000), 315.

148　"Lord of the Shoulders": Mahamedi, "Wall as a System of Frontier Defense," 157.

148　Moat of Shapur: Frye, "Sasanian System of Walls," 8–9, relying on the Persian historian Yāqūt.

148　"panic and bloodshed": Jerome, ep. 77.8.

150　defending both empires: For example, Priscus fr. 41.1, 47.

150　"bleeding their country": Moses Dasxuranci, *The History of the Caucasian Albanians by Movses Dasxuranci*, trans. C. J. F. Dowsett (New York: Oxford University Press, 1961), 83. He nevertheless described the walls as "wonderful works."

151　entire Merv oasis: Andrej Bader, Vassif Gaibov, and Gennadij Koselenko, "Walls in Margiana," in *In the Land of the Gryphons: Papers on Central Asian Archaeology in Antiquity*, ed. Antonio Invernizzi (Firenze: Le Lettere, 1995), 39–50, supplanting Frye, "Sasanian System of Walls," 14, who earlier dated the 250 km oasis walls to Antiochus I. Balkh: Azad, *Sacred Landscape*, 92–95. The Balkh walls encircled not only the walled city but also outlying farms and villages within its 72-km (45-mile) perimeter. Bukhara: The rampart dated from the fifth century and encompassed the entire oasis, including some fifteen districts and numerous villages. Its length is also estimated at 250 km. See Ciro Lo Muzio, "An

Archaeological Outline of the Bukhara Oasis," *Journal of Inner Asian Art and Archaeology* 4 (2009): 46. Although Lo Muzio dates the wall somewhat later, more recent fieldwork indicates that the Bukhara oasis wall dates to the fifth century. See Sören Stark et al., "Preliminary Results of the Field Season 2013," www.isaw.nyu.edu/research/bukhara -project/2013-field-season. Additional description at W. Barthold, *Turkestan down to the Mongol Invasion* (London: Oxford University Press, 1928), 98, 113–16. Bayhaq: Ira Lapidus, "Muslim Cities and Islamic Societies," in *Middle Eastern Cities: A Symposium on Ancient, Islamic, and Contemporary Middle Eastern Urbanism*, ed. Ira Lapidus (Berkeley: University of California Press, 1969), 68. Tashkent: The "stone city" was sheltered by three layers of walls, the outermost of which enclosed the entire oasis. See Guy Le Strange, *The Lands of the Eastern Caliphate: Mesopotamia, Persia, and Central Asia from the Moslem Conquest to the Time of Timur* (Cambridge: Cambridge University Press, 1905), 480–81. Nur: Aleksandr Naymark, "The Size of Samanid Bukhara: A Note on Settlement Patterns in Early Islamic Mawarannahr" in *Bukhara: The Myth and the Architecture*, ed. Attilio Petruccioli (Cambridge: Aga Khan Program for Islamic Architecture, 1999), 46. Samarkand: Naymark, "Size of Samanid Bukhara," 46. Naymark believes that the oasis wall of Samarkand functioned throughout the early Middle Ages, whereas it is the opinion of Stark et al., "Preliminary Results," that the Samarkand oasis wall, identified as Divar-i-Qiyamat, should be dated to the time of Abu Muslim in the mid-eighth century.

151 twenty new walls: Murtazali Gadjiev, "On the Construction Date of the Derbend Fortification Complex," *Iran and the Caucasus* 12 (2008): 2, 12.

151 Archaeologists believe that the walls: Muhammed-Yusuf Kiani, *Parthian Sites in Hyrcania: The Gurgan Plain* (Berlin: Dietrich Reimer, 1982), 11–38, who attributes construction to Mithradates II (123–87 BC), has been sharply criticized by archaeologists, who have firmly established a date shortly before or after AD 500. See James Howard-Johnston, *East Rome, Sasanian Persia and the End of Antiquity* (Burlington, VT: Variorum, 2006), 194n79; and Jebrael Nokandeh et al., "Linear Barriers of Northern Iran: The Great Wall of Gorgan and the Wall of Tammishe," *Iran* 44 (2006): 121–73.

152 water for brick making: Hamid Rekavandi et al., "Secrets of the Red Snake: The Great Wall of Iran Revealed," *Current Archaeology* 27 (2008): 12–22.

153 five barriers: After a crushing defeat in the late fifth century AD, the Sasanids enhanced their fortifications in the region. Around 500, they added the Ghilghilchay Wall, south of Derbent in the Siyazan region of Azerbaijan, and the main defenses at Derbent and Ghilghilchay

were then supplemented by three long earthen ramparts—one north of Derbent, another between Derbent and Ghilghilchay, and a third south of Ghilghilchay. See Howard-Johnston, *East Rome*, 192. Khosrow was probably responsible for constructing the spectacular stone wall that replaced the mud-brick original at Derbent. Archaeology confirms the statements of early medieval geographers who credit the 50 km (31 mile) mud-brick wall to Kavadh I (r. 488–531). Standing up to five meters (sixteen feet) high and resting on a base some eight meters (twenty-six feet) thick, the Ghilghilchay Wall formed a key part of the broader Caspian defense system. See Asker Aliev et al., "The Ghilghilchay Defensive Long Wall: New Investigations," *Ancient West and East* 5/1–2 (2006): 143–77; Howard-Johnston, *East Rome*, 192, gives the length as only 30 km. The Ghilghilchay Wall, here given the name that derives from the river it follows, is also occasionally known as the Shirwan Wall or the Gilginsky Wall.

153 Russian republic of Dagestan: In Armenian sources, Derbent is known as Cor, and it figures in Byzantine sources as Tzour, Chorytzon, or Tzon. It is also written as "Darband," and was constructed during the reign of Yazdigerd II (439–57). Aliev et al., "Ghilghilchay Defensive Long Wall," 144–48; Gadjiev, "On the Construction Date," 1–15. *Derbent* means "locked gate" in Persian, and towns by that name are liberally scattered across the mountains of the old empire.

153 "Alans and other barbarians": John Barker, *Justinian and the Later Roman Empire* (Madison: University of Wisconsin Press, 1966), 116; Gadjiev, "On the Construction Date," 13.

153 "Great Caucasian Wall": The improved Derbent fortifications began as two parallel walls that reached from the sea to the Caucasus, then continued for more than 40 km (25 miles) into the mountains. As always, scholars disagree as to the length. Gadjiev, "On the Construction Date," 2; Howard-Johnston, *East Rome*, 192; see also the older account of V. Minorsky, *A History of Sharvan and Darband in the 10th—11th Centuries* (Cambridge: W. Heffer and Sons, 1958), 13, 86–89. For a nineteenth-century traveler's account, see William Ainsworth, ed., *All Around the World: An Illustrated Record of Voyages, Travels, and Adventures in All Parts of the Globe*, 2 vols. (London: W. Collins, 1866), 294–98.

153 cursed name: Alexander was "considered the third of the trinity of evil spirits which according to Zoroastrian belief was created by Ahriman to vex the Iranian race." *The Shahnameh of the Persian Poet Firdausi*, trans. James Atkinson (London: Oriental Translation Fund, 1832), 338.

153 Gog and Magog: Alexander appears as Iskander, and Gog and Magog as Yajuj and Majuj. On the reception of the Alexander myth in the *Shahnameh*, see Haila Manteghi, "Alexander the Great in the *Shanameh*

of Ferdowsi," in *The Alexander Romance in Persia and the East*, ed. R. Stoneman, K. Erickson, and I. Netton (Groningen, Netherlands: Barkhuis, 2012).

154 Divar-i-kanpirak, or Kempirak: Stark et al., "Preliminary Results." Many scholars have identified Kanpirak with Bukhara's oasis wall. However, recent excavations make identification with the long wall more probable. Locals know the wall as Kempir-Duval. See Barthold, *Turkestan down to the Mongol Invasion*, 113.

154 northeast of Tashkent: Barthold, *Turkestan down to the Mongol Invasion*, 172–73. This later wall began at the mountains and followed the Chirchiq River to the Syr-Darya, demarcating cultivated land from steppe. Like other long walls in Central Asia, it was built in the eighth century and, curiously, is known to locals by the same name, Kempir-Duval, as the long wall at Bukhara. Local tradition holds that the wall once extended much farther than its surviving traces.

154 against the Turks: The account is from Abu Bakr Muhammed ibn Jafar Narshakhi, *The History of Bukhara*, trans. Richard Frye (Cambridge, MA: Medieval Academy of America, 1954), 33–34.

156 "they departed": On the fate of Bukhara, see 'Ala-ad-Din 'Ata-Malik Juvaini, *The History of the World-Conqueror*, trans. J. A. Boyle (Cambridge, MA: Harvard University Press, 1958), 1:75–85.

156 1.3 million: Ibid., 1:119–32.

156 numbers of the slaughtered: Morgan, *Mongols*, 74–78.

157 "fearful, hungry, and cold": Hend Gilli-Elewy, "Al-Hawadit al-gami 'a: A Contemporary Account of the Mongol Conquest of Baghdad, 656/1258," *Arabica* 58 (2011): 368.

157 "hunger and fear": Ibid.

158 canals still functioned: Jacob Gruber, "Irrigation and Land Use in Ancient Mesopotamia," *Agricultural History* 22/2 (1948): 73.

158 hydraulic infrastructure: S. Frederick Starr, *Lost Enlightenment: Central Asia's Golden Age from the Arab Conquest to Tamerlane* (Princeton: Princeton University Press, 2015), 465.

159 the number of wandering tribes: D. T. Potts, *Nomadism in Iran: From Antiquity to the Modern Era* (New York: Oxford University Press, 2014), 258.

159 ate up the entire harvest: Norman Lewis, *Nomads and Settlers in Syria and Jordan, 1800–1980* (Cambridge: Cambridge University Press, 1987), 8–9.

159 abandoned villages came to outnumber inhabited ones: Ibid., 11–23. By the mid-nineteenth century a growing number of tribes occupied Iraq as well. This movement became a "temporary flood" after World War I.

159 "Turkoman towers": Potts, *Nomadism in Iran*, 316–17.

The Horrible Bombard

165 "Give me Constantinople": Steven Runciman, *The Fall of Constantinople, 1453* (Cambridge: Cambridge University Press, 1965), 74.

Beyond the Pale

177 "his sword beside him": Samuel Johnson, *A Journey to the Western Islands of Scotland* (London: T. Cadell and W. Davies, 1816), 113–14.

178 "like second nature": Gerald of Wales, *Topography of Ireland*, 3:10, in *The Historical Works of Giraldius Cambrensis*, ed. Thomas Wright, trans. Thomas Forester and Sir Richard Colt Hoare (London: George Bell, 1905).

178 stone towers for residences: Terry Barry, "The Last Frontier: Defence and Settlement in Late Medieval Ireland," in *Colony and Frontier in Medieval Ireland: Essays Presented to J. F. Lydon*, ed. T. Barry, R. Frame, and K. Simms (London: Hambledon Press, 1995), 217–28.

185 Ukrainian Line: John LeDonne, *The Grand Strategy of the Russian Empire, 1650–1831* (Oxford: Oxford University Press, 2004), 48–49. This line followed the Bereslovaia River before crossing overland to the Bereka River, which was followed to the Donets at Izium.

185 progress in Siberia: The Siberian Line, eventually consisting of the Orenburg, Usinskaya, Presnogor'kovskya, and Irtysh Lines, is described in I. Stebelsky, "The Frontier in Central Asia," in *Studies in Historical Geography*, vol. 1, ed. J. H. Bater and R. A. French (New York: Academic Press, 1983).

185 sixteen hundred miles in length: Course described in LeDonne, *Grand Strategy*, 286–87.

186 "savage in character": Emeri Van Donzel and Andrea Schmidt, *Gog and Magog in Early Eastern Christian and Islamic Sources: Sallam's Quest for Alexander's Wall* (Leiden, Netherlands: E. J. Brill, 2009), 44.

Fort Brokenheart

191 "Young Indians": Thomas Forsyth, "An Account of the Manners and Customs of the Sauk and Fox Nation of Indians Tradition," in *The Indian Tribes of the Upper Mississippi Valley and Region of the Great Lakes*, vol. 2, ed. Emma Blair (Cleveland: Arthur H. Clark Co., 1912), 194.

192 "(death-whoop)": Henry Schoolcraft, *The Indian Tribes of the United States: Their History, Antiquities, Customs, Religion, Arts, Language, Traditions, Oral Legends, and Myths*, ed. Francis Drake, 2 vols. (Philadelphia: J. B. Lippincott, 1884), 184.

192 Warrior customs prevailed: "Even a cursory review of the literature reveals that one of the most highly prized social distinctions available

to Native American males was that specific to the warrior tradition. To be considered a fierce warrior ready and willing to battle in defense of the people was the ultimate honor." Richard Chacon and Rubén Mendoza, "Ethical Considerations and Conclusions Regarding Indigenous Warfare and Violence in North America," in *North American Indigenous Warfare and Ritual Violence*, ed. Richard Chacon and Rubén Mendoza (Tuscon: University of Arizona Press, 2007), 227.

193 "tenderest years": Charles Bishop and Victor Lytwyn, "'Barbarism and Ardour of War from the Tenderest Years': Cree-Inuit Warfare in the Hudson Bay Region," in Chacon and Mendoza, *North American Indigenous Warfare*, 37.

193 mature into elite warriors: R. F. Heizer and M. A. Whipple, *The California Indians: A Source Book*, 2nd ed. (Berkeley: University of California Press, 1971), 433–34.

193 "apprentice warrior": Antoine Simone Le Page Du Pratz, *The History of Louisiana, or of the Western Parts of Virginia and Carolina* (1774; repr., New Orleans: Pelican Press, 1947), 308.

193 thrown in the air: Helen Rountree, *The Powhatan Indians of Virginia: Their Traditional Culture* (Norman: University of Oklahoma Press, 1989), 79.

193 inserted in the wounds: To George Catlin, that tireless advocate of Indian causes and sensitive recorder of Indian customs, it was almost too painful to watch. He recalled the awful ripping sounds made by the knives and how the tortured youths had smiled at him, proud of their ability to withstand pain. George Catlin, *O-Kee-Pa: A Religious Ceremony; and Other Customs of the Mandans* (Philadelphia: J. B. Lippincott, 1867); also George Catlin, *Letters and Notes on the Manners, Customs, and Conditions of the North American Indians*, 3rd ed. (New York: Wiley and Putnam, 1844), 158ff.

193 demonstrating valor: On war dances, both preparatory and celebratory, see Marian Smith, "The War Complex of the Plains Indians," *Proceedings of the American Philosophical Society* 78/3 (1938): 449–52. A Dakota warrior with a kill to his credit was awarded an eagle's feather marked with a red spot. If he had slit his victim's throat, he could wear an even more prestigious ornament, a red feather that had been notched. Chippewa warriors wore two feathers for bloodying their weapons, three for killing and scalping an enemy, and five for having taken a wounded prisoner. Schoolcraft, *Indian Tribes of the United States*, 1:184–85.

193 sacred protection: One of the earliest English observers of Native Americans, Arthur Barlowe, noted of the Indians of Virginia in 1584, "When they goe to warres, they carry about with them their idol, of whom they ask counsel, as the Romans were woont of the Oracle of Apollo."

Arthur Barlowe, "The First Voyage to Roanoke, 1584," https://archive
.org/details/firstvoyagetoroaoobarl. The custom of warriors carrying
bundles of charms into battle was later observed among Algonquians,
Pawnee, Iowa, Osage, Omaha, Kansa, Blackfoot, Gros Ventre, Sioux,
and Crows, among others. Smith, "War Complex," 446–47.

193 Scalps: James Axtell and William Sturtevant, "The Unkindest Cut;
or, Who Invented Scalping?," *William and Mary Quarterly*, 3rd ser.,
37/3 (1980): 451–72.

193 Tribal military societies: Robert Lowie, "Military Societies of the
Crow Indians," in *Societies of the Plains Indians*, ed. Clark Wissler (New
York: Trustees of the American Museum of Natural History, 1916),
143–218; as well as William Meadows, *Kiowa, Apache, and Comanche
Military Societies* (Austin: University of Texas Press, 1999).

193 shown cowardice: John Stands in Timber and Margot Liberty, *Cheyenne
Memories*, 2nd ed. (New Haven, CT: Yale University Press, 1998), 63.

194 women did all the work: See, for example, the remarks of Schoolcraft,
Indian Tribes of the United States, 1:22: "The greatest obstacle to the
success of agricultural life among them has hither to been a haughty
spirit of pride and the unqualified laziness of the men and boys, who
will not work. The men hunt a little in summer, go to war, kill an enemy,
dance, lounge, sleep, and smoke. The women do everything—nurse,
chop wood and carry it on their backs from a half to a whole mile,
hoe the ground for planting, plant, hoe the corn, gather wild fruit,
carry the lodge, and in winter cut and carry the poles to pitch it with,
clear off the snow, etc: and the men often sit and look on."

196 "unmistakably primitive people": For the history of these women, as
well as those men who made similar expeditions, see Ure, *In Search
of Nomads*.

196 "I go dance on Broadway": Merian C. Cooper, *Grass* (New York: G. P.
Putnam's Sons, 1925), 53.

The Last Battles

203 gypped in a heroin deal: Upton Close, "Hot Water along the Great
Wall," *Saturday Evening Post*, April 8, 1933, 6–7, 31–36.

203 "Great Wall is glorious!": Lovell, *Great Wall*, 312.

203 "come to us on bended knee": "On Bended Knee," *Time* 21/4 (January
23, 1933): 25.

203 "Lives are our ammunition!": "War of Jehol," *Time* 21/10 (March 6,
1933): 23.

204 "at some deer": "Glorious 16," *Time* 21/11 (March 13, 1933): 24.

206 "monument to fear": Lovell, *Great Wall*, 279.

206 "Chinese love of enclosing walls": Ibid., 15.

206 "incompatible with them": Owen Lattimore, *Studies in Frontier History: Collected Papers, 1928–1958* (New York: Oxford University Press, 1962), 98.

206 "Wall is what makes China": Jeffrey Meyer, cited in Dee Mack Williams, *Beyond Great Walls: Environment, Development, and Identity on the Chinese Grasslands of Inner Mongolia* (Stanford, CA: Stanford University Press, 2002), 63–64.

206 "the national psyche": Ibid., 64.

209 "new Wall of China": Brent Sterling, *Do Good Fences Make Good Neighbors? What History Teaches Us about Strategic Barriers and International Security* (Washington, DC: Georgetown University Press, 2009), 212.

209 "Great Wall of France": Ibid., 232.

211 "concrete labyrinth": Harold Rosen, "Maginot Line," *Changing English* 11/2 (2004): 243.

"A Hell of a Lot Better Than a War"

220 "it was blank": Peter Wyden, *Wall: The Inside Story of Divided Berlin* (New York: Simon and Schuster, 1989), 682.

222 "better than a war": Frederick Taylor, *The Berlin Wall: A World Divided, 1961–1989* (New York: HarperCollins, 2006), 220.

Epilogue: "Love Your Neighbor, but Don't Pull Down Your Hedge"

236 "biggest exporter of cages in the world": "Israel: Walled In," *Financial Times*, June 29, 2016, https://www.ft.com/content/ccf4b532-3935 -11e6-9a05-82a9b15a8ee7?mhq5j=e3.

236 "crossed the border": Chris Helman, "What Trump Can Learn from the Man Who Built Israel's Border Walls," *Forbes*, February 1, 2017, https://www.forbes.com/sites/christopherhelman/2017/02/01/what -trump-can-learn-from-the-man-who-built-israels-border-walls/.

240 "nor particular efficient": Langerbein, "Great Blunders?," 10.

242 "control your borders": Daniel Halper, "Hillary: I Voted for Border Fence to Keep Out Illegal Immigrants," *Weekly Standard*, November 10, 2015, http://www.weeklystandard.com/hillary-i-voted-for-border -fence-to-keep-out-illegal-immigrants/article/1061753.

242 "Koch brothers' proposal": Peter Beinart, "How the Democrats Lost Their Way on Immigration," *Atlantic*, July–August 2017, https:// www.theatlantic.com/magazine/archive/2017/07/the-democrats -immigration-mistake/528678/.

Index

Numbers in italics with the letter m *refer to pages with maps.*